W9-APV-679

At the Heart of the Liturgy

Edited by
Maxwell E. Johnson
Timothy O'Malley
and
Demetrio S. Yocum

Foreword by
Mary Catherine Hilkert, OP

At the Heart
of the Liturgy

Conversations with Nathan D. Mitchell's
"Amen Corners," 1991–2012

A PUEBLO BOOK

Liturgical Press   Collegeville, Minnesota
www.litpress.org

A Pueblo Book published by Liturgical Press

Excerpts from the English translation of *The Roman Missal* © 1973, International Commission on English in the Liturgy Corporation (ICEL); excerpts from the English translation of *Ceremonial of Bishops* © 1989, ICEL; excerpts from the English translation of *The General Instruction of the Roman Missal* © 2002, ICEL. All rights reserved.

Excerpts from documents of the Second Vatican Council are from *Vatican Council II: The Basic Sixteen Documents*, by Austin Flannery, OP, © 1996 (Costello Publishing Company, Inc.). Used with permission.

Unless otherwise indicated, Scripture texts in this work are taken from the *New Revised Standard Version Bible* © 1989, Division of Christian Education of the National Council of the Churches of Christ in the United States of America. Used by permission. All rights reserved.

© 2014 by Order of Saint Benedict, Collegeville, Minnesota. All rights reserved. No part of this book may be reproduced in any form, by print, microfilm, microfiche, mechanical recording, photocopying, translation, or by any other means, known or yet unknown, for any purpose except brief quotations in reviews, without the previous written permission of Liturgical Press, Saint John's Abbey, PO Box 7500, Collegeville, Minnesota 56321-7500. Printed in the United States of America.

1   2   3   4   5   6   7   8   9

Library of Congress Cataloging-in-Publication Data

At the heart of the liturgy : reflections on Nathan D. Mitchell's Amen corners, 1991–2012 / edited by Maxwell E. Johnson, Timothy P. O'Malley, and Demetrio S. Yocum.
   pages   cm
   Includes index.
   "A Pueblo book."
   ISBN 978-0-8146-6309-7 — ISBN 978-0-8146-6334-9 (ebook)
   1. Mass—Celebration—Meditations.   2. Catholic Church—Liturgy—Meditations.   3. Mitchell, Nathan.   I. Johnson, Maxwell E., 1952– editor of compilation.

BX2169.A8   2014
264'.02—dc23

                                                        2014010551

In Memoriam

R. Kevin Seasoltz, OSB

(1930–2013)

Contents

Chapter 4: *Beauty*

Chapter 5: *Justice*

Chapter 6: *Unity*

Foreword

At the heart of the liturgy is the God of Love, poured out in Spirit and Word, who prepares a banquet where strangers and sinners—which is to say, all of us—are welcome. At the heart of liturgy is the God of compassion who nurtures us at her own breast. At the heart of liturgy is the God who sends us forth to testify to what we have seen and heard, to become what we eat, to be a blessing in and for God's beloved and broken world.

For over two decades, Nathan Mitchell offered his own testimony to that mystery in his "Amen Corners" in *Worship*. Although this book is not a complete collection of those poetic and prophetic essays, it offers a welcome sampling of a feature readers eagerly anticipated. We knew that we would find trustworthy historical and theological scholarship, as well as some hidden treasures. Likewise, we expected to find an assessment of the current state of a question which reframed past insights and opened up future possibilities. We knew, too, that we were in for a literary treat. Nathan would "tell the truth, but tell it slant" (Emily Dickinson).

With the soul of poet himself, Nathan was always on the lookout for the turn of phrase, the image, stanza, or metaphor from other classic wordsmiths that could capture the liturgical insight he wanted to explore. His essay on women and worship became "A 'Mansion' for the Rat." T.S. Eliot's reminder that "in my beginning is my end" persuaded readers to attend to details of liturgical history and complex philosophical distinctions, both medieval and postmodern. Church architecture became "the poetics of space" and the "geometry of prayer." Nathan's final column gathers images from sources as diverse as Zora Neale Hurston, Gerard Manley Hopkins, T.S. Eliot, Marge Piercy, Robert Farrar Capon, Wallace Stevens, Li-Young Lee, Flannery O'Connor, and Ellis Peters, among others. But Nathan wove the threads of their insights into his own tapestry, in this case a farewell eucharistic litany which draws the readers' attention back to the heart of liturgy: "We come to you, God, with praise and thanksgiving."

The introductions to each section of this volume, written by a new generation of liturgical scholars, clearly demonstrate that Nathan's students became apprentices in that same art. Instead of repeating or explaining Nathan's insights, yet clearly inspired by them, his former students whom he proudly claims as colleagues now, voice their own. Nathan opened doors and pointed to ways forward. He led expeditions into history and mystery with maps that had been discarded by others or that remained unfinished. In their own creative scholarship his companions have continued the journey, but they have also departed from the familiar trails and begun to explore new pathways of their own.

Nothing could delight a true teacher more. As Nathan's colleague, I witnessed his skills as a mentor in the classroom, a member of examination boards, and the director of dissertations. At times I marveled as he performed the academic version of the wisdom Catherine of Siena advocates in her *Dialogue*: "snatch the rose from between the thorns." Students treasured his insights in the classroom, but he treasured theirs even more. He showed a way forward in a writing project with a well-placed question in the margins of a text. During an examination process others found tedious, there was genuine delight on Nathan's face when students grasped something they had misunderstood, responded in a way that moved beyond his expectations, or offered an astute critique.

The fruits of some of those initial insights are evident in this volume, beginning with Kimberly Belcher's reflections on "the flesh as the hinge of salvation" in ways that neither Nathan nor Tertullian could have imagined. Likewise, Joél Schmidt exercises his own creative imagination in highlighting how effective preaching generates new possibilities of enfleshing the word of God in the world. Anne McGowan draws on a surprising discovery in an unfamiliar pastoral setting to show how the Spirit enables imperfect communities to "make room and make welcome." Celebrating all forms of genuine beauty as "portals to transcendence," Clare Johnson focuses on the subversive manifestation of God's beauty in the icon of the crucified one who calls us to recognize, and respond to, the image of God in the lost and the least. Katharine Harmon illustrates that "real presence is not only the gift but also the goal and work of Eucharist" through stories drawn from her original research on women's roles in the liturgical movement prior to Vatican II. Melanie Ross summons Anne Tyler and Wendell Berry, among others, to join Nathan in celebrating the grace of unconditional forgiveness and second chances, a gift which is at the same time a charge to every Christian gathering.

Readers of this volume will give thanks not only for Nathan's creative scholarship, pastoral commitment, and love of liturgy, all of which are reflected in his final hymn of praise and thanks, but also for the voice lessons he offered to this chorus of creative scholars. Together they celebrate that at the heart of liturgy is the heart of God.

Mary Catherine Hilkert, OP
University of Notre Dame

Acknowledgments

"The Wall" from THE AWFUL ROWING TOWARD GOD by Anne Sexton. Copyright © 1975 by Loring Conant, Jr., Executor of the Estate, renewed 2003 by Linda G. Sexton. Reprinted by permission of Houghton Mifflin Harcourt Publishing Company. All rights reserved. (United States and Canada.)

"The Wall" from THE AWFUL ROWING TOWARD GOD by Anne Sexton. Reprinted by permission of SLL/Sterling Lord Literistic, Inc. Copyright by Anne Sexton. (World excluding North America [print]; world electronic.)

"Nishmat," "The Wine," "House Built of a Breath," and "The Hunger Moon" from THE ART OF BLESSING THE DAY: POEMS WITH A JEWISH THEME by Marge Piercy, copyright © 1999 by Middlemarsh, Inc. Used by permission of Alfred A Knopf, an imprint of the Knopf Doubleday Publishing Group, a division of Random House LLC. All rights reserved. (United States, its territories and possessions, Philippines, Canada, Open Market [including EU].)

Excerpt from "One Art" from THE COMPLETE POEMS 1927–1979 by Elizabeth Bishop. Copyright © 1979, 1983 by Alice Helen Methfessel. Excerpt from "Easter 1989" from NEGATIVE BLUE: SELECTED LATER POEMS by Charles Wright. Copyright © 2000 by Charles Wright. Reprinted by permission of Farrar, Straus and Giroux, LLC, by permission of Farrar, Straus and Giroux, LLC.

"Hymn." Copyright © 1960 by A. R. Ammons, from COLLECTED POEMS 1951–1971 by A. R. Ammons. Used by permission of W. W. Norton & Company, Inc.

Excerpt from "For My People" from THIS IS MY CENTURY: NEW AND COLLECTED POEMS by Margaret Walker © 1989. Used by permission of The University of Georgia Press.

Li-Young Lee, "From Blossoms" from ROSE. Copyright © 1986 by Li-Young Lee. Reprinted with the permission of The Permissions Company, Inc., on behalf of BOA Editions, Ltd., www.boaeditions.org.

In process:

"Nishmat," "The Wine," "House Built of a Breath," and "The Hunger Moon" from THE ART OF BLESSING THE DAY: POEMS WITH A JEWISH THEME by Marge Piercy, copyright © 1999 by Middlemarsh, Inc. Used by permission of Wallace Literary Agency. (United Kingdom and Commonwealth [excluding Canada].)

"The Images." Copyright © 1981 by Adrienne Rich, from A WILD PATIENCE HAS TAKEN ME THIS FAR: POEMS 1978–1982 by Adrienne Rich. Used by permission of W. W. Norton & Company, Inc.

Introduction

My first encounter with Nathan D. Mitchell's scholarly work occurred not in conjunction with "The Amen Corner," which he composed for each issue of *Worship* from 1991 through 2012, but actually several years before that. Like many of us in the field of liturgical studies, my first encounter was with Nathan's still influential and widely read *Cult and Controversy: The Worship of the Eucharist Outside Mass*,[1] which he had completed in 1981 for a publication in 1982. I read *Cult and Controversy* for the first time as a Masters student in liturgical studies at Saint John's School of Theology, Collegeville, Minnesota, immediately after its publication. It was at that time also where R. Kevin Seasoltz, OSB (+2013), who was to become the editor of *Worship* over those same many years, suggested to me Nathan's essay, "The Once and Future Child: Toward a Theology of Childhood,"[2] something no one else was thinking about at the time, for a research project I was doing on the rites for infant baptism.

From those initial encounters with Nathan's work it has, of course, been a great pleasure over the years in my own academic development and career not only to continue reading his erudite insights into everything liturgical, from baptism and confirmation, Eucharist and ministry, language and catholic inclusivity, all the way to ethics, ecumenism, and eschatology, but to learn from him directly as a dear colleague in the Department of Theology at the University of Notre Dame for the past several years.

---

[1] Nathan Mitchell, *Cult and Controversy: The Worship of the Eucharist Outside Mass* (New York: Pueblo, 1982).

[2] Nathan Mitchell, "The Once and Future Child: Toward a Theology of Childhood," *Living Light* 12 (1975): 423–37.

All of us I am sure have our particular favorite Nathan quotes, those that would make a "Nathan's Greatest Hits" collection. Those I have found to be particularly helpful and informative for my own teaching and scholarship fall generally into four areas: (1) the meaning of liturgy; (2) the relationship between liturgy and theology; (3) liturgical history and its implications, the largest of these four, given the nature of my own work; and (4) liturgy and ethics or justice. In each of these, however, it is in fact difficult to separate his words into such distinct categories since there is a great deal of overlapping between them, a testimony to Nathan's own expertise in synthesis.

(1) *The Meaning of Liturgy*

As an important corrective to the popular notion one still all too frequently encounters about the meaning of liturgy as "work of the people" or "people's work," a true-enough, though extremely limited, definition, Nathan juxtaposes the following, what might be called a "Benedictine," definition, which underscores that the *work* of liturgy is primarily *God's*. He writes:

> Liturgy is God's work for us, not our work for God. Only God can show us how to worship God—fittingly, beautifully. Liturgy is not something beautiful we do for God, but something beautiful God does for us and among us. Public worship is neither our work nor our possession; as the Rule of St Benedict reminds us, it is *opus Dei*, God's work. Our work is to feed the hungry, to refresh the thirsty, to clothe the naked, to care for the sick, to shelter the homeless; to visit the imprisoned; to welcome the stranger; to open our hands and hearts to the vulnerable and the needy. If we are doing those things well, liturgy and the Catholic identity it rehearses will very likely take care of themselves. Liturgical art is our public gratitude that God is doing for us what we cannot do for ourselves. And there, perhaps, is where ethics and aesthetics together can begin to change the face of worship.[3]

[3] Nathan Mitchell, "The Amen Corner: Being Good and Being Beautiful," *Worship* 74, no. 6 (November 2000): 557–58.

(2) *The Relationship between Liturgy and Theology*

Aidan Kavanagh, OSB (+2006), one of Nathan's teachers both at Saint Meinrad's School of Theology and at Notre Dame, is probably best known today in the academy for his work *On Liturgical Theology*.[4] Therein, Kavanagh argues from the ancient formula of Prosper of Aquitaine, *"ut legem credendi lex statuat supplicandi,"* often appearing in the popular form, *"lex orandi, lex credendi,"* that liturgy is to be construed as *theologia prima*, first-order theology that is expressed in the liturgical life of the church, in distinction to *theologia secunda*, which has to do with systematic reflection and dogmatic clarification. In response to Kavanagh's work, the meaning of liturgical theology today is undergoing considerable debate, well summarized in recent articles by Michael Aune[5] and Robert F. Taft, SJ.[6] Nathan's own contribution to this whole puzzle of the relationship between *lex orandi* and *lex credendi*, while taking Kavanagh seriously, moves us beyond the either-or alternatives of most contemporary approaches:

> [T]he ancient, binary formula *lex orandi, lex credendi* ("the rule of prayer is the rule of faith")—though often invoked to assert the priority of doxology over doctrine—is in fact something of a red herring. The formula is flawed from the get-go, because its reasoning is circular: "We *believe*," it asserts, "that the church's public prayer shapes what (and how?) we believe." But such a statement *already expresses* fundamental *convictions—beliefs—*about the nature of both Christ and church, beliefs that make liturgy possible (and obligatory) in the first place. There is a sense, of course, in which it is quite true to say that liturgy is where theology is born—where the church is "caught in the act of being most overtly itself as it stands faithfully in the presence of the One who is both object and source" of its faith—and hence that liturgy alone deserves the moniker *theologia prima*. Still, the *lex orandi, lex credendi* formula suffers from the same

[4] Aidan Kavanagh, *On Liturgical Theology* (New York: Pueblo, 1984).

[5] Michael Aune, "Liturgy and Theology: Rethinking the Relationship," *Worship* 81, no. 2 (2007): 46–68, 141–69.

[6] Robert Taft, "Mrs. Murphy Goes to Moscow: Schmemann, Kavanagh, and the Byzantine Synthesis," *Worship* 85, no. 5 (2011): 386–407.

limitations that beset all such closed-circuit, binary oppositions. If doxology checks doctrine, might not the reverse be true as well, viz., that doctrine checks doxology?[7]

(3) *Liturgical History and Its Implications*

Trained at Notre Dame in classic *Liturgiewissenschaft* or "comparative liturgiology," Nathan's understanding of liturgy is imbued with an astute historical-critical sense of the various liturgical traditions and historical periods of East and West, and is permeated concomitantly with his first-hand familiarity with the liturgical sources of those traditions. Frequently in his writings this historical sense comes to bear on several distinct contemporary issues. For example, in response to a 1997 comment by then Josef Cardinal Ratzinger about the "damage" that the *Missale Romanum* of Pope Paul VI had allegedly inflicted upon the Church when "the old [Tridentine liturgical] structure was dismantled, and its pieces were used to construct another," with the result that the current Missal represented a "wholesale replacement" of one liturgy with another,[8] Nathan had this to say:

> Ironically, however, one could turn this argument with equal— indeed *superior*—force against the reforms that followed the Council of Trent. History will show, I believe, that *no* ecumenical council prior to Trent had ever commissioned a pope to reform the "breviary" and "missal," thereby creating a single, standard, invariably "uniform" liturgy for the entire Latin West. But that is precisely what Trent did, as Pope Pius V confirms in *Quo Primum* (the Apostolic Constitution printed in all official editions of the Missal of 1570). "As is fitting and suitable," wrote the pope, "the Missal should correspond to the Breviary, for as there is *one way* of celebrating the Office in the church of God, so there ought to be *one* rite of celebrating Mass." This was, of course, an unheard-of-innovation, a novelty that flew directly in the face of more than 1500 years of local diocesan

[7] Nathan Mitchell, *Meeting Mystery: Liturgy, Worship, and Sacraments* (Maryknoll, NY: Orbis Books, 2006), 223.

[8] "Pope Paul VI 'Damaged Church,'" *The Catholic Messenger* (Davenport, IA) 115, 17 (April, 1997), 1, 10.

diversity and liturgical pluralism in the West. As any study of the historical evolution of the Latin lectionaries, sacramentaries and pontificals can demonstrate, the Western rites were characterized—until well into the Middle Ages—by a constant cross-fertilization and migratory hybridization, with (for example) "Frankish" books influencing "Roman" ones and vice versa . . . Even after Rome moved to seize the initiative, and the liturgy of the papal court began to supplant local (variable) "usages" in the twelfth and thirteenth centuries, the development of the Roman liturgy into a recognizably "unified" rite was very gradual . . . What Trent did can only be described—to borrow Cardinal Ratzinger's phrase—as a "wholesale replacement" of cherished local liturgies by a strange "new" rite concocted by "specialists" and promulgated by persons with "juridical competence" . . . .

One could thus make the case, I think that the liturgical reforms prompted by the Council of Trent were far more drastic, unprecedented, and untraditional than those which followed Vatican II. Prior to Trent, liturgical "normalcy" in the Western churches was characterized by local variation. Thus, Augustine of Canterbury complained to Pope Gregory the Great, "If there is only *one* faith, why are the customs of the churches so different? The holy Roman church celebrates Mass one way, while the churches of Gaul celebrate another way." But Gregory responded: "You know the custom of the Roman church in which you were brought up; cherish it lovingly. But as far as I'm concerned, if you've discovered something more pleasing to almighty God—in the Roman or the Gallican or any other church—choose carefully, gathering the best customs from many different churches, and arrange them for use in the church of the English. . . . For we should love things not because of the places where they're found, but because of the goodness they contain." (Latin text in L. Hartmann, ed. *Monumenta Germaniae Historica*, Epistolae, II. Berlin: Weidmann, 1899, 344, lines 3–5 and 5–12; my translation.) . . . Here, Gregory epitomized the "classic" Roman tradition: *a generous acceptance of cultural difference and liturgical variation within the unity of faith*. In important respects, Trent's "one-size-fits-all" reforms represented a backing away from this classic tradition of respect for local usage and historical evolution. To Gregory, it seemed perfectly natural (and theologically necessary) to countenance and even to cultivate a *diversity* of custom—pastoral and liturgical—within that *communion* of churches whose ultimate bond is the *sacramentum fidei*. . . . In sum, the classic Roman tradition—formulated by popes like Gregory—was respect for diversity and local custom. *This* was "liturgical normalcy" for the Latin West. What is "abnormal" was the attempt to standardize a single rite (excluding all others) by "executive fiat"—a phenomenon that first emerged *not* (as Ratzinger suggests) at Vatican II, but at the Council of Trent![9]

Two years later, in response to those, especially Roman Catholic seminarians, clamoring for new standards of "orthodoxy" and the "restoration" of more "traditional" liturgical expressions and pieties, Nathan returned again to the development of the Roman Rite in the Middle Ages, with the clarification that such a designation actually could be used, originally, to describe at least *four* different liturgical usages at *Rome* itself:

> In short, "the" Roman Rite evolved as a loose confederation, a confluence of urban and papal practices that were further hybridized, especially—though not exclusively—by Gallican and Germanic material imported from north of the Alps. The whole idea of "a" Roman Rite is in many respects the invention of nineteenth-century liturgists like Prosper Guerangér, from whom allegiance to a single liturgical tradition (papal, Roman) offered stability in a Europe plagued by political and religious fragmentation. That is why van Dijk asserts: "Research into the ecclesiastical history of medieval Rome still labours under the assumption that, from the time when liturgical documents are available, the city had a single rite. This assumption is so long-standing that it has become almost venerable, not to say venerated. To put forward another point of view is like driving a wedge into the foundations of an ancient monument; it forebodes destruction." ([S.J.P. van Dijk, "The Urban and Papal Rites in Seventh and Eighth-Century Rome," *Sacris Erudiri* 12 (1961), 411–87], 415) . . . .
>
> . . . . Never one to be intimidated by uncomfortable facts, van Dijk continued his research. And he arrived at conclusions that might well cause today's restorationists to tremble. He concluded,

[9] Nathan Mitchell, "The Amen Corner: Rereading Reform," *Worship* 71, no. 5 (1997): 464–66.

for example, that in the late thirteenth century (ca. 1275), the city of Rome knew four different customs (or liturgical "rites," if you will (Ibid., 416). These four—the liturgy of the papal court (used by the papal staff at the Lateran *palace* and in the pope's own private chapel); the basilical liturgy of St. Peter's in the Vatican (a revision of the Old-Roman rite); a new urban liturgy that combined elements from earlier urban and papal rites; and the liturgy of the Lateran *basilica* (served by a group of Canons Regular)—coexisted and "influenced each other thoroughly." (Ibid., 416–21) Eventually, the liturgy of the papal court became, for a complex set of political and pastoral reasons, the one that most decisively shaped what we now call "the" Roman liturgy. . . .

Ironically, perhaps, the *roots* of this rite are not particularly "Roman" at all. As historian Jeffrey Richards notes, Rome had experienced a "dramatic influx" of Greek-speaking monks and clerics during the first half of the seventh century—many of them refugees from "Arab invasion and Monothelite persecution." (*The Consul of God: The Life and Times of Gregory the Great* [London: Routledge & Kegan Paul, 1980], 121) "In their wake," Richards continues, "there came a large-scale introduction of the cults of the Greek saints, Greek ecclesiastical rites and rituals, and even Greek church institutions into Rome. . . . *Ordo Romanus I* records the pope asking on Easter morning: 'How many infants were baptized in Latin and how many in Greek?'" (Ibid.) No wonder Pope Gregory had to defend himself against the charge that he had permitted the Roman liturgy to be usurped by Greek customs![10]

And, as the result of what might be called this Byzantinization of Roman liturgy, including the import of "caesaropapism" into the West, Nathan summarized further:

"The" Roman liturgy was thus well on its way to becoming a spectacle performed by trained specialists rather than common public prayer celebrated by people and ministers together. Rigid etiquette, Byzantine grandiosity and a refusal to permit any variation, change or improvisation thus became "symbols of Papal sovereignty in the West,

[10] Nathan Mitchell, "The Amen Corner: Back to the Future?" *Worship* 73, no. 1 (1999): 64–65.

turning the congregation into spectators and listeners. The distinguishing feature of the old urban rite, which was symbolic of the Roman community and was here displaced, was participation in the ritual by the congregation as well as the clergy. The new papal rite excluded the congregation and was built around the glorification of the pope." (Richards, *The Counsel of God*, 121]. . . . In short, "the" Roman Rite was becoming a sort of infomercial aimed at focusing attention on the awesome person, power, prestige, and prerogatives of the pope. Not surprisingly, our first surviving description of a solemn papal Mass (*Ordo Romanus I*, probably produced in Rome sometime in the early eighth century) reveals precisely this kind of liturgy rooted in a "cult of personality."[11]

If the above two examples are concerned with the contemporary relevance of the liturgical reforms of the Council of Trent and earlier medieval liturgical history questions, the final example for this section is rooted more in Nathan's own lived history of the transition from the pre–Vatican II rites to the present. In response this time to the 2007 *motu proprio* of Pope Benedict XVI, *Summorum Pontificum*, and the accompanying "Letter of Benedict XVI" sent to bishops, Nathan challenges Pope Benedict's allegation that after the *Missale Romanum* of Paul VI appeared, "in many places celebrations were not faithful to the prescriptions of the new Missal. . . . which frequently led to deformations of the liturgy which were hard to bear." ("Letter of Benedict XVI," 21) In response to this assertion, Nathan writes, displaying his own wonderful sense of humor:

> No one would deny that the postconciliar liturgy—like the early eucharistic liturgy described by Paul in 1 Cor 11—has suffered its share of improprieties and indignities. Yet the use of MR [*Missale Romanum*] 1962 does nothing, in itself, to immunize either the liturgy or the faithful against such indignities and "deformations." I too remember the preconciliar *Missale Romanum*; it was the only Mass liturgy I knew throughout my childhood and young adulthood. That preconciliar missal (beautifully commented on by the likes of Pius Parsch and Aemiliana Löhr) shaped and nurtured my own

---

[11] Ibid., 66–67.

lifelong love of the Roman Rite. I have no personal animus against it, but I recognize that it needed a thorough *instauration*. Moreover, I well remember preconciliar "deformations" that were every bit as excruciating as any encountered after Vatican II's reform. I still remember the eighth-grade children's choir screeching its way through the Gregorian *"Missa de angelis"* at Sunday morning "High Mass," while a would-be organist accompanied the chant with harmonization that can only be called Brahmsian. I remember pitifully scaled-down Masses (which commanded higher stipends than low Masses!) with their propers "chanted" in an incomprehensible *recto tono* because the solo singer did not dare "delay Father at the altar." I remember nightmarish preconciliar Holy Week liturgies (including a Holy Saturday "celebration" that involved a pastor whose idea of what we now call the "light service" of the Easter Vigil was a five-minute quickie performed at a card table hastily erected in the sanctuary, using a birthday-cake candle and a cigarette lighter whose flint was blessed to light the "new fire."). . . . The postconciliar liturgy, therefore, hardly has a monopoly on "hard to bear," "arbitrary," liturgical "deformations." There were plenty to go around during the four hundred years between MR 1570 and MR 1970.[12]

(4) *Liturgy and Ethics or Justice*

In his definition of liturgy above, in describing "our work" in the world, the connection was made already between liturgy and justice in Nathan's thought. This connection, a traditional hallmark of the Liturgical Movement itself, is perhaps best illustrated in Nathan's most recent book on sacramental theology, *Meeting Mystery*. Here Nathan calls for the verification of Christian liturgy in the "liturgy of the neighbor." Further, he articulates here what can only be called a *theologia crucis* as a hermeneutical key for Christian ethics.

> Christian ritual is best understood as tablature or musical score—and that liturgical scores are "rhizomal, nomadic," limitlessly multiple in meaning and internally "indeterminate," that is, capable of verification only through the *exteriority* of ethical action. Christian liturgy

[12] Nathan Mitchell, "The Amen Corner: Summorum Pontificum," *Worship* 81, no. 6 (2007): 558–59.

begins as ritual practice but ends as ethical performance. Liturgy of the neighbor verifies liturgy of the church, much as a composer's score makes *music* only through the risk of performance . . . The slogan *lex orandi, lex credendi* does not, then, offer as much light as it may seem to promise. In spite of the tension between them, doxology and doctrine remain a cozy *ménage à deux,* each partner in the pair defining itself in terms of the other. But the deeper question is not whether faith controls worship, or vice versa, but whether either of them can be verified in the absence of a *lex agendi* (a rule of action or behavior), an ethical imperative that flows from the Christian's encounter with a God who is radically "un-God-like," a God who, in the cross of Jesus and in the bodies of the "poor, the hungry, the thirsty, the naked, the imprisoned," has become everything we believe a God is *not.* The ethical imperative implied by the phrase *lex agendi* breaks apart our comfortable "faith and worship" duo by introducing that subversive element of *indeterminacy.*[13]

In her introduction to Nathan's 2003 *Festschrift,* entitled *Ars Liturgiae: Worship, Aesthetics, and Praxis,* editor Clare Johnson, herself a contributor to this volume, had this to say about Nathan and "The Amen Corner":

> Nathan's is the persistent voice that has sounded forth from the pages of "The Amen Corner" bimonthly since 1991 in the liturgical journal *Worship.* In his tenure as author of "The Amen Corner" Nathan has provided informed and insightful commentary on myriad topics. Always abreast of the latest liturgical developments, Nathan effortlessly weaves together everything from politics, papacy, and pop stars to arts, aesthetics, and architecture, offering his readers a measured and critical view of the most recent happenings and topic issues of both a secular and sacred nature . . . Among Nathan's many gifts, arguably his greatest is his aptitude for synthesis. The ability to interlace artistically the historical, theological, ritual, aesthetic, and pastoral dimensions of liturgical studies is something that seems to come naturally to Nathan . . . A self-described "card carrying Vatican II progressive," Nathan has made no apology for

[13] Nathan Mitchell, *Meeting Mystery: Liturgy, Worship, and Sacraments* (Maryknoll, NY: Orbis Books, 2006), 38–40, 223–25.

his unceasing promotion of the ideals and vision of the Second
Vatican Council in his writings and work. He never hesitates to take
the opportunity to affirm the liturgical principles outlined by the
council, frequently advocating a vision of liturgy that recognizes the
active agency of the assembly in the liturgical event as both subject
and recipient of the sacramental action. Nathan has also been an
advocate for the use of inclusive language, the inculturation of the
liturgy, and the need for an active ethical response to flow from
the liturgy into the world.[14]

Johnson's words could easily serve as an introduction to this
volume, concerned as it is precisely with "The Amen Corner."

This volume, however, is not a *Festschrift* for Nathan written by
others in his honor, but a celebration of his own thought as he has
worked out his own liturgical theology in the pages of "The Amen
Corner" over the more than twenty years of his writing the column.
In part, this volume intends, as I have been doing in a smaller way
so far in this introduction, to let Nathan's words speak for themselves by means of reprinting some of his significant "Amen
Corners." But more than that, by means of introductory essays to
various "Amen Corners," by six of Nathan's former Notre Dame
doctoral students, five of whom wrote their PhD dissertations
under his direction, and five of whom, of great significance for the
future of liturgical studies, are *women* (!), Nathan's thought is put
into dialogue with their own developing theological reflections.
Hence, as the contributors were told, their introductory essays
were to be something like thirty percent Nathan and seventy
percent their own critical reflections on where Nathan's thought
had led them and where it might go in the future.

Reflecting that approach, this volume is organized into six
sections or chapters around various themes that appear from the
selected "Amen Corners" themselves. These "themes" have been
designated by a single word with the result that chapter 1 is entitled

---

[14] *Ars Liturgiae: Worship, Aesthetics and Praxis: Essays in Honor of Nathan D. Mitchell*, ed. Clare V. Johnson (Chicago: Liturgy Training Publications, 2003), x–xi.

"Body," chapter 2 is "Word," chapter 3 is "Spirit," chapter 4 is "Beauty," chapter 5 is "Justice," and chapter 6 is "Unity." In her introductory essay to chapter 1, "Body," encompassing themes of Eucharist and Real Presence so often considered by Nathan in many published forms, Kimberly Belcher's "Can a Mother Forget her Nursing Child? Flesh, Blessing, and the Eucharist" compares and contrasts her own experience of breastfeeding with being fed by Christ's own flesh in the Eucharist. But this experience does not become for her a "privileged *locus theologicus*" for the Eucharist, or some kind of arbitrary or exclusive model to be emulated by others as a superior method of mothering. It is, rather, the other way around, that the Eucharist illumines *this* experience of nurture and feeding with one's own flesh. She writes: "the ontological presence of Christ in the Eucharist enjoins on us a willingness to recognize the traces of presence elsewhere. A theology that seeks to find Christ in the Eucharist to the exclusion of Christ elsewhere will end with a Christ that remains nowhere. Rather, a living Eucharistic theology will lead to the conviction that God is remembered everywhere, that the whole universe, by which we are nourished, is the flesh of the Word, bearing the ineradicable traces of God's constant love. The Word so longed for the world, as Julian [of Norwich] sees it, that he fell into the Virgin's womb, becoming our Mother, and counts the suffering of the cross as nothing compared to the joy of being united with his beloved humanity."[15]

Joél Schmidt's introductory essay to chapter 2: "Word": " 'There is a Christ Who is to be Made:' Paradoxes in the Sacramentality of Preaching,"[16] takes as its focus the challenge of contemporary Christian preaching, a concern near and dear to Nathan's heart as well, given the rather poor quality of much modern preaching. Herein Schmidt writes that: "preaching is by its very nature a *creative* act. Preaching does not simply recite word-for-word the biblical texts or provide an historical exposition of Jesus' life in its original context, but rather relates the character of God revealed in Jesus' life "then" to the "now" of the congregation. This is an

[15] Below, 11.
[16] Below, 36–47.

imaginative, creative act that generates new meanings relevant to the current context which were emphatically not part of the biblical authors' original intentions. More specifically, such creative applications rely upon a schematizing function of the productive imagination in a kind of metaphorical transfer, that allows the preacher to see analogous similarities between Jesus' life then and the world situation now. Such an act, argues Schmidt with Nathan, is the creation of "fiction." That is, "Christ's presence in preaching is not primarily a matter of overcoming an inconvenient absence by re-presenting an identical lost Christ object. It is rather a question of how Christ is mediated through an *invented* object, what Ricoeur refers to as "fiction" since it does not have a referent in existing reality. As Ricoeur wrote, '*Fiction* addresses itself to deeply rooted potentialities of reality to the extent that they are absent from the actualities with which we deal in everyday life.'"[17]

Anne McGowan introduces chapter 3: "Spirit," with her essay, "Inspired Bodies in Action: Tracing the Spirit through Metaphor, Materiality, and Motion." Herein she underscores what might be termed a liturgical pneumatology, noting that: "while the Spirit has no concrete incarnation of its own and is often described using impersonal imagery, part of the Spirit's work in the world appears to be building bodies and drawing them together, demonstrating that matter *matters* to God. Finally, the Spirit emerges as an active force in almost constant motion, inciting dynamism in all it touches and prompting contemplation of the movement within the life of the triune God and the call of those caught up into this life through the sacraments (especially baptism and Eucharist) to be active participants in God's mission in the world."[18]

As noted above, Nathan's own definition of Christian liturgy contains reference both to ethics and aesthetics, that is: "liturgical art is our public gratitude that God is doing for us what we cannot do for ourselves. And there, perhaps, is where ethics and aesthetics

---

[17] Below, 43.
[18] Below, 65.

together can begin to change the face of worship."[19] Chapter 4: "Beauty," focuses on this relationship in greater detail. Clare Johnson's essay, "Portals to Transcendence," provides a theological foundation for this relationship as well as drawing implications from it for "beautiful" liturgical celebrations, namely, for the importance of a worthy *"ars celebrandi."* She writes that

> if liturgy is beautiful because it is an encounter with Christ the expression of God's beauty, and if liturgy is the expression of faith of those created in the image and likeness of the Beautiful, an assembly of the beautiful (as Christ's body at worship), then it can be argued that the faithful have a right to beauty in worship, and a right to become cocreators of beauty in worship by participating in the work of God which is the liturgy. What is less-than-beautiful in the manner of celebrating the liturgy thus must be avoided at all costs. If what is at stake is the faith life of believers, which poor celebrations risk weakening or destroying, then good celebrations, beautiful celebrations, are vital because the encounter with Christ's beauty in the liturgy is that which changes us/opens us up to desire the promotion of what we have experienced: exposure to God's beauty prompts us both to promote and emulate that beauty beyond the realm of the liturgical.[20]

Chapter 5: "Justice," is introduced by Katharine Harmon's essay, "Linking Cult to Care: Social Transformation and the Liturgical Movement." Herein Harmon picks up on Nathan's strong commitments to the relationship between liturgy and ethics, as noted already above. Reflecting her own doctoral work on the liturgical movement in the United States, Harmon writes that: "the vision of the liturgical movement never ended in its media, be it worship aids, missals, microphones, or vernacular translations. The liturgical movement was a *social movement*, seeking to bring the faithful to a deeper realization of their role in the great Mystical Body of Christ, both within the act of worship and as faithful members of

---

[19] Nathan Mitchell, "The Amen Corner: Being Good and Being Beautiful," *Worship* 74, no. 6 (November 2000): 557–58.
[20] Below, 96–97.

the baptismal priesthood in the world."[21] Such a social transformation, she notes, included a vast array of women, whose own roles in the American liturgical movement she summarizes and highlights.[22]

The final chapter, chapter 6: "Unity," is introduced by Melanie Ross's essay, "Church of the Second Chance: Reconciliation Among the Saint Maybes," a response to the selected "Amen Corner" for this chapter, namely, Nathan's 2011 column, "Gathering as an Act of Reconciliation."[23] Christian unity presupposes some form of reconciliation not only between but within churches today, and Ross asks the question: "Can we worship next to those with whom we vehemently disagree? Will reconciliation as Nathan describes it—a making *different,* a making *otherwise,* an at/one/ment, which results in a new relationship that changes both progressives and conservatives—be possible? This is the question of our age."[24] She answers her own question in the affirmative, saying: "T.S. Eliot beautifully captures this tension in his final quartet: 'From wrong to wrong the exasperated spirit/ Proceeds, unless restored by that refining fire/ Where you must move in measure, like a dancer.' We assemble around the eucharistic table week after week for precisely this reason: to be restored 'by that refining fire.' Ultimately, however, our gatherings can only be understood as acts of reconciliation insofar as we allow the light and heat of the liturgy to burn away our comfortable pretenses. . . . Like a dancer, the church must move in measure between the "already" of what God has accomplished through Christ by the power of the Spirit, and the "not-yet" of unjust inequalities and ongoing divisions. The steps of reconciliation are complicated, and the company of "saint maybes" is prone to stumble. Thanks be to God for prophets like Nathan

---

[21] Below, 134. Emphasis added.

[22] See her recent book, *And There Were Also Many Women There: Lay Women in the Liturgical Movement in the United States, 1926–59,* Foreword by Nathan D. Mitchell (Collegeville, MN: Pueblo, 2012).

[23] Nathan Mitchell, "The Amen Corner: Gathering as an Act of Reconciliation," *Worship* 6 (2011): 542–53.

[24] Below, 167.

who lead the way, singing the truth and reminding us that Christianity is a cockeyed religion of atonement, complete forgiveness, and second chances."[25]

Here, then, is a celebration of Nathan Mitchell as poet, liturgical theologian, historian, prophet, and wordsmith as he is revealed, especially, though not exclusively, through "The Amen Corner." And here as well in the introductory essays in this volume is reflected the fruit of Nathan's many years as a teacher and mentor of graduate students at the University of Notre Dame as they now take his insights and develop them further in their own work and academic careers. It is nothing other than a sheer delight to be part of this celebration.

Finally, on behalf also of the other editors, Timothy O'Malley and Demetrio Yocum, I wish to thank especially Mary Catherine Hilkert for her foreword, to all the contributors themselves, some of whom were not yet born, when Nathan first began writing "The Amen Corner," and, of course, to Hans Christofferson and Lauren Murphy of the Liturgical Press for accepting this volume from us and for seeing it through to publication under the Pueblo imprint.

Maxwell E. Johnson
University of Notre Dame
November 13, 2013
All Saints of the Benedictine Order

---

[25] Below, 172–73.

Chapter One: *Body*

Can a Mother Forget Her Nursing Child?: Flesh, Recognition, and the Eucharist

Kimberly Hope Belcher

The Problem of Sacramental Presence

I distrust magical thinking. My thoughts do not change material entities; the universe is not persuaded by my desires. Thus it is always with some doubt, as well as with some faith, that when I am away from my infant daughter and need to express milk for her to drink, I pause to remember her face, the smell of her skin, her sleepy cry. It seems like magical thinking—and then suddenly there is a familiar tightening, and milk flowing into the bottle. My flesh remembers her, and my conscious discipline of remembering her, remembering her sensual presence, seems to be only a way of entering into this deeper memory with which I cannot forget her.

Our culture, too, distrusts magical thinking, fears that God's presence to us is a subjective projection of our desires; yet the flesh of the world remembers God, even as God remembers the world and draws it deeper into the mystery of salvation. Such thinking is not magical thinking, but sacramental thinking, which dares to remember the trace of God's presence on the flesh of the world.

From *Cult and Controversy* to *Meeting Mystery*, Nathan Mitchell has been focused on two key questions that limn the boundary between liturgical and sacramental theology: how do we understand God's presence to us and our presence to God in Christian worship? And how do the sacraments provide a paradigm for the

Christian experience of grace?[1] Both these questions prove to be problematic in richly productive ways. On the topic of presence, God's omnipresence makes it difficult to discuss in what way the sacraments provide a salvific, experiential "real presence" of God. On the sacramental "difference," it is difficult to give an apology for a special role of the sacraments in the Christian life without provoking sacramental minimalism and a divorce between liturgical life and piety. Nathan's answer to both questions is an emphasis on the dynamic of "recognition," not as a merely subjective and intellectual phenomenon, but as a relational crisis to which both God and humanity respond.

If we envision the public acts of liturgy as a garden lattice that structures the vine of Christian identity, Nathan is really interested in the vine. Nathan saw that the theological vision historically applied first to baptism and Eucharist, then to the seven sacraments, then to the public liturgies and the church structure, would also apply, *mutatis mutandis,* to other aspects of Christian life. Thus, in Nathan's work the interstices of liturgy and Christian spiritual life shrink, until, for example, the rosary, once the ultimate competitor with the active participation aimed at by the liturgical movement, can be seen as a mediating practice by which liturgical celebrations become embodied and internalized by practicing Catholics and thereby influence doctrinal consensus and emphasis.[2]

Nathan's project is to eradicate our barriers between the sacred and the ordinary, the holy and the hopeless, God and the world, until Christians can recognize God breaking into the world in all things, and become food for the rest of humanity.

Blessing: A New Starting Point

If we are to seek "a new starting point" to think of sacramental presence, as Nathan suggests in his 2006 essay, we must reject facile

---

[1] Nathan Mitchell, *Cult and Controversy* (Collegeville, MN: Liturgical Press, 1990); *Meeting Mystery* (Maryknoll, NY: Orbis Books, 2006).

[2] Nathan Mitchell, *Mystery of the Rosary* (New York: New York University Press, 2009).

but false dichotomies between self and other, presence and absence, spirit and body, and liturgy and popular devotion. We must also discard the temptation of easy answers, and resolve instead to live within the difficult, even scandalous questions that provoke us to change. For the Christian life, and thus the sacraments, is *metanoia*, repentance, the turning toward God, "rooted—like dance—in physical craving and desire, in the body's urge to turn, to extend, to lift and stretch itself toward another."[3] This desire requires that presence always be balanced by a sense of distance, a space for another.

Nathan's reconfiguring of sacramental discourse depends on the insight that God's presence in the sacraments is, relatively speaking, a mundane thing. It is no great gift for God to become present in the things of creation. After all, as the Psalm says, "the earth is the Lord's, and all that is in it"; nevertheless, the Psalm goes on to ask, "Who will ascend to the hill of the Lord?" (Ps 24:1, 3). This paradox represents the incalculable gift offered in the sacraments: the challenge and the power to recognize God's presence. For God to be present is ordinary, but for God to be *revealed*—that is the sacramental gift. This does not mean that God's presence in the sacraments can be reduced to the ordinary presence in all creatures; if the sacraments differed from the ordinary only by our imagination, we could not *recognize* but only *project* God's presence. Sacramental presence is distinct from God's ontological presence in all creation in that it reaches out, addresses itself to human beings, and perhaps even shakes them by the shoulder and demands that they attend! To reveal God's presence, liturgy, like Jesus's parabolic teaching and action in the gospels, "summons recognition and response,"[4] and thus it is not incompatible with language that highlights the sensible absence, as well as the definitive and objective presence, of God among humanity.

Nathan turns to Jean-Luc Marion for a theological category that can accommodate both presence and absence, and returns with the

---

[3] Nathan Mitchell, "The Poetics of Space," *Worship* 67, no. 4 (July 1993): 363.

[4] Nathan Mitchell, "Present in the Sacraments," *Worship* 80, no. 4 (July 2006): 358.

concept of gift. A gift, for Marion, is not primarily a present nor a presence, but is a space opened where the other can come-into-presence, that is, where I recognize the other's presence to me. Certainly this way of thinking of gift is appropriate to the sacramental gift being given, whether we think of sacrament as Christ's power, as Thomas Aquinas did, or as Christ's promise, as John Calvin preferred, for both mean the participation in Christ's Gospel, which was marked by a radical kenosis, a "giving himself away." This giving occurs, as Marianne Sawicki argues, "at three tables simultaneously: the table of his word (in the gospel narratives), the table of his bread (broken for and among those gathered 'in his name'), and the table of the poor, where hunger and thirst become the 'baseline competence' needed to experience the Risen One."[5] Sacramental presence, then, is a participation in this radical gift-giving, a space opened for hospitality not only to my neighbor, but also to a God who may exceed but will certainly never meet my expectations.

If sacramental grace, then, is the grace of recognition, the prophetic gift to recognize what God is doing in the world, how does the liturgy nurture this grace? It requires of us the seemingly passive capacities for "hunger and thirst"[6] and for listening.[7] Yet the passivity is deceptive, for hunger and thirst (or more broadly, humility, a recognition of our own neediness) and listening are skills of potentially infinite depth that can be fully developed only through long practice. It is an act, a word that paradigmatically provokes our listening, our hunger, and our thirst for God's presence in creation: a word of blessing.

It is important to recover the concept of blessing in its most fundamental Judeo-Christian sense, as first a "good word" offered for God's goodness, and secondarily a recognition of the goodness of an object that comes forth from God and a prayer that God may continue to be manifest in this object. "Blessed are you, Lord, our God, King of the universe, who has brought forth bread from the

---

[5] Ibid., 355.
[6] Ibid.
[7] Mitchell, "The Poetics of Space," 367.

earth": to bless is first an act of recognizing God's presence, God's good gifts, among the fruits of the earth. This opens a space within our vision for God to continue to come-into-presence, for us and for all creatures.[8]

In the Eucharist, in the extended act of blessing that the sacrament is, the three tables of Christ's presence come together: "Book is bread is the needy little ones."[9] In the eucharistic feast, the word is proclaimed over the bread and heard by the needy; the bread is recognized to be the flesh of Christ given for the needy; the rich hear the word and take the bread and recognize that they are the needy, called to be slaves to the poor ones of God. This experience should reveal that all tables are God's table and call for every word we speak to be God's word. It should throw light on the ecclesial body of Christ revealed in all the rites of the Church, and the crucified body revealed in all human need. In this sense, "the presence of Christ in the Eucharist does, in fact, illumine the fundamental nature of *all* [human] presence."[10]

At the Margins of Life: The Work of Recognition

In fact, however, the transition from sacramental to mundane is not so simple. Human beings are always building up barriers to the full experience of God, always developing restrictions on what kind of God they will recognize. And, unfortunately, it is easy for these barriers to be imported into our eucharistic celebrations. In our complacency, we can even become bored with the table of God, and fail to recognize God's work precisely where it is most recognizable, as the Israelites did in the wilderness: "we detest this miserable food!" (Num 21:5). It is imperative, for a robust liturgical spirituality, not only that the eucharistic experience inform our

---

[8] See Lawrence A. Hoffman, "HaMotzi: The Deeper Significance of the Blessing over Bread," http://www.myjewishlearning.com/practices/Ritual/Prayer/Blessings/HaMotzi.shtml, accessed November 13, 2013.

[9] Mitchell, "Present in the Sacraments," 357, quoting Marianne Sawicki, *Seeing the Lord* (Minneapolis, MN: Augsburg Fortress, 1994).

[10] Mitchell, "Present in the Sacraments," 359.

quotidian life, but for the quotidian to inform our experience of God in the Eucharist.

This is where my experience of breastfeeding is helpful to me. Breastfeeding is quotidian, even tedious at times. Not every parent, not every mother, has the opportunity and ability to do it, however, and so it is a gift. Yet the gift can be concealed, quite effectively, at three in the morning when the baby has eaten every two hours for the past seven days and is now crying again. To reclaim it as a gift requires an act of recognition on my part, a blessing, an opening of this space and time as a gift I offer to another, to this other. No doubt this act of recognition is always imperfect. Yet an imperfect recognition suffices, because it is not my mind that nourishes the baby, but my flesh, and my flesh remembers yesterday's space and time, and the day before, and the day before. My flesh is much better at listening, hungering, and thirsting, than my restless mind.

Like music and pain, the act of nourishing can become "coded in the body." It can become a part of identity that may ignore—but also transcend—my conscious choices. If I awaken the "skin's memory" of my child, of her need, I run the risk of becoming a body out of control, milk flowing not into the sanitary confinement of a bottle but all over my clothes, my body, and perhaps my sense of self. Matter out of place. But Jesus's saying, "Anyone who does not come to the kingdom like a child will not enter," encouraged early Christians to see God as an out of control mother as well, grace pouring sweet and free and messy all over the face of creation, blessedly ignorant of the obvious distinctions between Jew and Greek, slave and free, man and woman.[11] Nathan, too, reminds us to see God's grace pouring out all over creation, messing up the boundaries we have made to clean it up, to keep things and people in their places. At the table of "God's breast," common sense boundaries are erased and threatening scandal is reinterpreted as nourishing freedom.

---

[11] Sawicki, *Seeing the Lord*, 27–50.

At its best, sacramental practice is a reminder that the whole world is God's breast. In the psalms, creation is not only God's artistry and playground, but perhaps most of all God's table, with food and drink fit for human beings and for all the other creatures. Psalm 104:20-23 even praises God's wisdom for the cycles of the day, which allow times for the predators to prowl and be fed by God as well as times for human beings to labor safely for their bread. The generosity of this recognition of the needs of dangerous animals is at odds with the usual human strategy of eliminating predators who threaten us or our sources of food.[12] If we allow this generosity, this willingness that others be nourished, to become encoded in our flesh, we will be able to resist the temptation to see the world as a zero-sum game, where for me to be fed, another must go hungry. We will be called to recognize the world as a place of nourishment and work so that all may be fed.

Is breastfeeding, then, a privileged *locus theologicus* for understanding the presence of Christ in the Eucharist, and by extension in all the sacraments? No! Such privileged points need to be strictly eradicated from our thinking. For such locations pit us against one another, reducing the mystery of parenting to "breast or bottle feeding?", the church to progressives vs. traditionalists, and even the celebration of our unity in Christ to a meal *or* a sacrifice. Rather, the celebration of the Eucharist is at the center, and is the only privileged place for interpretation. In order to verify that center (to "make it true"), we must follow the traces of the celebration outwards, until it touches even the margins of human existence, rendering the quotidian holy. Only then will we be able to return to the center with a restored desire for communion. How can we develop and interpret these outer traces, the places where the eucharistic life blossoms in the mundane? I propose that in order to do this, we need to see the Eucharist not only as Christ's body but as Christ's flesh.[13]

---

[12] Rosie Woodroffe, "Predators and People: Using Human Densities to Interpret Declines of Large Carnivores," *Animal Conservation* 3, no. 2 (2000): 165–73.

[13] On the early Christian use of "flesh," "fragments," and other words for the Eucharistic meal, see Paul Bradshaw, "Did Jesus Institute the Eucharist at the

Flesh: Presence in the World

Jean-Luc Marion assigns the limit of Cartesian anthropology to the notion that the human person is soul and body, where the body is mere matter like other matter, and the soul is a spiritual principle inhabiting it. This notion is flawed in that every observer exists in the world because of the "feeling flesh, never felt otherwise than as originally feeling."[14] Without flesh, there can be no body; that is, I only have access to any body as body (rather than as inert matter) inasmuch as my feeling flesh has "attach[ed] me to a body of the world, because first it will feel it, therefore it will be able to feel it like its own, indeed appropriate it as its own."[15] When I look at other human beings, I may be able to envision them as material bodies animated by spiritual souls, but when I examine my own experience I should see that the fleshy character of perception and the perceptive character of my flesh goes all the way down: "My flesh . . . before even being able to perceive itself as a possible external object in the world, it perceives; before even making itself be felt, it allows one to feel; in short, before making itself be seen and appearing, it makes me feel (myself) and appear."[16] Because my subjectivity is inscribed in the irreducible materiality of my flesh, I experience time, Marion suggests, not as "passing," but as "accumulating" in my flesh, especially in my face where I am revealed to the world. "Only time can draw the portrait of a face, since it alone sketches it. . . . [A]ccomplished time only manifests itself in taking flesh in mine, which it defeats, affects, marks. It takes flesh in me."[17] We can only perceive the past, Marion suggests, because both we and the world (faces and buildings) have been marked and altered by time taking flesh.

Last Supper?" in *Issues in Eucharistic Praying in East and West*, ed. Maxwell Johnson (Collegeville, MN: Liturgical Press, 2010), 1–19.

[14] Jean-Luc Marion, "The Flesh or the Givenness of the Self," *In Excess* (New York: Fordham University Press, 2004), 88.

[15] Ibid.

[16] Ibid., 87.

[17] Ibid., 95.

In the scriptures, too, the God who does not alter has allowed Godself to be marked by the taking of the flesh of the world. Of course this is true of the incarnation, but it is also a theme of Isaiah 66, where God is identified with the nursing mother Jerusalem:

> Rejoice with Jerusalem, and be glad for her,
> all you who love her;
> rejoice with her in joy,
> all you who mourn over her—
> that you may nurse and be satisfied
> from her consoling breast;
> that you may drink deeply with delight
> from her glorious bosom.
> For thus says the Lord:
> I will extend prosperity to her like a river,
> and the wealth of the nations like an overflowing stream;
> and you shall nurse and be carried on her arm,
> and dandled on her knees.
> As a mother comforts her child,
> so I will comfort you;
> you shall be comforted in Jerusalem.

Here Jerusalem nourishes the returned exiles of Judah, becoming the flesh of God's care, which is like that of "a woman [for] her nursing-child . . . the child of her womb" (Isaiah 49). The Christian proclamation of astonishing divine mercy was grounded in this recognition of the world as evidence of God's compassion, and such a cosmic spirituality is embedded in the Eucharist from the outset.[18]

Christians have embedded their memory in inanimate things; recently in smartphones, but more deeply in liturgical things: pilgrimage Madonnas, huge cathedrals, even God. "Lord, remember your church," we plead, knowing that we are the ones who have forgotten. Poets and mystics remind us of the immanence of the

---

[18] In the early period, eucharistic theology implied a nondocetic Christology and a contra-Gnostic anthropology; see, e.g., Louis-Marie Chauvet, *Symbol and Sacrament* (Collegeville, MN: Liturgical Press, 1995), 449–50.

spirit in the mundane stuff of the world. Julian of Norwich is even able to see excretion as the proof of God's care: "A man goes upright, and the soule [waste!] of his body is spared [hidden] as a purse full fair. And when it is time of his necessary, it is opened and spared again full honestly. And that it is [God] that does this, it is showed there where he says he comes down to us to the lowest part of our need." [19] The use of the word "soule" for waste here challenges, as does much of Julian's work, the notion that God cares for the soul, not the body.

Instead of a duality of mind and body, Julian proposes that human beings are made of substance and sensuality; the substance is like to and enclosed in the whole Trinity, and the sensuality was assumed by and is enclosed in "Christ our Mother" in his taking flesh, so that humans are "oned" to God in their entirety (chaps. 57–61). "Sensuality," like Marion's "flesh," implies the human experience of existence in a spiritual and sensory relationship to the world. The daring continuity of the flesh, that unity between soul and body, exemplifies Julian's theology of creation, which is all "beclosyd" (enclosed, enveloped) in God by its very nature. This radical anthropology is the unparalleled foundation for the theology of God's motherhood so often remarked in her work:

> The mother may give her child suck of her milk, but our precious Mother Jesus, he may feed us with himself, and does full courteously and full tenderly with the blessed sacrament that is precious food of very life. . . . The mother may lay her child tenderly to her breast, but our tender Mother Jesus, he may homely lead us into his blessed breast by his sweet open side and show us therein part of the Godhead and the joys of heaven. [20]

In the very fleshly body of Christ, inside the wound that is Christ's "breast" in medieval iconography and in Julian's vision,

[19] Julian of Norwich, *Showings* (New York: Norton, 2005), chap. 6, spelling modernized.

[20] Ibid., chap. 60, spelling modernized.

the whole spiritual realm is revealed.[21] The Eucharist is the ultimate witness that Jesus has taken flesh, not only that of the Virgin, but our flesh, and by the extension the world through which we know ourselves as flesh. The whole world is enclosed in God as the world is enclosed in the human body; notice how the image of "soule" as digested food in the intestines erases the boundaries between the matter that is the human person (body) and that coming from and going to the whole cosmic cycle (food, waste).

A theology of eucharistic presence that attended to this radical anthropology and the Christology it implies would recover the idea that the Eucharist, as the *flesh* of Christ, cannot be reduced to an inanimate object. Rather, we must take seriously the act of blessing in Christ's name that inaugurates his presence and the symbolic microcosms of the universe nourishing animal life that bread and wine are. The ontological presence of Christ in the Eucharist enjoins on us a willingness to recognize the traces of presence elsewhere. A theology that seeks to find Christ in the Eucharist to the exclusion of Christ elsewhere will end with a Christ that remains nowhere. Rather, a living eucharistic theology will lead to the conviction that God is remembered everywhere, that the whole universe, by which we are nourished, is the flesh of the Word, bearing the ineradicable traces of God's constant love. The Word so longed for the world, as Julian sees it, that he fell into the Virgin's womb, becoming our Mother, and counts the suffering of the cross as nothing compared to the joy of being united with his beloved humanity.

Conclusion

If both the God of the sacramental economy and the world blessed by it are "half clod, half sun, alive from the root," sacramental theology needs to be willing to go through the sacramental rites to find the places where the world, even in its characteristic worldliness, is busy remembering the presence of God. The common

[21] For a broader context on the understanding of Christ's wounded side as a breast, see, e.g., Caroline Walker Bynum, *Holy Feast and Holy Fast* (Berkeley: University of California Press, 1987).

table, the domestic church, the nourishing breast; none can be a privileged locus, but none can be excluded, either, from the task of remembering grace. For the act of recognition that epitomizes sacramental grace—"this, here! is the flesh of Christ"—is a radically inclusive act of blessing that dares to open mundane matter to the substance of God, knowing that the Word has dared to unite himself to human flesh. It is the Holy Spirit that empowers us to make this identification, to listen to one another as we follow this elusive presence out into the world, rendering it in different ways.

The sacramentality of the world does not make the sacraments *less* sacramental; rather, the sacramental act of blessing makes the world sacramental. Any definition of sacraments that begins from the desire to distinguish sacraments categorically from things that are not sacraments will end by dividing the church, for it is the defining characteristic of sacraments, paradoxically, to drag those things that are not sacraments in, to bless them, and to recognize in them and transform them into mediations of God in the flesh of the world.

"The Poetics of Space"[1]

This Earth is the honey of all Beings, and all Beings
Are the honey of this Earth . . . O bright immortal Lover
That is incarnate in the body's earth—
O bright immortal Lover Who is All!

This Water is the honey of all Beings, and all Beings
Are the honey of this Water . . . O the bright immortal Lover
That is in water and that is the seed
Of Life . . . O bright immortal Lover Who is All!

This Fire is the honey of all Beings, and all Beings
Are the honey of this Fire . . . O bright immortal Lover
That is in fire and shines in mortal speech—
O bright immortal Lover Who is All!

This Air is the honey of all Beings, and all Beings
Are the honey of this Air . . . O bright immortal Lover
That is in air and is our Being's breath—
O bright immortal Lover Who is All![2]

In this poem from her "Bee Oracles," Edith Sitwell imagined
Earth as a good-humored old woman—half clod, half sun, alive
from the root—who leans her dusty ear to the hive, where she hears
"her sisters of the barren lives," the "priestesses and prophetesses,"
sing their golden "hymn of being to the lost." It is an ecstatic hymn,
huge with hope, sweetened by the honey of earth, air, fire, water,

---

[1] This essay originally appeared in "The Amen Corner," *Worship* 67, no. 4 (July 1993): 360–67.

[2] Edith Sitwell, "The Bee-Keeper," in *The Canticle of the Rose: Poems 1917–1949* (New York: Vanguard Press, 1949), 238.

thunder, sap and sun. Sitwell seemed to know, as all poets do, that earth is an oracle—and our consciousness of it, a great poem spun over centuries by bards and balladeers. Sitwell recognized, too, that even in its most natural, unspoiled condition, earth is never simply "empty"—it is always *composed, arranged* by wind and sun, rain and ice, snowfall and footfall. We never get nature "pure." We get it processed by priestesses and prophetesses spinning nectar into honeycomb. We get it pounded and beached as white-sand silicone along Carmel's shoreline. We get it sifted, heaped and molded as dunes along the southeastern coast of Lake Michigan. We get it reddened by aeons of pressure, fire and wind in the Sangre de Cristo range, mountains crimson as Christ's blood.

Even the magnificent repose and stillness of the Japanese imperial gardens at Katsura are not *natura pura,* but deftly arranged landscapes of light and stone, green and grey, form and freedom. Nature is never empty—it is always *claimed* by the presence of something or someone. That presence is so fragile, yet so filling, that it seems, often, not to be there at all. Hence the Westerner's discomfort at the apparent "emptiness" of a Zen garden or a room prepared for the tea ceremony. In fact, of course, those spaces are so crowded with presence, so rich and rightly balanced in beauty and bounty, that to *add* one single branch or blossom would arrest the movement and ruin everything.

There is, in sum, a *poetics* of space, a perfect economy of rest and motion, presence and "emptiness," light and shadow—which transfigures our experience of rooms and buildings—and landscapes. We first feel such a poetics arising within our bodies, for we are instinctively, powerfully drawn *toward* some spaces (a river's waters rearranged by rocks and rapids) and just as instinctively repelled by others (a refuse-littered landfill). Our bodies know which spaces welcome the human and the humane. Unfortunately, the body's wisdom is often overruled by minds which tell us that burnt-brown naugahyde is beautiful and that "what this room really needs" is another chain-lamp or a painted-velvet portrait of Elvis.

As that superb—though much-maligned and often-ignored— document *Environment and Art in Catholic Worship* (hereafter EACW) puts it: "Our words and art forms cannot contain or confine God, [but] they can, like the world itself, be icons, avenues of approach, numinous presences, ways of touching without totally grasping or seizing. Flood, fire, the rock, the sea, the mountain, the cloud, the political situations and institutions of succeeding periods—in all of them Israel touched the face of God, found help for discerning a way, moved toward the reign of justice and peace." Like the covenant itself, the liturgical celebrations of the faith community (church) involve the whole person. They are not purely religious or merely rational and intellectual exercises, but also human experiences calling on all human faculties: body, mind, senses, imagination, emotions, memory. Attention to these is one of the urgent needs of contemporary liturgical renewal (EACW, ## 2; 5).

The church's worship is *embodied* worship; its spaces for celebration are shaped and served by *enfleshed* creatures, by the touch of skin against stone, and weight against wood. This essay will explore three aspects of what I'm calling (after Gaston Bachelard) "the poetics of space": the skin's memory, the body's wisdom, and the geometry of prayer.

The Skin Remembers: Anyone who has ever played a musical instrument (keyboards, at least) knows that remembered music is buried in the skin. I first learned Robert Schumann's A-minor piano concerto thirty-five years ago, and I've played it rarely since. But if I were to sit down at a piano today, my hands, arms, feet and back would quickly remember how that music goes—much more (and more reliably) than my mind. Musical memories are coded in the body as motion and sequence, pitch and timbre, rhythm and repetition. The same can be said of pain. There comes a moment, in suffering, when the mind refuses any longer to recollect its source or beginning:

> After great pain, a formal feeling comes—
>
> > The Nerves sit ceremonious, like Tombs— . . .
> > The Feet, mechanical, go round—
> > Of Ground, or Air, or Ought—
> > A Wooden way
> > Regardless grown,

A Quartz contentment, like a stone—
This is the Hour of Lead—
Remembered, if outlived,
As Freezing persons, recollect the Snow—
First—Chill—then Stupor—then the letting go—[3]

It is the nerves "sitting ceremonious like tombs" that remember pain's name and nature, its stupefying sameness and dull duration. Ask any amputee. She or he will tell you that the lost limb still feels pressure and pain.

Traditional Christian liturgies (and newly emergent ones as well) appeal strongly to the body's memory, to its tactile inventory. For in embodied rites, so much depends on what is *done*, not what is said. The liturgies of Lent, for instance, begin on Ash Wednesday with a ritual act of physical "disfigurement" that rearranges the head and face, painting them with ashes. In the northern hemisphere, these charcoal drawings, etched on winter-weathered skin, may well resemble death-camp art. As indeed they should. For repentance is not a state of mind, but the body's slow and deliberate turning toward the fire that burns, consumes, and cleanses. Unless you are willing to be "burnt, burnt alive, burnt down / to hot and flocculent ash," wrote D. H. Lawrence, you will never really change. *Metanoia*, repentance, is rooted—like dance—in physical craving and desire, in the body's urge to turn, to extend, to lift and stretch itself toward another. As *Time* magazine reported in a 1975 essay on the art of Mikhail Baryshnikov, "When he launches his perfectly arched body into the arc of one of his improbably sustained leaps—high, light, the leg beats blurring precision—*he transcends the limits of physique and, it sometimes seems, those of gravity itself.* . . . He is an unbelievable technician with invisible technique. Most dancers, even the great ones, make obvious preliminaries to leaps. *He simply floats into confounding feats of acrobatics and then comes to still, collected repose.* He forces the eye into a double take;

---

[3] Emily Dickinson, "After great pain, a formal feeling comes—," *The Complete Poems of Emily Dickinson*, ed. T. H. Johnson (Boston: Little, Brown & Company, 1960), 162.

did that man actually do that just now?"[4] *Transcending the limits
. . . "defying gravity" . . . floating into confounding feats . . . coming
back to still, collected repose*: isn't that what repentance is all about?

Or consider the liturgy of Christian initiation, where the body's
slumbering memories are abruptly awakened by the deep, cold
shock of water, aroused by the warmth of oil-slick fingers, and
enveloped by the welcome tastes of bread and wine. The theologians of the East sometimes likened the Spirit, at work in such
sacraments, to a skillful painter with brush in hand. And there is
probably no student of sacramental theology who has not, at one
time or another, read these words of Tertullian: "The flesh is the
hinge of salvation (*caro cardo salutis*) . . . For the flesh is washed
that the soul may be cleansed; the flesh is anointed that the soul
may be consecrated; the flesh is sealed that the soul may be
strengthened; the flesh is overshadowed by the laying on of hands
that the soul may be illumined; the flesh is fed by Christ's body
and blood that the soul may fatten on God. Since they have been
joined in such [saving] deeds, they cannot be separated in their
destined reward" (*De Resurrectione Mortuorum*; 8:2-3).

Or recall the old rites of consecrating a church and altar. As
EACW wisely notes, the Christian assembly's building is not a
barricade (keeping world out and *sacra* in), but "a shelter or 'skin'
for liturgical action. It does not have to 'look like' anything else,
past or present. Its integrity, simplicity and beauty, its physical
location and landscaping should take into account the neighborhood, city and area in which it is built" (EACW, # 42). Like skin, a
church *breathes*, interacts continually with its environment, becoming somehow (if nonverbally) "conscious" of the play between
light and shadow, open and closed, this season and that. And because it is skin, because it is a body, the old consecration liturgy
dealt with the building in ways profoundly personal and violently
physical. Like a public sinner or a heretic in some macabre
medieval fantasy, it was ritually set afire; like a neophyte, it was
washed with water and anointed with perfumed oil; like a slave, its

---

[4] Cited in Michael Murphy, *The Future of the Body* (Los Angeles: Jeremy
Tarcher, 1992), 111.

skin was indelibly branded with the marks of its Owner—wounds forever lit by cross and candle. The church was named, like any newborn—Mary, Ann, Elizabeth; John Mark, Matthew. Its consecration (as a body for the Body) was annually celebrated with dancing and feasting. For like the assembly itself, the church's skin remembers.

The Body's Wisdom: As a species and as a church, then, our deepest aspirations and secrets are inscribed in the skin, carved into the body. This is a source of both gall and grandeur for us. The galling aspects of the body's modes of memory are well recorded in this poem of Anne Sexton:

> We are all earthworms
> digging into our wrinkles.
> We live beneath the ground
> and if Christ should come in the form of a plow
> and dig a furrow and push us up into the day
> we earthworms would be blinded by the sudden light
> and writhe in our distress.[5]

But the body is not only a chronicler of pain; it is also a chamber of grandeur which opens onto the whole history of our species' search for truth and meaning. For these latter are not simply objects of the mind; they arise within the body. What Carl Gustav Jung first called "archetypes" (in 1919) are not only patterns of thought and cognition, they are patterns of *bodily* action that dispose us toward *ritual* explorations of our conflicts and *ritual* solutions to our problems. As Jung himself noted, archetypes are not only "images and emotions," they are "*systems of readiness for action.*" Archetypes are more than "inherited ideas"; they are *patterns of bodily behavior*—biologically rooted, inborn responses that cause certain kinds of wasps to sting the motor ganglion of caterpillars, that help certain species of eels to find their way to Bermuda, that cause seven-week-old human babies to wave their arm *for purely*

---

[5] Anne Sexton, "The Wall," in *The Awful Rowing toward God* (Boston: Houghton Mifflin, 1975), 46–47.

symbolic reasons. Each of us, as Anthony Stevens has noted, is born with an "archetypal endowment," a built-in biological clock that encompasses the whole life-cycle of our species—"being mothered, establishing a place in the social hierarchy, courting, marrying, child-rearing, hunting, gathering, fighting, participating in religious rituals, assuming the cultural responsibilities of advanced maturity, senility, and preparation for death."[6]

As Stevens explains elsewhere, the *ritual embodiment* of archetypal images and patterns—in puberty rites, for instance, or in other initiatory scenarios—breaks through psychic "log jams," overturns the *status quo* and so promotes the personal and social changes necessary for the survival of individuals and groups.[7] Such initiatory rites, Stevens notes, evidently became essential in the evolution of human cultures because "individual willingness to submit to the demands and disciplines of outer reality is not something which occurs automatically with the normal processes of growth. It has to be imposed with sufficient determination to overcome . . . 'the renegade tendency,' that combination of inertia, fear, and resistance to change which characterizes the Trickster, who clings to the *status quo* and . . . accepts no discipline other than his own experimental attitude to life."[8]

Somewhere along the line, in other words, the micro-history of the individual has to be grafted onto the macro-history of the tribe. This grafting is first and foremost a *physical* act. "Bring the body— the mind will follow." That is the reason why, in many traditional cultures, pubescent boys are taken into the bush to be circumcised (new identity, carved in the flesh), painted white (the color of death), and taught all the rites of adult manhood. It is the reason why young girls, at their first menstruation, are secluded, instructed in the mysteries of womanhood, then feted extravagantly. It is also the reason why Christians are initiated by means of an

[6] Anthony Stevens, "Thoughts on the Psychobiology of Religion and the Neurobiology of Archetypal Experience," *Zygon* 21, no. 2 (1986): 12.

[7] See Anthony Stevens, *Archetypes: A Natural History of the Self* (New York: Morrow, 1982), 147–49.

[8] Ibid., 148.

embodied ritual process rather than by means of a syllabus. In all these cases, what the tribe has to teach resides in its skin. As an old Zen proverb puts it, "There are some things that can be known only by rubbing two people together."

The Geometry of Prayer: In spite of all our rhetoric about prayer as a "spiritual" experience, then, it is in fact a celebration of the skin and senses. Perhaps this is no more clearly evident than in the postures we bring to prayer. Kneeling, for instance, does not call up the "idea" of humility or the "attitude" of adoration; it is the very act of humble adoration itself, inscribed in the body's motion. Lifting the arms in petition and praise does not describe a mental state; it *enacts* a relational reality, puts humans in touch with God—Giver of bread and breath, Shining Source of bone and sinew. As EACW (## 2–8; 55–62) suggests, ritual postures are not idle or optional movements intended to "heighten," "dramatize," or "solemnize" actions; they *are* the rite—they *are* the way the assembly experiences God in this time and space. A procession is not "about" God's presence or revelation; it is an epiphany of the Holy One, who marches before and behind a people—a Column of Cloud by day, a Pillar of Fire by night. Every movement through space *reconfigures* space, redraws the world's map, redefines the terms of our turning, in love and longing, toward God.

Ritual prayer is, then, a holy geometry—of intersecting bodies, processional motion, departures and arrivals; of smoke swirling in spiraling circles from censers swung in arcs; of bodies bent, arms extended, voices lifted. I am reminded, in this connection, of a wonderful essay by Robert Lawlor that appeared fifteen years ago in an issue of *Parabola* (Vol. 3:1 [1978], 12–19). Entitled "Geometry at the Service of Prayer: Cistercian Mystic Architecture," the essay discussed the extraordinary architectural qualities of twelfth-century monastic churches (such as the one near the tiny southern French village of Le Thoronet). So exquisitely constructed were these buildings that a pin dropped in the church's nave produces a full set of harmonic overtones. As the monks sang in those spaces, the walls quite literally breathed in speech and sound, vibrated with the pitches of rising and falling voices. Song set the building in motion. And even though Cistercian ideology championed the suppression of the *visual* sense (through whitewashed walls, clear-glass windows), it subtly fostered the acoustic and tactile. In effect, the monks, whose singing bodies vibrated in concert with the church's walls, received an acoustic massage! Perhaps that is why St. Bernard was convinced that if we are to see God "face to face," our vision must first be restored through *hearing*. "You should know," he told his monks in a chapter sermon, "that the Holy Spirit educates hearing before leading you to vision. 'Listen my child,' says the Spirit, 'and see.' Why are you straining to see? First, it is necessary to lend the ear. Hearing will restore vision to us if our attention is devout, faithful and vigilant. For only hearing attains the truth, since only hearing perceives the Word." For the early Cistercians, ascetic austerity was balanced by sensual singing, by the skin's recognition that God is known in the marrow before being known in the mind. For them, sound became light and food, charging the body with energy and infusing it with knowledge. Acoustically perfect spaces initiated those monks into the geometry of prayer. We should be so lucky!

"Present in the Sacraments"[1]

"In my beginning," wrote poet T. S. Eliot famously, "is my end."[2] Departures beget arrivals, and starting points shape conclusions. Such is the case not only if we probe the riddles of faith and life—where, Eliot assures us, "the end of all our exploring / Will be to arrive where we started / And know the place for the first time"[3]—but also if we try to think theologically. Where we start goes a long way toward determining where we will end.

This is particularly true, I think, when we begin to ponder if or how Christ is "present in the sacraments" (*Sacrosanctum Concilium* 7). Thus, for example, in his *Commentary on John's Gospel*, St. Augustine thinks sacrament starting from Christ's own power and agency: "Even though many ministers—just or unjust—may baptize, the power of baptism should be attributed to Christ alone, on whom the dove descended and of whom it was said 'This is the one who baptizes with the Holy Spirit.' Peter may baptize, but it is really Christ who baptizes. Paul may baptize, but it is Christ who baptizes. Judas may baptize, but still it is Christ who baptizes."[4] Eight

---

[1] This essay originally appeared in "The Amen Corner," *Worship* 80, no. 4 (July 2006): 347–60.

[2] Just as famously, Eliot reverses his aphorism at the end of his second Quartet, "East Coker" ("In my end is my beginning"). See *Four Quartets* (New York: Harcourt, Brace, Jovanovich Harvest, 1971), lines 1 and 209, pp. 23 and 32, respectively.

[3] Eliot, *Four Quartets*, "Little Gidding," lines 240–42, p. 59.

[4] *Tractatus in Ioannem*, 6.7; my translation. Clearly, Augustine was concerned about both the unity of baptism (many different ministers do not signify many different baptisms) and its efficacy (independent of the minister's personal life and character). This is the text on which the bishops at Vatican II based

centuries later, in the third part of his *Summa Theologiae,* Aquinas thinks sacrament starting from sign and cause.[5] And because Thomas sees a strict coherence between his Christology and his sacramental theology—sacraments flow and derive their efficacy from the incarnate Word—Christ is the indispensable source of a sacrament's power to sanctify.[6] In contrast, a sixteenth-century Reformer like John Calvin thinks sacrament starting from sign and covenant (promise). A sacrament, writes Calvin in the *Institutes,* "is an outward sign by which the Lord seals on our consciences the promises of his good will toward us."[7] Far from being an empty gesture, sacrament is, for Calvin, "a sign whereby God effects in us the promise that God signs and seals to us with that sign."[8] For that reason, he can write that in "the sacred mystery of the Supper," the Lord "inwardly fulfills what he outwardly designates."[9]

---

their assertion that "by his power," Christ is "present in the sacraments so that when anybody baptizes it is really Christ himself who baptizes" (SC 7).

[5] See *Summa Theologiae* (ST), IIIa Pars, 60.1; translations from the *Summa* are mine unless otherwise noted. As Louis-Marie Chauvet notes, this very first question in Thomas' treatise on the sacraments in the *Summa* reveals significant maturation and innovation in his thinking, particularly in his view of the relation between sign and cause. See *Symbol and Sacrament: A Sacramental Reinterpretation of Christian Existence*, trans. Patrick Madigan and Madeleine Beaumont (Collegeville, MN: Pueblo, 1995), 9–21.

[6] See the prologue to *ST*, IIIa Pars, 60: "After considering those things that pertain to the mysteries of the incarnate Word, one must ponder the church's sacraments, which derive their efficacy from the incarnate Word himself." See also *ST*, IIIa Pars, 60.3, corpus: "The word 'sacrament' is properly used for what is de-signed to signify our sanctification, about which three things may be considered: First, the very cause of our sanctification, which is the passion of Christ (*ipsa causa sanctificationis nostrae, quae est passio Christi*)." See also Chauvet, 20.

[7] *Institutes of the Christian Religion*, Book IV; xiv.1. English translations of the *Institutes* are taken from: John Calvin, *Institutes of the Christian Religion*, ed. John T. McNeill, trans. Ford Lewis Battles, 2 vols.; Library of Christian Classics, vv. 20–21(Philadelphia: Westminster Press, 1960).

[8] Nicholas Wolterstorff, "Not Presence But Action: Calvin on Sacraments," *Perspectives* (March 1994): 16–22; here, 16.

[9] *Institutes of the Christian Religion*, Book IV, xvii.5.

Each of these writers—Augustine, Aquinas, Calvin—shows us not simply a different starting point for thinking sacrament, but also a distinct view of liturgy. Hence, Augustine can tell his people that when they eat and drink the Eucharist they "become what they receive" and "say Amen to what they are," while Aquinas is preoccupied about the *dissimilar* way priests and people participate in the one priesthood of Christ—and hence about their dissimilar relation to sacraments and worship. "Liturgy," writes Aquinas, "consists either in *receiving* certain divine realities or in *giving* them to others. In each case, a different power [*potential*] is required, for giving to others demands action, while receiving requires only passive power."[10] Priests *give*; people *receive*. But Calvin's thought moves in another direction. Not surprisingly, he emphasizes the essential relation between sacrament and preaching, and is critical of what he perceives as late-medieval mumbling of the mysteries: "They [papists] thought it enough if the priest mumbled the formula of [eucharistic] consecration while the people looked on bewildered and without comprehension. Indeed, they deliberately saw to it that . . . nothing of doctrine should penetrate to the people."[11] Both preacher and people are actively engaged in sacramental liturgy because in each "what increases and confirms faith is precisely the preparation of our minds by [the Holy Spirit's] inward illumination to receive the confirmation [the seal of the covenant promise] extended by the sacraments."[12] So, Calvin concludes, a sacrament "requires preaching to beget faith."[13] The view of liturgy that emerges from Calvin's account of sacrament is clear. "To enter the liturgy, as Calvin understands it, is to enter the sphere not just of divine presence but of divine action. God, in Calvin's way of thinking, is less a presence to be apprehended in the liturgy than an agent to be engaged."[14]

---

[10] *ST*, IIIa Pars, 63.2. See also *ST*, IIIa Pars, 63.5, corpus.

[11] *Institutes of the Christian Religion*, Book IV, xiv.

[12] Ibid.

[13] Ibid.

[14] Wolterstorff, "Not Presence But Action," 21. Wolterstorff's essay explores several interesting affinities between the sacramental thought of Calvin and that of Aquinas.

Calvin's doctrine of God in the liturgy—an agent to be engaged rather than a presence to be apprehended—is actually far closer to Aquinas's than we might expect. In his mature discussion of sacraments in the *Summa*, Aquinas seems almost to avoid the discourse of *presence*, a point often missed by commentators. When he begins to discuss what we commonly call Christ's "real presence" in the Eucharist, for instance, Aquinas carefully poses his theme as follows: "Now let us consider how Christ exists [*existit*] in this sacrament by asking" (the eight questions that follow).[15] One could of course argue that existence and presence amount to the same thing, but Thomas is subtler than that. He knows that presence is a richly multivalent reality that can be used of God, human persons, and material objects.[16] Moreover, he understands that while we typically equate presence with place (with "being in a place"), such a common-sense equation is dangerously misleading. As counter-intuitive as it may seem, presence for Aquinas has no necessary connection with spatial location. Thus, for example, "what's known exists in the knower" and "what's desired in the one who desires," and hence God exists [*est*] in a special way in rational creatures who know and love him—but not as in a place (e.g., as water is physically contained in a glass).[17] In fact, Aquinas argues that while God "exists in everything [*est in omnibus*],"[18] this existence happens in distinct (but related) modes. Hence "God exists in everything by *power* inasmuch as everything is subject to his power, by *presence* inasmuch as everything is naked and open to his gaze, and by *substance* inasmuch as he exists in everything causing their existence."[19] God's "being in (persons and) things" is real, yet obviously not bound by space or time. Moreover, presence, power, and substance are not identical, and so Aquinas explicitly rejects the

[15] *ST*, IIIa Pars, 76.

[16] See, for example, *ST*, Ia Pars, 8.2-3. Aquinas assumes that these diverse uses of presence are related analogically.

[17] *ST*, Ia Pars, 8.3, corpus.

[18] Ibid.

[19] Ibid. English translation by Thomas Gilby in Thomas Aquinas, *Summa Theologiae*, vol. 1: *The Existence of God; Part One: Questions 1–13* (New York: Doubleday Image Books, 1969), 133; emphasis added.

idea that for God "to exist in everything by substance and by presence are the same thing."[20] It would be much more accurate, therefore, to say that "things exist in God rather than God in things (*'magis res sunt in Deo, quam Deus in rebus'*)."[21]

My point is that Thomas's thought about how God acts in the sacraments is complex and dynamic. As in Calvin's doctrine of God in the liturgy, sacrament has more to do with "an agent to be engaged" than with "a presence to be apprehended."[22] Thus, as we have seen, Thomas's discussion of how God is present (he says, "exists") in everything is grounded on an understanding of God's causality as *dynamic agency* rather than mere "efficient instrument" or "static (unchanging) source."[23] Presence must not be confused with place, time, power, or substance.[24] Moreover, Aquinas does not define either sacrament or liturgy starting from "presence," and even the phrase "real presence" is more our term than his. He thinks sacrament starting from *action* (God's agency at work in signs that "cause"),[25] and he thinks liturgy starting from *common participation* (by priests and people) *in the one priesthood of Christ.*[26] Thus, though we usually think presence means "occupying space (place)," it does not. And this has important implications for how God is met in liturgy. First, God's "self-presence" is *relational* (constituting the persons of the Trinity), rather than physical and spatial. As a result, God's self-communication happens not by filling up a place but, as Catherine Pickstock puts it, by *pre-occupying* space. God "occupies space even before there is a space, and occupies it more than it occupies itself. God is also preoccupied in rela-

---

[20] *ST*, Ia Pars, 8.3, obj. 2; English translation by Gilby (n. 18), 132.

[21] *ST*, Ia Pars, 8.3, reply to obj. 3; English translation by Gilby (n. 18), 134.

[22] Wolterstorff, "Not Presence But Action," 21.

[23] *ST*, Ia Pars, 8.3. See also ST, Ia IIae Pars, 32.3, corpus (where Thomas outlines the fundamental ways "something may be present to us [*est aliauid praesens nobis*]."

[24] This has significant ramifications for Thomas' later treatment of transubstantiation and Christ's distinct mode of presence in the eucharistic species. The issue of "eucharistic real presence" will be the focus of a later "Amen Corner" column in this series on "revisiting presence."

[25] *ST*, IIIa Pars, 60.1, 3.

[26] *ST*, IIIa Pars, 63.5, 6.

tion to space because He is displaced. He is permanently concerned with the Other. In Himself, [God] . . . is ecstatically preoccupied. So although God is not in a place . . . He is not non-spatial, for He situates sites themselves. And therefore He is the eminent (or pre-eminent) space of preoccupation, which gives space its job in advance of itself, which is to make space for worship."[27]

In short, God's kenotic "self" is always a going-out toward others, and God's "place" is the opening of space for worship, doxology, praise. God's "presence" in the liturgy is thereby revealed as a "making room for others," as opening a hospitable "doxological domain" where *others* may meet. Presence is, therefore, a relational category; it is always presence *of*, presence *to*, presence *for*, and hence it inevitably implies "otherness," a point to which I will return later in this column.

A New Starting Point for Sacrament

What I have just written suggests some of the possibilities and perils of thinking sacrament by starting from Christ's power and presence, from sign and cause, or from sign, seal, and covenant. Reviewing the tradition of scholastic sacramental theology, Louis-Marie Chauvet argues, in *Symbol and Sacrament*, that by seeing sacraments as a "direct prolongation of Christology," theologians like Aquinas produced a system that was logically coherent but reductive: pneumatologically weak, "excessively separated from ecclesiology," and obsessed about juridical and institutional matters (e.g., the priest's power to confect the Eucharist; the precise moment of consecration).[28]

A better starting point, Chauvet suggests, is the Pasch of Christ. "One of the most fundamental lessons of the Church's liturgical tradition from its earliest antiquity," he writes, "is that the point of departure for sacramental theology is not to be sought in the hypostatic union, but in the Pasch of Christ taken in its full scope

---

[27] Catherine Pickstock, *After Writing: On the Liturgical Consummation of Philosophy* (Oxford, UK: Blackwell Publishers Ltd., 1998), 229.

[28] See the discussion in Chauvet, *Symbol and Sacrament*, 453–76.

(including, as a consequence, the Church or the Christian fact)."[29] It is Easter that illumines all other Christian mysteries (including the incarnation) and helps to explain both the formation of the gospels and the churches' diverse but related liturgical traditions. Both gospel and liturgy read history "*backwards . . .* starting from the resurrection of Jesus, the Crucified."[30] In thinking sacrament we should begin from Christ's Pasch and so "locate the sacraments within *the dynamic of a history,* that of a Church born, in its historic visibility, from the gift of the Spirit at Pentecost and always in the process of becoming the body of Christ all through history. To start from the Pasch is to be obliged to build sacramental theology not only on the *Christological* but also on the *pneumatological principle.*"[31]

A Question not an Answer

Starting from Easter, however, does not mean beginning with trumpets, lilies, and shouts of victory. It means, instead, that *sacraments begin in scandal*—not the Christological scandal of two natures hypostatically united without confusion or separation, but a more radical crisis: "How must it be with God if we can confess God's full revelation in the human being Jesus, put to death in the name of the very law of God?"[32] Yet the crisis precipitated by Jesus' crucifixion and death cannot be separated from its twin: his *dis-appearance*, his *empty* tomb.[33] Easter is a question, not an answer.

[29] Ibid., 476.
[30] Ibid., 486, 489.
[31] Ibid., 487.
[32] Ibid.

[33] It is possible that the empty tomb narrative, which we first encounter in Mark 16:1-8, was not the oldest way for Christians to grapple with Jesus' fate after his death. Daniel A. Smith suggests that the Sayings Gospel Q may have employed ancient Jewish speculation about the "assumption" of a prophet or sage as the prelude to that person's later eschatological mission (as God's "Coming One"). Assumption and resurrection reflect different theologies (and also different conclusions about the fate of Jesus' body), though in some early Christian sources, such as the Gospel of Luke, these are combined. Acts 2:23-24 and 4:10 suggest resurrection as God's post-mortem vindication of Jesus; Acts 2:31-35 suggests the theme of assumption as "exaltation," and

Given the religious expectations of many of Jesus' contemporaries, an empty tomb would have meant no corpse available to be purified by decomposition, no bones to be readied for resurrection by the rotting process.[34] In a word, Easter deepened and amplified—it did not resolve—the scandal facing Jesus' followers in the aftermath of the cross.

What must it mean, moreover, "that God raised this Jesus who had been crucified in the name of God's law? *Who*, then, is God if God has justified him who was . . . condemned for having blasphemed against God's own law? *Does God then contradict God?*"[35] A sacramental theology that begins with Christ's Pasch challenges our assumptions about God's very identity, requires us "*to reach back to our presuppositions about God with a critical attitude*," and prompts us to ask "What sort of God are we . . . speaking about if we . . . maintain, in faith, that God offers God's very self to be encountered through the mediation of the most material, the most corporeal, the most institutional of the Church's actions, the [liturgical and sacramental] rites?"[36]

In a nutshell, the challenge facing the earliest Christians was how to "redesign" the figure of Jesus after his death and disappearance. As Marianne Sawicki suggests, the eucharistic table became the site where a significant amount of such "redesigning" went on as the gospel traditions were shaped and transmitted.[37] The table became, then, not only a cultic center where eucharistic thanksgiving

---

Acts 1:11 points to assumption as "expressive of eschatological significance" (Jesus who "went away" will come again). See Smith's article, "Revisiting the Empty Tomb: The Post-Mortem Vindication of Jesus in Mark and Q," *Novum Testamentum XLV* (2003): 123–37; here 133.

[34] See the discussion in Marianne Sawicki, *Seeing the Lord: Resurrection and Early Christian Practices* (Minneapolis, MN: Fortress Press 1994), 280–89.

[35] Chauvet, *Symbol and Sacrament*, 488.

[36] Ibid., 498.

[37] Sawicki, *Seeing the Lord*, 263. To speak of "redesigning" Jesus does not dispute the reality of his bodily resurrection, but asks how Christians came to understand his availability—and their access to him—following God's "raising him up, releasing him from the throes of death, because it was impossible for him to be held by it" (Acts 2:24). For an example of how such redesigning may have shaped Mark's gospel, see ibid., 294–95.

is made, but a site of recognition where Jesus himself is met "in the breaking of bread," and where bewildered disciples could gather in fear and hope. It was not a peaceful place. For if, on one hand, the table was "God's breast, where even little children may rest their heads" and Jesus' feet "where instruction flows sweet as kisses and clean as tears," that same site was also a "slippery slope"—at once a grapevine, a cup, a jar, a well of living water, an altar.[38] The Christian table became something "people have in common who think they have nothing in common": "It is the leveling of all flesh by the body's innate fragility and the ravages of time. It is a tabulation of race, class, and gender that reduces privilege to naught. It is the lowest common human denominator—hunger, disability, need—depicted in a riveted tableau of the universal death-bound condition. The Christian table is the home of the homeless, the larder of the poor. And theirs only."[39]

The table was thus a place of *risk*—for Jesus and for Christians. After all, *Jesus gave himself away at table*—and hence "table transactions signal the start of the diffusion of Jesus' body: in word and narrative, in cult and sacrament," and in surprising new social circumstances where the "first are last and the last are first."[40] By saying "This is my body . . . this cup is the covenant in my blood," Jesus began giving himself away at three tables simultaneously: the table of his word (in the gospel narratives), the table of his bread (broken for and among those gathered "in his name"), and the table of the poor, where hunger and thirst become the "baseline competence" needed to experience the Risen One. At these three tables, Marianne Sawicki suggests, we acquire competence to "see the Lord," an embodied, "composite competence" arising from the "new literacy of God's kingdom."[41] That third table—solidarity with the poor—is especially risky, for Christians are in the habit of viewing the poor as problems to be solved, clients to be managed and made more like us, eyesores to be cleaned up or cleared out.

[38] Ibid., 296.
[39] Ibid., 296–97.
[40] Ibid., 297.
[41] Ibid.

"We do not see," writes Sawicki, how the poor "are flesh of our flesh," transformed now "into the body of Christ, indispensable to the possibility of our ever looking Jesus in the face."[42]

To think sacrament starting from Christ's Pasch is thus to begin with Christian *praxis,* where alone we can discover the living site of Easter faith, the place where "resurrection show[s] up in what the early Christians habitually did."[43] "Briefly and broadly," writes N.T. Wright, "they behaved as if they were in some important senses already living in God's new creation. They lived as if the covenant had been renewed, as if the kingdom were in a sense already present, though . . . future as well."[44] This resulted in a refiguring not only of Jesus, but of that "symbolic world" which Christians now "focused upon Jesus himself" and ritually embodied in "baptism and eucharist . . . consciously undertaken with reference to him."[45] Christians thus received their identity from the "Easter sacraments," much as Jesus's own identity as God's Word made flesh was established by "working backward" from cross and empty tomb. The *praxis* of Easter in the symbol-rich rites of word, water-bath, and table gave early Christians "a set of resurrection-shaped answers": "Who are we? Resurrection people: a people that is formed within the new world which began at Easter and which has embraced us, in the power of the Spirit, in baptism and faith. Where are we? In God's good creation, which is to be restored; in bodies that will be redeemed. . . . What's wrong? The work is incomplete: the project which began at Easter (the defeat of sin and death) has not been finished. What's the solution? The full and final redemption of the creation, and ourselves with it . . . when Jesus reappears . . . What time is it? In the overlap of the ages: the 'age to come,' longed for by Israel, has already begun, but the 'present age' still continues."[46] Far from immunizing Christians

---

[42] Ibid.

[43] N. T. Wright, *The Resurrection of the Son of God* (Minneapolis, MN: Fortress Press, 2003), 578.

[44] Ibid.

[45] Wright, *The Resurrection*, 580.

[46] Ibid., 582.

from history or liberating them from its concerns, the new life embodied in sacramental praxis committed them "to living and working within history, not to living in a fantasy-world where history had in principle already come to a stop and all that remained was for this to be worked out through the imminent end of the space-time universe."[47]

Easter Disrupts

But one must be cautious about concluding that the church's sacraments somehow "recapitulate" the resurrection or that they represent the Christian's own "personal Easter." As Jean-Luc Marion argues, Easter *innovates,* and does so radically—so radically, in fact, that it "throws us forward" into "a world too new for us," where we "must relearn everything" like children or the old, "overcome by newness."[48] The fact that early Christians created *multiple* narratives about Jesus' postmortem fate—appearances, ascension, assumption, exaltation, empty tomb, church-foundation stories—disables the fiction that we can fully comprehend what it means to say God "has glorified his servant Jesus" (Acts 3:13). Thus, the gospels' Easter narratives not only "establish" structures, practices, and beliefs, they also disrupt and destabilize those "institutions."[49] As Marianne Sawicki puts it,

> The Gospels set things in order, but in a disruptive way. Jesus is copied [into stories] not in order to close the book on him but *so that he can overwrite* an ever-expanding community of human bodies. To imagine this, one has to keep in mind the superimposition of the 'three' Christian tables. Book is bread *is* the needy little ones. Each one keeps the others from closing in upon itself. Because of the book, we know that the bread is more than bread. Because of the bread, we know that the book is not about the past. Because of the needy little ones, we know what to do with the book and the bread.

[47] Ibid.

[48] Jean-Luc Marion, "The Gift of a Presence" in *Prologomena to Charity,* trans. Stephen Lewis (New York: Fordham University Press, 2002), 124.

[49] Sawicki, *Seeing the Lord,* 316.

The availability of Jesus as Risen Lord has to be understood as a relation of these three.[50]

Thus, our accessibility to the Risen Christ depends on breaking open "the tomb of text," an action accomplished day by day in the Christian liturgy, where the Lord's promise to "be there" (Matt 18:20) takes flesh in suffering and hoping members, in the "least likely," the littlest and most vulnerable.[51]

Traditional approaches to sacrament assume that the relation between word (sign) and reality (signified) is one of *reference*, and hence requires some sort of *causality* (whether instrumental/efficient or "symbolic") if sign is ever to *effect* signified and so result in a *presence*. But another way to think presence is possible, one that begins not with signs and signification, but with *gift*. As I have noted often in this current series of columns, Jesus' post-Easter "presence" is paradoxical; it is narrated through a discourse of departure, distance, disappearance, and absence. Luke's gospel, for instance, ends with Jesus departing (Luke 24:51); yet at the same time the evangelist provides an important detail. Jesus *blesses* (Greek, ευλογησεν) his disciples, and immediately after his being "taken up," they return to Jerusalem *"blessing* (Greek, ευλογουντες) God"* (Luke 24:53). In this scene, framed by acts of blessing, Jean-Luc Marion sees a new model for understanding presence. "The presence of Christ," he writes, "discloses itself by a gift: it can therefore be recognized only by a blessing"; it is a presence that can be seen only by being received, and can be "received only in being blessed."[52]

Christ's departing act of blessing thus beckons repetition on our part: "Presence depends directly on blessing: there where men do not bless the Father, the Father cannot make himself present. . . . There is no presence of God among men, if men do not bless him and the one he has sent. . . . Not that the blessing of men functions as the condition for the possibility of the presence of Christ . . . [Rather,] His blessing by men constitutes the condition for the

---

[50] Ibid., 318, emphasis added.
[51] Sawicki, *Seeing the Lord*, 316.
[52] Marion, "The Gift of a Presence," 129.

possibility not of the presence of Christ, but of Christ's being recognized by them. Christ can give the present of his presence without any condition; but so long as men do not bless God, this presence offered remains . . . rejected and disfigured."[53] The challenge facing disciples, then, is to "do as Jesus did," to repeat, "to bless to the point of acknowledging the gift of God. . . . Henceforward the disciples, that is to say the Church, that is to say humanity, finally reconciled with its destiny, . . . has but one function and one mission in a thousand different attitudes: to bless, so as thereby to welcome and acknowledge, the gift of the presence of God in and as his Christ."[54]

In sum, Christ's departing act of blessing discloses, paradoxically, the gift of his bodily presence, of his bodily belonging to God in the glory of resurrection, of his being "exalted at the right hand of God" (Acts 2:33). In the very act of blessing (and departure), Christ makes himself "recognized" by his disciples: *full disclosure and absence/disappearance coincide.*[55] Thus, "the blessing, at the heart of which the Ascension is accomplished, cannot be separated from the Eucharistic blessing."[56] The connection between absence (ascension, departure) and presence (blessing) is crucial. What Christ does at table cannot directly manifest itself as an "object" (i.e., an artifact at the disposal of onlookers and participants). Jesus' action is *provocative*; it summons recognition and response. The given gift that blesses (Christ's glorified, ascended body) awakens our own act of blessing (repetition). Our eucharistic praise and thanksgiving thus embody our grateful "recognition of the gift of the presence of God in *this* man [Jesus the Christ], because this man can give himself to the point of abandoning himself like bread [that is broken and] distributed, abandoning himself like bread, like *this* bread, can concentrate all his presence in a gift, whether in a fleshly body or by taking body of the bread, always without any reserve whatsoever. In blessing, Christ makes himself recognized as gift of

[53] Ibid., 129; the lack of inclusive language is present in Lewis' English translation.

[54] Ibid., 130.

[55] Ibid., 133.

[56] Ibid., 132.

presence; the consecrated bread incarnates the perfectly abandoned gift of a 'body given for [us]' (Luke 22.19)."[57]

So the presence of Christ in the Eucharist does, in fact, illumine the fundamental nature of *all* sacramental presence. The ascension, notes Marion, "does not signify the disappearance of Christ into the closed heavens, but the opening of heaven by a retreat that remains a mode of return. . . . The withdrawal of Christ does not make him less present, but more present than his physical presence permitted. Or rather, the new mode of his bodily presence (as the Eucharist) assures us, in the very withdrawal of the former body, a more insistent presence."[58]

To think sacrament starting from gift means that our sacramental action is, then, neither an attempt to retrieve the past nor a self-congratulatory "summons" of Christ to indwell our present. In sacramental worship we recognize God's *gift given* as recognizable only in the "liturgy of the neighbor," only if we seek the face of Jesus in the least and littlest, in "one who stands among you whom you do not know" (John 1:26). As a result, Louis-Marie Chauvet is quite right to say that sacraments (especially, but not only, Eucharist) proclaim "the irreducibility of God . . . to our concepts, discourses, ideologies, and experiences."[59] Sacraments "disclose, even while concealing it, the difference of God."[60] They are thus "the most dangerous of the ecclesial mediations of the faith," for "nothing is nearer to us than the other in its very otherness . . . nothing is more present to us than what, in principle, escapes us."[61] Because sacraments "resist every attempt at a definitive understanding" by the thinking human subject, they remain "the most radical mediation of the real's resistance to every attempt at a subjectivist reduction."[62]

---

[57] Marion, 133.
[58] Ibid., 138.
[59] Chauvet, *Symbol and Sacrament*, 403.
[60] Ibid.
[61] Ibid., 404.
[62] Ibid., 400–401.

Chapter Two: *Word*

"There Is a Christ Who Is to Be Made": Paradoxes in the Sacramentality of Preaching

Joél Schmidt

"As I write this column the days have grown visibly shorter, and the diminishing light seems to gather itself, morning and evening, into tight knots of mellow warmth that protest—however gently— the numbing approach of cold and darkness."[1] These words, drawn from the very beginning of Nathan D. Mitchell's career of writing the "Amen Corner," struck me as a very apt way to begin this short essay. For not only do they in fact accurately describe the meteorological conditions under which I myself am writing this chapter, but they provide a small glimpse of the creative artistry, the feel for the physicality of language, that Nathan consistently evinces in his writing and with which his regular readers are surely familiar. Not only did Nathan regularly incorporate poetry into his "Amen Corners" and other scholarly writing, he himself is a poet. Focusing our attention in this manner upon language and its evocative capacities seems appropriate in an essay devoted to a consideration of the language act of preaching. However, at the outset I must offer the caveat that this essay will in no wise venture a poetic tribute on a level with Nathan's own considerable linguistic *élan*. Rather, in this essay I shall attempt a more straightforwardly analytic approach, centered upon Nathan's emphasis in the "Amen

[1] Nathan D. Mitchell, "Sunday Morning," *Worship* 65, no. 6 (1991): 54.

Corner" that follows that preaching should express itself in "popular language." When carefully examined, this central affirmation in fact contains within itself indications of a number of important interrelated qualities that should be considered in future reflection upon Christian preaching, including: its historical/prophetic/incarnational character; its inherently innovative quality; the role of the productive imagination in preaching; the centrality of "fiction" in the sacramental mediation of preaching; and the physicality of language.

Perhaps the most central theme of the "Amen Corner" on preaching included in this volume is Nathan's argument that it is necessary to use popular language in preaching so as to enliven it, to give to preaching its requisite dynamism. Drawing upon the reflections of Fr. Walter J. Burghardt, Nathan protests against "the insufferably dull, bland, and abstract character"[2] of so much of the preaching at Sunday Mass, and argues that "[t]he church's official pronouncements do not *have* to be a pitiful pastiche of clichés and abstractions."[3] This is evinced by historical periods in which not only the words of novelists and poets, but even those of preachers (!) were considered creative, evocative, and exciting. In analyzing the reason for this, Burghardt argued that the preaching of this period was so engaging in part because it "built upon popular language."[4] The price of ignoring this necessarily imaginative quality of preaching is, according to Nathan, very high, for he links the ongoing dramatic loss of Roman Catholic adherents in the United States to the church's failure to meaningfully connect its preaching to people's experience of "ongoing life."[5]

Nathan's appeal to popular language involves more than simply "getting down" with the prevailing argot. It serves rather to highlight the essentially historical, prophetic, and ultimately incarnational quality of preaching. This historical/prophetic/incarnational quality of preaching is evinced in the "Amen Corner" that follows

---

[2] Nathan D. Mitchell, "The Art of Preaching," *Worship*, 82, no. 3 (2008): 270.
[3] Ibid., 271.
[4] Ibid.
[5] Ibid., 270.

in a recurring bipartite relation between a relatively fixed term and the historical dynamism of the contemporary situation. For example, Burghardt's analysis of the efficacy of mid-nineteenth century preaching is bipartite: the preaching of this period was exciting and creative because it "was rooted in a religious tradition and built upon popular language."[6] In like manner, when reflecting upon his priestly role, Burghardt commented that it simultaneously requires fidelity to "demands that are unchanging," and responding "to a church in motion."[7] In preaching, this double fidelity to that which endures and that which is changing often takes the form of an application or contextualization of the reality of God to the particular situation of the preacher and her or his congregation. This communication of what exceeds the present situation in the terms of the present situation is prophetic, for in the biblical sense prophecy is not primarily concerned with forecasting the future, but with interpreting the current situation from the perspective of God's enduring fidelity, love, and call to justice. Moreover, relating the reality of God to the particulars of a given situation is itself fundamentally an incarnational dynamic, in that there is a revelation of the divine excess in finite particulars. It is thus fitting that both in his comments on Catholic devotionals and toward the end of his essay Nathan turns to the theme of the incarnation, commenting in the latter case that the Ash Wednesday liturgy reveals how "God himself has strewn his own head with the dust of the earth . . . [God] has become flesh, flesh that suffers even unto death, transitory, fleeting, unstable dust."[8] What Nathan's turn to an incarnational theme suggests is that in preaching the Word takes on flesh in the words of the preacher, entering our lives here and now and making its home among us in the gifts and challenges of our everydayness.

Demonstrating the intrinsically historical/prophetic/incarnational quality of preaching naturally leads one to recognize its inherently innovative quality. As authors as diverse as Yves Congar and Paul Ricoeur have argued, relating the fixed text of the Scrip-

[6] Ibid., 271.
[7] Ibid., 262.
[8] Ibid., 274.

tures to the contemporary situation is a creative, analogizing act that generates new meaning.[9] According to Ricoeur, a distinctive characteristic of the biblical narrative is the interpretation of the significance of new historical situations in the light of past paradigmatic events. This is a kind of "typological" interpretation, the key feature of which is an insight into analogical similarity. As Ricoeur commented, what is crucial about the paradigmatic is precisely its generative power, its ability to inspire a following-after by means of "a transposition in situations which would be understood as analogical."[10] Moreover, such an interpretation is creative of new meaning, since the analogical insight opens new possibilities not present in either the original paradigmatic event, or in the current historical situation. On the one hand, issues such as genetic engineering, the ongoing crisis of the sixth mass extinction, and the particular configuration of structured inequalities in our present context were not envisioned in the original meaning of the biblical materials, and so to the extent that the preacher engages them she or he "adds" to the meaning of the Scriptures. As Gregory the Great succinctly stated, "The Scripture increases with those who read it."[11] On the other hand, to the extent that the paradigmatic pattern of Jesus' life and ministry clashes with existing historical realities, it liberates new possibilities in the present.

The necessarily creative nature of preaching offers some important implications for theological reflection. For example, consideration of the sacramentality of preaching will have to reflect upon how preaching, to the extent that the "matter" or *sacramentum tantum* is constantly changing, differs considerably from a number of the official sacraments in which the "natural resemblance" at

[9] For Congar's perspective on typology, see for example Yves Congar, *La Tradition et les Traditions*, vol. 1 (Paris: A. Fayard, 1960), 79ff.

[10] Paul Ricoeur, David Pellauer, and John McCarthy, "Conversation," in *The Whole and Divided Self*, ed. David E. Aune and John McCarthy (New York: Crossroad Publishing, 1997), 227, 240.

[11] Paul Ricoeur, "L'Enchevêtrement de la Voix et de l'Écrit dans le Discours Biblique," in *Lectures 3*, ed. Olivier Mongin (Paris: Éditions du Seuil, 1994), 325.

work is very stable, e.g., water's cleansing in baptism, or the nourishment of food and drink in the Eucharist. Here we are dealing with sacramental matter that constantly changes in relation to the vicissitudes of the historical situation, and that must constantly take new forms if it is to accomplish its intended sacramental mediation.

In addition, recognizing the necessarily creative nature of preaching calls for increased attention to the role of the imagination in preaching, in dialogue with perspectives in relevant disciplines such as philosophy and psychology. Such attention will move beyond general exhortations to be "imaginative" that generally construe the imagination's contribution to preaching in merely decorative terms, and instead develop greater specificity by identifying productive imaginative operations constitutively involved in the act of preaching on the sides of both the hearers and the listeners. For example, some contemporary psychologists have explored the role of imagination in analogy as "the fuel and fire of thinking,"[12] and in philosophy Paul Ricoeur's tension theory of metaphor can be used as an extended explanation of how the application of scriptural passages to new situations in preaching necessarily results in semantic innovation.[13]

Recognizing the operation of the productive imagination in the inherently innovative quality of preaching in turn has profound consequences for theological reflection upon the sacramentality of the word. Specifically, one of the most important directions for future reflection on preaching and its sacramentality will consist in moving beyond the consideration of sacramentality in terms of "presence" and "absence," to deal instead with the category of "fiction."

In some sense the themes of "presence" and "absence" constitute intrinsic and ineradicable components of any sacramental theology, from the biblical period onward. There is of course the experience of Christ on the road to Emmaus, in which the recognition of

[12] Douglas Hofstadter and Emmanuel Sander, *Surfaces and Essences: Analogy as the Fuel and Fire of Thinking* (New York: Basic Books, 2013).

[13] Paul Ricoeur, *The Rule of Metaphor*, trans. Robert Czerny, Kathleen McLaughlin, and John Costello (New York: Routledge, 2008).

Christ occurs in the breaking of the bread and at the very moment of his corporeal disappearance. There is the inward presence of the Spirit made possible, according to Johannine testimony, only by Jesus' absenting himself from normal, intra-mundane forms of being-there.[14] There is the ostensibly (but as the travails of Berengar indicate not actually) self-evident sacramental principle that it is precisely because Jesus is not now physically present in the same manner as during his earthly life that a sacramental re-presentation is possible.

Nathan has extensively explored the sacramental dynamics of "presence" and "absence" in his writing, from at least two distinct perspectives. On the one hand, the fact of Jesus' physical absence, twinned with the believer's *experience* of union with him, gives rise to intellectual efforts to elucidate the manner of Jesus' ongoing presence. The work of Odo Casel is one ultimately unsuccessful example of trying to overcome the "absence" of Jesus by speaking of the way in which not only his person but even his very historical acts are made present again, "re-presented" in Christian liturgy.[15] On the other hand, the fact of Jesus' absence, twinned with the believer's *desire* for union with him, can sometimes give rise to misplaced psychological attempts magically to overcome this experienced absence in the mode of a direct experience of him. According to Louis-Marie Chauvet, such attempts are the religious equivalent of a Freudian primary process by which people simply hallucinate the presence of the absent but desired Christ-object.[16] In contrast, Chauvet argues that part of spiritual maturity is consenting to "the presence of the absence of Christ," associated with recognizing the unavoidably mediated, sacramental quality of Christ's presence. Jesus must be absent (in one way) so that he can be present (in another).

[14] Significant in this connection is the fact that for Paul the Holy Spirit is precisely the Spirit of Christ, the inward presence of the risen Lord. See, for example, Romans 8:9-10.

[15] Nathan D. Mitchell, "Christ's Presence in the Assembly," *Worship*, 80, no. 3 (2006).

[16] Nathan D. Mitchell, "But Only Say the Word," *Worship* 80, no. 5 (2006).

Viewed from a philosophical perspective on the imagination, both Casel's and Chauvet's positions—notwithstanding their very different theoretical perspectives—operate within the same frame of reference of the image as copy. In his essay "The Function of Fiction in Shaping Reality," Paul Ricoeur used the language of "copy" versus "fiction" to limn some of the important distinctions between a reproductive and productive functioning of the imagination. For at the time of writing this article, Ricoeur judged that no one had yet provided a coherent theory of the imagination that adequately distinguished between these two very different imaginative functions.[17] The reproductive functioning of the imagination had been amply described, both in relation to memory's re-presenting of objects once present but now absent (Casel), and also in relation to the human tendency to hallucinate the presence of absent-but-desired objects (Chauvet). Both of these imaginative functions revolve around issues of "presence" and "absence." The fundamental commonality between such ostensibly disparate imaginative functions lies in the following: "If we put the problem in terms of a general theory of denotation or reference . . . we have to say that the image as copy raises no specific question of reference, since it is the same thing, by hypothesis, that is to be perceived *in praesentia* or imagined *in absentia*. Image and perception differ only as regards their *modes of givenness*."[18] Or again, "This defines the status of absence. Absence and presence are modes of givenness of the same reality."[19]

Such a notion of sacramental presence as "copy" is questionable in relation to any sacramental mediation (and is one which Nathan himself has critiqued by arguing instead for the futural eschatological dimension of sacramental mediation),[20] but it is particularly inadequate when applied to the question of the sacramentality of

[17] Paul Ricoeur, "The Function of Fiction in Shaping Reality," *Man and World* 12, no. 2 (1979): 123.

[18] Ibid., 124.

[19] Ibid., 126.

[20] See for example: Nathan D. Mitchell, "Christ's Presence in the Assembly," 255–56, 264–265; Nathan D. Mitchell, "Real Presence," *Worship* 80, no. 6 (2006): 557–59.

preaching. This is the case because as described above, preaching is by its very nature a *creative* act. Preaching does not simply recite word-for-word the biblical texts or provide an historical exposition of Jesus' life in its original context, but rather relates the character of God revealed in Jesus' life "then" to the "now" of the congregation. This is an imaginative, creative act that generates new meanings relevant to the current context which were emphatically not part of the biblical authors' original intentions.

More specifically, such creative applications rely upon a schematizing function of the productive imagination in a kind of metaphorical transfer that allows the preacher to see analogous similarities between Jesus' life then and the world situation now. As mentioned above, preaching thus evinces semantic innovation in at least two ways. First, it generates new meanings beyond those envisioned by the biblical authors. Second, it innovates vis-à-vis present reality since what preachers describe is generally not what "exists" but rather what "could be," namely, possibilities for action that could be realized in the present situation. When preachers exhort congregations to act on behalf of the oppressed, to greater interpersonal warmth and mutual aid within the congregation, and to a deeper spiritual life, they are identifying things that people could do, situations that could be, if people would allow the seed of the proclaimed word to bear fruit in their lives. Or, in less theological language, in their proclamation preachers project new possibilities that can change one's interpretation of, and engagement with, reality. What is at stake is the actualization of possibilities, a giving flesh to proclaimed virtualities.

But if this is true, then Christ's presence in preaching is not primarily a matter of overcoming an inconvenient absence by re-presenting an identical lost Christ object. It is rather a question of how Christ is mediated through an *invented* object, what Ricoeur refers to as "fiction" since it does not have a referent in existing reality. As Ricoeur wrote, "*Fiction* addresses itself to deeply rooted potentialities of reality to the extent that they are absent from the actualities with which we deal in everyday life."[21] Ricoeur wished

---

[21] Paul Ricoeur, "The Metaphorical Process as Cognition, Imagination, and Feeling," *Critical Inquiry* 5, no. 1 (Autumn, 1978): 154–55.

very clearly to distinguish between the *unreality* adhering to invented possibilities, as compared to the *absence* of something that really exists, or existed in the past, but at the moment is not present. Considered within a referential framework, in the latter case "absence" and "presence" have an identical status with respect to their reference to reality, the two terms differing only with respect to the givenness of the referred-to object. In contrast, the unreality generated by fictions is of a very different kind, in that the objects to which they refer do not presently and never did exist in reality as given. "In that sense, the non-existence of the object of the fiction is the true form of unreality. There is no symmetry between absence as a mode of givenness of the real, and non-existence as the contrary of the real."[22] Or in other words, in fiction we have to do with the "nothingness" of its referent.

The upshot of these reflections for sacramental theology is that beyond the paradoxes of Christ being made in some ways "present" as a result of his being in other ways "absent," in the sacramentality of preaching we have to say that Christ's presence is mediated by the "nothingness" of the preacher's fictive inventions. "Fictive" here has a very particular meaning, not at all to do with any resonances of "false" or "misleading." It rather refers to the fact that the new applications to current situations generated by preachers very often have a subjunctive status, being possibilities and not instantiated actualities. They identify things that people *could* do, situations that *could* be, in other words "potentialities of reality to the extent that they are absent from the actualities with which we deal in everyday life." Thus, "fiction" here does not connote or denote falsity but rather potentiality, undergirded by the conviction that the possibilities invented by the preacher function as an uncovering or dis-covery of more faithful ways of being conformed to the image of Jesus as the Second Adam, which simultaneously mediate the character and reality of God. Beyond issues of presence and absence, the paradox here is that the sacramental presence of Christ is mediated by the nothingness of invented/discovered fictional possibilities. Here we could cite the theme of the "plenifi-

---

[22] Paul Ricoeur, "The Function of Fiction in Shaping Reality," 126.

cation" of Christ in Yves Congar's writings, which is succinctly summarized in the provocative statement that "there is a Christ *who is to be, who is to be made.*"[23] What can it possibly mean to say that in preaching there is a Christ who is "to be made"? How is it that *our invention* can coincide with the discovery of *God's reality*? This is the paradox which haunts all preaching as a creative application and interpretation, and requires us to investigate how the sacramental presence of Christ can be mediated by the "nothingness" of the preacher's inventions.

Finally, as Nathan himself has acknowledged,[24] it will be important for future intellectual reflection on preaching to engage in more searching analyses of the dimensions and functioning of language in dialogue with relevant disciplines, including especially the physicality of language. As a poet, Nathan of course makes mention of this aspect of language at various points in his writing. We see this, for example, in the comments that "Poetry begins with a deliciousness of our senses . . . poetry is a way of thinking with our skin,"[25] and that there is a "music" to words that cannot be separated from their "meaning."[26]

In relation to the major themes previously outlined, recognizing the materiality/physicality of language draws our attention to a further paradox in preaching and its sacramentality. Namely, if the inherently innovative quality of preaching requires us to recognize the fictive quality of the sacramentality of preaching, the physicality of language adds the further paradoxical stipulation that the "nothingness" at the heart of the sacramentality of preaching is mediated by the very materiality of our oral communication. It would in fact be entirely erroneous to think that sacraments mediate encounters with God via physical matter, whereas "the word"

---

[23] In the original French, "il y a un Christ qui est à être, qui est à faire." Yves Congar, *Jalons Pour une Théologie Du Laïcat*, Troisième édition augmentée (Paris: Cerf, 1964), 458.

[24] Nathan D. Mitchell, "But Only Say the Word," 458.

[25] Nathan D. Mitchell, "Being Good and Being Beautiful," *Worship* 74, no. 6 (2000): 556.

[26] Nathan D. Mitchell, "The Weight of the Word," *Worship* 77, no. 4 (2003): 357, and footnote 3 on 357.

does not. In preaching, in liturgical language, in the confessional, a person works with words themselves as a physical medium (sound waves heard by a physical ear) as much as any painter with his canvas, or any sculptor with stone. Any future consideration of preaching and its sacramentality cannot afford to overlook this basic yet profound fact.

Moreover, giving sustained intellectual attention to this aspect of language can shed light not only on the fact that the physicality of language contributes to its sacramentality, but also some of the means by which it does so. For example, a consideration of the density of the quasi-perceptual mental images evoked by poetic language could help us to understand how these images contribute to the suspension of our ordinary perceptions and experience of the world (as in reading), so as to create a space for the consideration of the new possibilities evoked by the preached word. Many people have the experience in reading of losing track of time, of entering another world. Here the de-realization of the objective world corresponds with an encounter with the world projected by the literary work, and the reader's imaginative entrance into such a world is facilitated by the "images" evoked by the author's writing. In this perspective, the physicality of language itself contributes to the *epochē*, the suspensive distanciation from what *is*, that facilitates a person's engagement with the fictive world of the text. In other words, the "nothingness" in preaching that paradoxically mediates the sacramental "presence" of Christ is itself paradoxically mediated by the very physicality of language.

Looking back upon the argumentative itinerary of this essay, I began by focusing upon Nathan's exhortation in the following "Amen Corner" to use popular language in preaching. A careful examination of the implications of this fundamental point revealed a set of interrelated qualities which should be considered in future reflection upon Christian preaching, including: its historical/prophetic/incarnational character; its inherently innovative quality; the role of the productive imagination in the creative interpretation and application of preaching; and the centrality of "fiction" in the sacramental mediation of preaching, as compared to the significant amount of attention recently devoted to issues of "presence" and "absence." Finally, I closed with some reflections on the need to recognize that it is through the physicality of language that the paradoxical mediation of Christ's presence through the nothingness of the preacher's inventions is itself paradoxically mediated.

The topics covered in this brief essay of course do not in any way exhaust the avenues that future reflection upon preaching will need to travel. For example, given the inherently innovative quality of preaching, attention to the work of the Holy Spirit in preaching represents just one such important trajectory not at all treated in this essay.

Whatever the myriad aspects of preaching remaining to be discovered and reflected upon, I think that Nathan has aptly expressed the ultimate purpose of our attempts to speak well of God in a Christian context. This is, of course, that we ourselves become "God's words, God's new language in the world."[27] When we ourselves enflesh the reality of God which the preacher attempts to communicate in his or her words, a new dimension of the theology of the word is revealed. Namely, a life transformed according to the image of Christ is itself iconic, theophanic, and remains perhaps the most powerful sacramental mediation of the reality of God in a world that rightly wearies of Christian preaching insofar as it remains "just talk."

---

[27] Nathan D. Mitchell, "Seeing Salvation," *Worship* 76, no. 2 (2002): 174–75.

"The Art of Preaching"[1]

This past February 16, the renowned Jesuit priest, preacher, teacher, and theologian, Fr. Walter J. Burghardt, died at the redoubtable age of 93. Widely admired for his incisive, eloquent, imaginative homilies, Burghardt also served from 1946 to 1990 as managing editor—then editor-in-chief—of the influential Jesuit journal *Theological Studies*. His passing marks the loss of yet another pioneer whose work helped prepare—then implement—the Second Vatican Council's mandate to reform and renew Catholic worship and preaching. Not only did *Sacrosanctum Concilium* (SC 56) teach that "the two parts . . . of the Mass, the liturgy of the Word and the Eucharistic liturgy, are so closely connected with each other that they form but one single act of worship," but the restoration of the homily at Sunday Mass was itself among the first fruits of the broad conciliar directive for "a general restoration of the liturgy" (SC 21). Little more than a month after the Liturgy Constitution appeared (4 December, 1963), Pope Paul VI's motu proprio *Sacram Liturgiam* (25 January, 1964) decreed that starting on the First Sunday of Lent (16 February, 1964), the "norms of [SC] article 52 shall take effect, namely, that there be a homily during Mass on Sundays and holy days of obligation."[2]

In a marvelous memoir published in 2000, Fr. Burghardt, reflected on his (then) 59 years of ordained ministry:

---

[1] This essay originally appeared in "The Amen Corner," *Worship* 82, no. 3 (May 2008): 262–75.

[2] For the text of *Sacram Liturgiam*, see International Committee on English in the Liturgy, *Documents on the Liturgy, 1963–1979: Conciliar, Papal, and Curial Texts* (Collegeville, MN: Liturgical Press, 1982), doc. 20, pp. 84–87; here, 85.

My half century and more of priesthood have told me at least two truths about priestly fidelity. First, we must be faithful to demands that are unchanging: Apostles, disciples, and presbyters, we must preach the word and preside at the Eucharist, help shape Catholic communities and serve the wider human family. Second—what is more difficult and perilous—we must respond to a church in motion, a church on pilgrimage, a church that has asked many of us, halfway through our lives, to change. To change the way we think, the way we worship, the way we live. And without guaranteeing that each change will bring certainty to our minds, peace to our souls, joy to our hearts. Quite the contrary, I would be amazed if changes in the church—liturgical directives, women servers, parish councils, closing of churches and schools, drastic drop in vocations, sacerdotal dropouts and priestly scandals, a host more—did not pose problems, rouse resentments, provoke many priests to ask if this is indeed the same church that washed our foreheads and oiled our fingers.[3]

A church in motion; a church on pilgrimage; a church "that has asked many of us, halfway through our lives, to change"—and to change without resentment, with no guarantee that the results will be uniformly pleasant, peaceful, or problem-free. This, Burghardt believed, constituted the heart of the council's call to ongoing conversion, a radical change that must take flesh in *public behavior*, and not merely in the private precincts of the heart. Make no mistake about it, he wrote, ours is "a strange age, a frightening age," where those who minister in church and society must "try desperately to respond, in new ways, to the needs of a whole little world with more colors and smells, more problems and pressures, more anxiety and despair than the very human Jesus himself experienced."[4] A favorite biblical text of Burghardt's was Hebrews 5:2, "He is able to deal gently with the ignorant and wayward, since he

---

[3] Walter J. Burghardt, *Long Have I Loved You. A Theologian Reflects on His Church* (Maryknoll, NY: Orbis Books, 2000), 257. Fr. Burghardt had been ordained on 22 June, 1941 (ibid., 234). At his death, therefore, he had served just shy of 67 years as a priest.

[4] Ibid., 258.

himself is subject to weakness."[5] Gentleness, he recognized, is a quality especially needed as "the years roll on," as

> the body that once gloried in its strength wastes slowly or speedily away; as the mind that was so keen and fertile dulls and forgets; as the spirit that once prided itself on its own achievements looks back on its infidelities and bends in sorrow and love beneath the gentle hand of God. Yes, it is so much easier now to deal gentle.[6]

Church and World in Motion

Walter Burghardt's love of gentleness did not blind him to the sometimes painful impingements of a rapidly changing order in church and world. A late and fascinating chapter of his memoir chronicled a series of developments in both that complicate both the preacher's task and the prospects for a continued pastoral renewal of church life. American society, Burghardt argued—gently though persuasively—is increasingly pluralistic, secularized, and gripped by a cunning self-concern; but it is also better educated and better connected (through media that are "instantaneous, universal, and total").[7] Similarly, the Catholic community in the United States is polarized in its theological and liturgical preferences and its views of church authority; often fragmented in its response to moral and ethical issues; conflicted over what choices are best for celebrating Sunday Eucharist (music, postures, solemnity vs. informality); less confident in the integrity of its clergy; uncertain about how to practice social justice and to affirm women's rights to share power and make decisions in the church; and

[5] Burghardt, *Long Have I Loved You*, 258. The phrase "deal gently" is how the NRSV translates the Greek verb *metriopathein*. The distinguished classicist Richmond Lattimore translates this verb by the phrase "be moderate." See *Acts and Letters of the Apostles* (New York: Farrar, Straus, & Giroux, 1982), 225. The NIV (New International Version) translation of Hebrews 5:2, follows the NRSV ("deal gently"). The NAB uses "deal patiently."

[6] Ibid.

[7] Ibid., 328–31.

doubtful about the church's ongoing commitment to the economic conditions of the poor and marginalized.[8]

Burghardt's list of changes in church and culture was not a self-indulgent threnody over the "sad state of the world." He noted helpfully, for instance, that "secularization" and "secularism" are not identical:

> Secularism is an ideology, a view of life based on the premise that the religious dimension of human living should be ignored or excluded, and . . . has no place in the public square, in politics or law, in medicine or education. Secularization . . . is a process of increasing differentiation in society that results in the legitimate autonomy of institutions that may, over time, fulfill tasks formerly assigned to the churches (e.g., care of the poor).[9]

"A secularized society is not a secularist society," as the blatantly high profile of religious affiliation and discourse in American politics and public life attests. (The people whose voices are rarely heard in public are self-avowed atheists, not devout believers.)

Yet real problems persist. Especially troubling, Burghardt maintained, is the neuralgic relation between *magisterium* ("teaching authority") and *obsequium* ("submission")—revisited in Vatican II's Constitution on the Church (*Lumen Gentium*, 25), yet still an unresolved issue shaping debates about assent and dissent within the American Catholic community. He noted that the "restrictive and exclusive meaning of *magisterium* as 'the teaching authority of the hierarchy' began to develop among German theologians and canonists in the eighteenth century, became widely accepted in the nineteenth, probably was first used in a papal document by Gregory XVI in 1835, found ample use in the schemata of Vatican I, and from that point on 'became a household term in Catholic theology.'"[10] Yet precisely what is meant by the "ordinary"

[8] Burghardt, *Long Have I Loved You*, 331–36.

[9] Ibid., 329.

[10] Burghardt, *Long Have I Loved You*, 337. Burghardt referenced an important article about the history of the term by Ladislas Orsy, "Magisterium: Assent and Dissent," *Theological Studies* 48 (1987): 473–97.

magisterium of the Church—and what degree of assent it requires—is not altogether clear:

> Two meanings emerge from our sources. In the standard theology textbooks before Vatican II, ordinary magisterium meant that a point of doctrine was determined as integral to Catholic faith not by an infallible decree of a general council or by a papal definition, but through its consistent affirmation as Catholic doctrine by popes and bishops. Such is the understanding retained in the 1983 Code of Canon Law, canon 750. A relatively new use, in particular by Roman authorities, applies the term simply to "the ordinary and usual teaching and preaching activity of the hierarchy, affirming a point of doctrine which (as yet) cannot be said to be part of our Catholic faith because as yet the Church has not affirmed it with a decisive judgment." But problems arise when the same absolute obedience is demanded in both instances.[11]

Burghardt's point was not to protest (still less deny) the church's authority to teach, but to counsel against an ill-advised rush to define as dogma what may only be recent opinion. He also wished to challenge the "public affirmation of a U.S. archbishop that 'all public dissent is illegitimate.' "[12] Theology today is—as it was in medieval Paris—"a public activity, a ceaseless interchange, published critique."[13] Especially injurious to a healthy theology "are the 'hit lists' that abound, unofficial but influential dossiers of suspect theologians," a practice at odds with the remarks Pope Paul VI made when he established the International Theology Commission in October of 1969, pledging "to respect the freedom of expression rightfully belonging to theological science and the need for research inherent to its progress."[14] Indeed, the church's long custom of making certain saintly theologians (women and men) "doctors [teachers] of the church" attests that the ecclesial charism of magisterium is best exercised "in a context of open collaboration among

[11] Ibid., 338–39. The internal quotation is from Ladislas Orsy's article, cited in my previous note.

[12] Ibid., 341.

[13] Ibid.

[14] Burghardt, *Long Have I Loved You*, 341. For the pope's comment, see *Acta apostolicae sedis* 61 (1969): 715.

the competent."[15] Thus, Burghardt himself was appointed to the first (1969) International Theological Commission, even though he had earlier (1968) dissented from certain aspects of Pope Paul VI's position on artificial contraception in *Humanae Vitae*. As a result of his dissent, an American bishop compelled a college in his diocese to rescind its speaking invitation—and a "Midwest monsignor" put Burghardt on a list of "dissenting Modernist maggots."[16] Yet Paul VI valued and deliberately sought the theological opinions of this "dissident" on an international body whose principal purpose was "to advise the pope in doctrinal matters!"[17]

At the end of the day, Burghardt suggested, we are surely part of a "church in motion, on pilgrimage," but our community's sometimes bumptious dynamism depicts not a crisis of faith but a crisis of culture. It's important that we not confuse the two, just as it's important that we not treat (legitimate) secularization as (pernicious) secularism. The church's faith, after all, is guaranteed by Christ's "first gift from the Father to those who believe" (see Eucharistic Prayer IV)—the Holy Spirit, Giver of life. A significant portion of the crisis in the church today flows from a conflict of cultures rather than from deep-seated disagreement (or denial) about matters of faith. As Burghardt's contemporary and fellow-Jesuit Bernard Lonergan wrote shortly after the conclusion of Vatican II:

> Classical culture cannot be jettisoned without being replaced; and what replaces it cannot but run counter to classical expectations. There is bound to be formed a solid right that is determined to live in a world that no longer exists. There is bound to be formed a scattered left, captivated by now this, now that new development, exploring now this and now that new possibility. But what will count is a perhaps not numerous center, big enough to be at home in both the old and the new, painstaking enough to work out one by one the transitions to be made, strong enough to refuse half-measures and insist on complete solutions even though it has to wait.[18]

[15] Ibid.

[16] Ibid., 342.

[17] Ibid.

[18] See *Collection: Papers by Bernard Lonergan*, ed. F. E. Crowe, (New York: Herder and Herder, 1967), 166–67.

Searching for the Center

Nevertheless, the emergence of the "perhaps not numerous center" Bernard Lonergan hoped for may prove more elusive than he imagined. Meanwhile, the Catholic community's complex relation to cultures, in the United States at any rate, has continued to change in ways that may intensify—rather than ease—conflicts between loyalists of the "right" or "left," between Catholics whose "mentalities" oscillate between " 'strict' and 'elastic.' " [19] An extensive new survey published by the Pew Forum on Religion and Public Life on 26 February of this year details "the religious affiliation of the American public and explores the shifts taking place in the U.S. religious landscape." [20] Its findings present a somewhat challenging (some might say "menacing") picture of Roman Catholics in the United States. Overall, the Pew Study confirms that the U.S. "is on the verge of becoming a minority Protestant country; the number of Protestant denominations now stands at barely 51%." Even that percentage may be somewhat misleading, because among other significant discoveries, the Pew Study found that:

- Traditional "mainline Protestant churches, which in 1957 constituted about 66 percent of the populace, now count just 18 percent as adherents"—a precipitous decline over the past half-century;[21]

- Although "one in three Americans are raised Roman Catholic, only one in four adults describe themselves as such." [22] As a

---

[19] Burghardt, *Long Have I Loved You*, 332. Burghardt preferred "strict" and "elastic" to labels such as "conservative" and "liberal," "progressive" and "traditionalist."

[20] See "Reports: Summary of Key Findings," available online at: http://religions.pewforum.org/reports?sid=ST2008022501236, accessed March 18, 2014. This report was based on interviews with over 35,000 Americans age eighteen and older. All quotations from the Pew Study in this section are taken from the online report. The full report, in pdf format, is also available online.

[21] See Julia Duin, "Catholic Tradition Fading in the U.S.," *Washington Times*, February 26, 2008, page 1 of 2, http://www.washingtontimes.com, accessed March 18, 2014.

[22] Ibid.

story on the Pew Study in *The Washington Post* put it, "no American faith group has lost more adherents" among adults in the U.S. than Roman Catholicism;[23]

- Evangelical Christians have now become the largest single religious tradition in the U.S., "supplanting Roman Catholicism, which is slowly bleeding members;"[24]

- Losses in the Roman Catholic community, the Pew Study reports, "would have been even more pronounced were it not for the offsetting impact of immigration." It has of course long been the case that Hispanics form the most rapidly growing portion of the Catholic population in this country. The Pew Study confirms this trend, but also notes that among those who leave the Church, "Hispanic Catholics leav[e] at higher rates; 20 percent of them end up in evangelical or Pentecostal churches." Meanwhile, "one out of every 10 evangelicals is a former Catholic."[25]

- Thus, while the "Catholic share of the U.S. adult population has held fairly steady in recent decades at about 25%," according to the Pew Study, this is due to "the disproportionately high number of Catholics among immigrants to the U.S." This suggests a great deal of dynamic "movement" within Catholicism—characteristic of a "church in motion"—but the overall trend may well be negative. The overall percentage of self-identified Christians in this country stands at 78.4%, with "evangelical churches" claiming 26.3%; mainline churches, 18.1%; and Roman Catholics, 23.9%.

Catholic researchers responding to the Pew Study like to point out that immigration has always had a major impact on the Catholic population in the United States, at least from the early to

---

[23] Michelle Boorstein and Jacqueline L. Salmon, "In Major Poll, U.S. Religious Identity Appears Very Slippery," *Washington Post*, February 26, 2008, http://www.washingtonpost.com, accessed March 18, 2014.

[24] Duin, "Catholic Tradition Fading in the U.S.," page 1 of 2.

[25] Ibid. Duin is citing Pew Forum director Luis Lugo.

mid-nineteenth century onward. Others would point out that surveys about religious affiliation or self-identity do not always distinguish adequately between "believing, belonging and behaving," between basic adherence to a doctrinal tradition and (regular or intermittent) participation in church practice (e.g., liturgy). Still others argue that Catholics have a "higher standard" for what makes one a "practicing member" of the church than some other Christian bodies do.[26]

"What is particularly striking" about the Pew Study, Richard P. McBrien recently observed, "is that those who were once pejoratively referred to as 'lapsed Catholics' now constitute one of the largest single 'religious' groups in the United States. This is a pastoral reality which the leadership of the Catholic Church cannot ignore."[27] The question naturally arises: what response can or should leadership make to such data? Frantic appeals to circle the wagons or to reinforce "tradition" will probably not be effective. As Fr. McBrien suggests,

> Simply turning up the volume or increasing the frequency of our doctrinal and moral pronouncements does not constitute an effective response. The thousands upon thousands of Catholics who have left the church have not done so because they were unfamiliar with, or confused about, its teachings and practices. On the contrary, they were generally aware of those teachings and practices, but no longer found them credible or practical as guides for their own thinking and behavior.
>
> Such an assessment will not be warmly embraced by pastoral leaders who have convinced themselves that the truth of the church's most frequently cited official teachings whether on birth control, divorce-and-remarriage, homosexuality, the ordination of women, or obligatory celibacy for priests is so clear and compelling

[26] For a summary of these reactions, see Boorstein and Salmon, "In Major Poll, U.S. Religious Identity Appears Very Slippery," page 2 of 3.

[27] Richard P. McBrien, "The Pew Study on U.S. Religion," *Essays in Theology* (nationally syndicated column, March 24, 2008). Special thanks to Fr. McBrien for making the text of his essay available to me in advance of its actual publication while I was preparing this "Amen Corner" column.

that only a person of bad will could possible disagree with them, in whole or in part.[28]

It is possible, moreover, that the statistics summarized in the Pew Study show a deepening split between what Catholics perceive as the church's way of proclaiming the Gospel in preaching and liturgy and their experience of "ongoing life." In saying this, I do not mean to claim that "liturgy (postconciliar, preconciliar, both, or neither) is the problem." I draw attention, rather, to the insufferably dull, bland, and abstract character of much that passes for "preaching" at Sunday Mass. (Allusions to the latest "reality show" on television, to the fortunes of a particular sports franchise, to the weather, or to the personal biography of the preacher do not, I'm afraid, qualify as interesting.) The split I'm speaking of here results not from a crisis in the liturgy, or from a crisis of culture, or from a failure of faith. It results from a failure of the imagination.

Feeding the Flame

And this point leads us back to Fr. Walter Burghardt's work. Almost a decade and a half ago, Burghardt published an essay entitled "Preaching in American Words and in American Symbols," in which he cited the opinion of a professor of literature who felt it was high time "to speak truthfully to the Church about the quality of its rhetoric."[29] Discourse in the church, the professor had mused, "is so dull. In sermons, in social-action statements, in all the communication we hear within the Church, the guiding principle seems to be blandness."[30]

The almost preternatural dullness of churchly discourse may be one reason why Catholics have often been more loyal to their devotions than to their liturgies. If one looks, for example, at the collections of pilgrim songs sung from early medieval times by

[28] Ibid.

[29] Walter J. Burghardt, "Preaching in American Words and in American Symbols," in Francis J. Butler, ed., *American Catholic Identity: Essays in an Age of Change* (Kansas City, MO: Sheed and Ward, 1994), 53–68.

[30] Ibid.

travelers from every part of Europe to the famous shrine of Santiago de Compostela in northwest Spain, one starts to grasp the point. These were songs filled with arresting images—sights, smells, shells, spices, savory foods, robbers, shysters, flimflam artists—encountered along a journey that stretched from the royal abbey of Saint-Denis, just outside Paris, through the heart of France, across passes in the Pyrenees, toward Spain's Atlantic coast. They are multilingual songs—punctuated by snatches of Latin, Catalan, Hebrew, and Arabic—that embody the diverse cultures that co-existed even in the West for many centuries. Or take the numerous prayers—medieval or modern—addressed to saints (real or imaginary). We liturgists despise them as hopelessly wordy—tangled in their rhetoric, suspect in their theology, craven or sentimental in their affections. Yet these prayers let people have *real* conversations about *real* matters (their exasperating spouses, their snotty children, their noisy neighbors, their beloved parents, their torn ligaments). In speech, song, and bodily gesture these prayers—and the rituals that accompanied them—opened a space where the devout could affirm their faith while still complaining loudly about the rotting meat in their stews or the high price of pepper.

Preaching, Burghardt believed, should offer people of every time, place, and condition, a similar opportunity. A homily at Mass—or a pastoral letter from a bishop—does not by definition *have* to be dull. The church's official pronouncements do not *have* to be a pitiful pastiche of clichés and abstractions. "In the middle of the nineteenth century," Burghardt observed, "not only novelists and poets but preachers as well were often exciting and creative. Why? Because discourse in the antebellum period was rooted in a religious tradition and built upon popular language."[31] Even in our own time, sermons in America have sometimes proved gripping and powerful—embodying rhetoric and images that remain astonishingly fresh and memorable after decades of repetition. "Black preachers from Martin Luther King, Jr.," until today still "stir spontaneous amens from the sophisticated and the simple, from college teachers and the untutored. Why? Because their

[31] Burghardt, "Preaching in American Words and in American Symbols," 54.

sermons are not only 'rooted in a religious tradition' but 'built upon popular language.' "[32] Who among us does not hear hope stirring anew when we recall Dr. King's words:

> I have a dream . . . I have a dream that one day out in the red hills of Georgia the sons of former slaves and the sons of former slave owners will be able to sit down together at the table of brotherhood. . . . I have a dream that one day every valley shall be engulfed, every hill shall be exalted and every mountain shall be made low . . . and the glory of the Lord shall be revealed and all flesh shall see it together.

It is surely possible, then, to be theologically sophisticated, doctrinally exact, and imaginatively engaged in the popular speech of everyday life while faithfully preaching the Gospel. Take, for instance, the homilies of still another distinguished, twentieth-century Jesuit theologian, Karl Rahner. When writing professionally, Rahner's essays were excruciating in their exactness and detail, as anyone who's ever struggled through his famous three lectures on the Mystery of God in Catholic Theology can tell you.[33] There, for instance, we read: "If we called the 'Whither' of transcendence 'object,' we should conjure up the misunderstanding that it was an object such as is present elsewhere in the act of knowledge, and that we were dealing with the Whither of transcendence as if it were expressly objectivated by secondary reflexion upon this immediate transcendence. . . . The Whither of transcendental experience is always there as the nameless, the indefinable, the unattainable."[34] Uh, yes. Rahner's point was no doubt a crucial contribution to the (post)modern effort at reaching beyond the language of predication (whether positive and cataphatic or negative and apophatic) in order to affirm that God's life is not a riddle to be solved but a Mystery to be contemplated in ever-increasing

---

[32] Burghardt, "Preaching in American Words and in American Symbols."

[33] See Karl Rahner, "The Concept of Mystery in Catholic Theology," in *Theological Investigations*, Vol. 4, trans. Kevin Smyth (Baltimore: Helicon Press, 1966), 36–73.

[34] Ibid., 50.

wonder and love. But the language is technical, abstract, and, as part of a homily or catechesis would more likely bewilder than illumine.

Yet Rahner was also a master of the image. A case in point comes from one of his homilies for Ash Wednesday, which focuses on the ritual action of sprinkling or smearing ashes on the bodies of would-be penitents while repeating an ominous threat from Genesis 3.19: "You are dirt, and to dirt you shall return" (NAB translation). (In the postconciliar liturgy, the priest places the ashes and says either "Remember . . . you are dust and to dust you will return," or "Turn away from sin and be faithful to the Gospel.") Rahner began by reminding his hearers that "dust can tell us a good deal."[35] Almost immediately, however, he ups the ante on the image by refusing to let us take comfort in the familiar notion that "though the body decays the soul is immortal." *Dust*—disorder, nothingness, the discomfiting state of being out of joint, "in the wrong place at the wrong time"—isn't merely about the body; it is "an image of the whole human being. . . . *The human person . . . is dust.*"[36]

From the get-go, then, Rahner warns us, the human situation in the world is far scarier, far less secure, than we thought. Dirt, dust—"image of the commonplace, image of anonymity"—deflates our self-importance, ridicules our proud confidence as the "pinnacle" of creation. Dust?

> One fleck is as good as the next . . . one fleck is like the next, and all are nameless. What does it matter whether it is this dust or that dust. It is all the same. Dust is the symbol of nothingness . . . it lies around so loosely, it is easily stirred up, it blows around blindly, is stepped upon and crushed—and nobody notices. It is . . . a nothing . . . the symbol of coming to nothing: it has no content, no form, no shape; it blows away, the empty, indifferent, colorless, aimless,

[35] Karl Rahner, "Ash Wednesday," in *The Great Church Year*, ed. Albert Raffelt, trans. Harvey Egan (New York: Crossroad, 1994), 121.
[36] Ibid., 122.

unstable booty of senseless change, to be found everywhere, and nowhere at home.[37]

Homelessness, dust whispers, is the human condition, and our existence as dirt is the terrible sign that we can't fully connect with what matters most: the ones we love, the ones we've lost, the ones we long for, the Creating One who first bent over our bodies to breathe in them the spirit of life. As T. S. Eliot put it in his poem "Ash Wednesday," we sit lonely and desolate, "torn on the horn between season and season, time and time . . . / In the last desert between the last blue rocks / The desert in the garden the garden in the desert / Of drouth, spitting from the mouth the withered apple-seed."[38]

It is not a pretty picture. Nevertheless, this same Ash Wednesday liturgy reminds us "that God himself has strewn his own head with the dust of the earth, that he fell on his face upon the earth, which with evil greed drank up his tears and his blood . . . [God] has become flesh, flesh that suffers even unto death, transitory, fleeting, unstable dust."[39] Sprinkled with dust—smeared with dirt and its derangements—we embittered humans hear the preposterous news that God has become everything we are: "nothingness that is filled with eternity; death that teems with life; futility that redeems; dust that is God's life forever."

What is it like to hear such an outlandish announcement? Perhaps our reaction resembles Sarah's (Gen 18:1-15), as memorably depicted in a homily by novelist Frederick Buechner:

> She is an old woman, and, after a lifetime in the desert, her face is cracked and rutted like a six-month drought. She hunches her shoulders around her ears and starts to shake. She squinnies her

[37] See Rahner, "Ash Wednesday," 122, for this and other quotations from Rahner's homily in this paragraph.

[38] T. S. Eliot, *Collected Poems, 1909–1962* (New York: Harcourt, Brace & World, Inc., 1970), 93.

[39] See Rahner, "Ash Wednesday," 124–25, for this passage and other quotations in this paragraph.

eyes shut, and her laughter is all China teeth and wheeze and tears running down as she rocks back and forth in her kitchen chair. She is laughing because she is pushing ninety-one hard and has just been told she is going to have a baby . . . and her husband can't control himself either . . . They are laughing because with part of themselves they do believe it . . . They are laughing because if by some crazy chance it should just happen to come true, they then would really have something to laugh about. They are laughing at God and with God . . .[40]

The absurd, the improbable, the laughable: a face "rutted like a six-month drought," a nonagenarian body—decaying dust suddenly shining as it shields the splitting cells of an infant unfurling in the dark emptiness of her womb. Surely there is something about Sarah's body, her laughter, and our own dust-covered faces that sees and loves the God who "has strewn his own head with the dust of the earth."

Walter Burghardt's legacy was and remains a many-faceted gift to the church. His love of preaching—its perils, it pleasures—was rooted in his love of the people he served for nearly sixty-seven years as a priest. He believed, ardently, that those people deserve to hear the Gospel fully, imaginatively, and in living color. His own words about the costly grace of preaching are worth repeated pondering:

I am convinced that within the Catholic Church preaching remains at a low ebb, is less effective than it should be, primarily because preachers of the Word, specifically those ordained to preach, either see the sermon as a product that comes cheap or, recognizing its high cost, are reluctant to pay the price. Effective preaching, preaching that moves hearts and changes minds, is costly because, like grace, it costs me my life. Literally. An outrageous thesis? Hardly. I preach at a great price because preaching costs me my mind, my spirit, my flesh and blood.[41]

[40] Cited in Burghardt, "Preaching in American Words and in American Symbols," 62–63.
[41] Burghardt, *Long Have I Loved You*, 335.

Chapter Three: *Spirit*

Inspired Bodies in Action: Tracing the Spirit through Metaphor, Materiality, and Motion

Anne McGowan

On a trip through the southeastern United States one Saturday before Pentecost Sunday, settling in to my hotel room for the night and thinking about the following day's activities, I came to the rather melancholy conclusion that I was more concerned with fulfilling my *obligation* to attend Sunday Mass than standing open to the profound in-breaking of the Holy Spirit that Pentecost is meant to represent. The mission statement posted on the website of one local parish promised a diverse community, vibrant and spiritual worship, and a commitment to outreach ministry in the local community. Saddled with fairly low expectations nonetheless, I unexpectedly stumbled into a community of expert "croodlers." This assembly was attuned to the formation of community through embracing difference. The body of Christ gathered to worship that morning was indeed one of the most ethnically and culturally varied congregations I have ever experienced. To this day, I have no real certainty what historical accidents, intentional leadership, or surprise workings of the Spirit caused this little community to exist and thrive, but I knew after only a few minutes that I had walked into something special. I encountered a mix of Asian, Caucasian, Latino and African-American parishioners (both American-born and immigrant), in a small, out of the way Georgia town, living spectacularly into the reality of God's life where hospitality and doxology are intimately intertwined.

Community members shared their gifts to make the simple worship space beautiful, lead the congregation in song, and "make room" for the "other" in their liturgy and in the ethical extension of their doxology through service ministries in the neighborhood. The kenotic thrust of God's trinitarian life flowed palpably through this community that so obviously sought holiness while simultaneously celebrating humanity through power and vulnerability. For example, the community enthusiastically supported its young members who had prepared special music to praise the Spirit on this feast. Yet the Spirit's presence was also pervasive in the shelter one recent first communicant found in her mother's arms after abandoning her role in the procession at the preparation of the gifts. This assembly had learned "[t]o discover the divine in the daily; to meet the holy in the homely; to reach up by reaching out; to confess the Creator's transcendence by 'croodling,' [and thus] to perform [its] identity as human and Christian."[1]

The Spirit and several other entities to which it is closely connected—God's trinitarian life, the assembly as the corporate subject of liturgical action, and the intersecting "bodies" of Christ which the Spirit animates and propels into the world—lend themselves to being treated in a rhizomatic manner.[2] The Spirit suffuses, more often surprises than settles, thrives on uniting the seemingly incompatible (as in the union of humanity with divinity through the incarnation), and, like ritual more generally, resists any "process that can be systematically planned, engineered, implemented, evaluated, and then improved."[3] In the reflections that follow I will use Nathan Mitchell's work as a springboard to consider the liturgical role of the Holy Spirit from the perspectives of metaphor, materiality, and motion. Metaphor capitalizes on *difference* and *unlikeness* to spark new insights; similarly, the Spirit's otherness

[1] See Nathan D. Mitchell, "Croodling," *Worship* 78, no. 2 (2004): 165–75; quotation from 174.

[2] On worship as "applied rhizomatics," see especially the first chapter of Nathan D. Mitchell, *Meeting Mystery: Liturgy, Worship, Sacraments* (Maryknoll, NY: Orbis Books, 2006).

[3] Nathan D. Mitchell, "Ritual as Ars Amatoria," *Worship* 75, no. 3 (2001): 259.

and elusive activity can be captured better through the tangential approach of metaphoric speech than the direct discourse of logical analysis. While the Spirit has no concrete incarnation of its own and is often described using impersonal imagery, part of the Spirit's work in the world appears to be building bodies and drawing them together, demonstrating that matter *matters* to God. Finally, the Spirit emerges as an active force in almost constant motion, inciting dynamism in all it touches and prompting contemplation of the movement within the life of the triune God and the call of those caught up into this life through the sacraments (especially baptism and Eucharist) to be active participants in God's mission in the world.

Metaphor: Speaking Spirit in Mystery

In many of his essays, Mitchell exploits the potential of poetic language to say something about God that would fall flat if cast in prosaic terms. Whether exegeting the symbolism of a short story by Flannery O'Connor or a painting by Caravaggio or a liturgical prayer or the native "speech" of the body, Mitchell attends to the capacity of metaphor to give voice, however inadequately, to what otherwise could not be said at all and to the metaphoric mode through which God's Word is inscribed on human bodies in the liturgical context.[4] For the paschal mystery irrevocably disrupts the normal chatter of human language and necessitates a different way of speaking. Mitchell writes, "The mystery of God's life is a communion based on *kenosis,* on mutual outpouring, one Person to Another: the Unsayable, the Said, and the Breath that unites them. . . . Through Christ's *kenosis,* through the Easter mystery, our human language has been forever—and irreducibly—revolutionized."[5]

As a rather nebulous entity in the Christian tradition, the Spirit especially breathes through the language of metaphor—since it

[4] For a fuller discussion of metaphor in Christian worship, see Mitchell, *Meeting Mystery,* 189–227.

[5] Nathan D. Mitchell, "The Unsayable Said," *Worship* 78, no. 3 (2004): 278.

would be nearly impossible to speak of the Spirit otherwise. Despite the availability of evocative biblical metaphors for the Spirit (e.g., wind, breath, fire) the Western tradition in general (and the Catholic tradition in particular) has often been accused of neglecting the Spirit in its theology and worship.[6] However, metaphors for the Holy Spirit that have flourished even in the Western tradition in the past can be explored as fertile avenues toward a more expansive understanding of the Spirit's role as making room for diverse people to gather and then sustaining these same people in their croodling communion.[7] For example, Catherine of Siena's image of the Holy Spirit as a waiter who serves the food of the incarnate Word at the table of God—both in this life and in the heavenly banquet—set against the backdrop of the eucharistic liturgy, underscores the intimate link between the "two tables" of Word and Eucharist and the Spirit's service in preparing the feast and whetting the appetite of the Christian people.

In addition to images that arise within the Christian tradition, other metaphors for the Spirit emerging from non-Western cultures might fruitfully be tapped to let the Spirit speak still more polyphonically to the life experiences and worldviews of Christians who belong to a truly global Church. Certainly, the resonance that "Holy Spirit" has in liturgical texts and elsewhere will be conditioned by the linguistic and cultural connotations of the concept of "spirit" in a particular society. As British theologian Kirsteen Kim notes based on her extensive experience with Asian spiritualities, awareness of "varied pre-understandings of 'spirit' [can] greatly enrich pneumatological reflection."[8] To cite just a few examples, Spirit metaphors drawn from the cultures of Asia, Latin America,

---

[6] For a critique of this view that insists on a more qualified assessment, see Teresa Berger, "Veni Creator Spiritus: The Elusive Real Presence of the Spirit in the Catholic Tradition," in *The Spirit in Worship—Worship in the Spirit*, ed. Teresa Berger and Bryan D. Spinks (Collegeville, MN: Liturgical Press, 2009), 141–54.

[7] See, for example, Elizabeth Dreyer, *Holy Power, Holy Presence: Rediscovering Medieval Metaphors for the Holy Spirit* (Mahwah, NJ: Paulist Press, 2007).

[8] Kirsteen Kim, *The Holy Spirit in the World: A Global Conversation* (London: SPCK, 2007), 141.

and Africa serve to illustrate how a metaphoric approach might contribute to a more capacious understanding of the Spirit as, respectively, a kettle that transforms its contents and sustains the life of those gathered around it, the liberator of the poor and oppressed and creator of just communities, and the bond which unites the communion of saints through *anamnesis* of ancestors in the faith.

"In a typical Asian view of life—if there is anything 'typical' in such a vast continent," observes Veli-Matti Kärkkäinen, "what is spiritual is primary while the material world is secondary, a feature that runs contrary to much in the West."[9] While characterized by a pluriformity of religious traditions, the idea of a God as Spirit or a Heavenly Spirit or as one spirit, perhaps the *supreme* Spirit, in a world inhabited by many spirits is quite at home in many Asian religions, and this provides a backdrop for understanding the *Holy* Spirit in the Christian tradition, especially the Holy Spirit in a Johannine mode—"God is spirit" (John 4:24).[10] The Korean theologian Jung Young Lee describes the Holy Spirit as a feminine principle, as a mother who sustains the world. One maternal metaphor that emerges in this context is the Spirit as kettle, alluding to the kettle's capacity to provide physical and spiritual nourishment. Furthermore, "[b]ecause food is cooked in the kettle, the kettle represents the nurture and transformation of all things."[11] Applied to the liturgical context, the Spirit could be seen as a gathering principle that inspires croodling around the sources of the community's sustenance and in turn empowers Christians to become nourishment for the world in which they live. For example, as a mother's meal brings her family together around the table, so the pneumaticized body of Christ which Christians are called to receive and become in the Eucharist unites those who share in the meal and forms them for a common mission.

---

[9] Veli-Matti Kärkkäinen, ed., *Holy Spirit and Salvation: The Sources of Christian Theology* (Louisville, KY: Westminster John Knox Press, 2010), 420.

[10] See Kärkkäinen, 417–18 and Kim, 67, 107.

[11] Jung Young Lee, *The Trinity in Asian Perspective* (Nashville, TN: Abingdon Press, 1996), 104.

Another sort of Spirit metaphor originates in Latin American liberation theology. In *The Holy Spirit and Liberation*, José Comblin observes that, "The Spirit is the one who gathers the poor together so as to make them a new people who will challenge all powers of the earth. The Spirit is the strength of the people of the poor, the strength of those who are weak. Without the Spirit, the poor would not raise their voices and conflict would not raise its head."[12] Without uncritically "baptizing" all aspects of liberation theology, the concept of the Spirit as the divine spokesperson for the poor, the creator of unity among people and of a more just community, and the agent of empowerment for change of unjust structures could emphasize the Spirit's place in the life of a God who "makes room" for welcoming the stranger as a prerequisite to authentic and hospitable doxology.

Finally, another dimension of the Spirit's activity is highlighted in the African concern for the links between the Spirit, the ancestors, and the communion of saints. If the Spirit invites "croodling" not just among the living but also among all those who have gone before us in faith, the metaphor of the Spirit as ancestor emphasizes the eschatological scope of the Spirit's mission. Addressing the "pillars of [traditional] African life" that merit incarnation in inculturated liturgical celebration, Chris Nwaka Egbulem draws attention to a unified understanding of reality (one in which divinity and humanity and the material and spiritual worlds are intimately interrelated), the vital role of community in African life, and the important role of the ancestors in most African cultures.[13] Egbulem explains that, "The ancestors (sometimes called 'the living dead') are those 'dead' members of the family or community whose lives left a great heritage and honor to the living, and who continue to influence their families through the legacy they left behind."[14]

---

[12] José Comblin, *The Holy Spirit and Liberation*, trans. Paul Burns (Maryknoll, NY: Orbis Books, 1989), 99.

[13] Chris Nwaka Egbulem, "An African Interpretation of Liturgical Inculturation: The Rite Zairois," in *A Promise of Presence*, ed. Michael Downey and Richard Fragomeni (Washington, DC: The Pastoral Press, 1992), 227ff.

[14] Egbulem, 240–41.

While not all the dead attain the status of "ancestor" in this specific sense, just as not all deceased Catholics are canonized saints, the ancestors play an important role in traditional African rites as intermediaries between God and people. In African Christian theology, the Holy Spirit is sometimes perceived as the "Grand Ancestor" who preserves the people and guides them spiritually. As the "ancestor par excellence," explains Nigerian theologian Caleb Oladipo, the Holy Spirit

> sustains the entire line of humanity by embracing the beginning as well as the end of human spiritual destiny. The Holy Spirit assumes the legitimate aspiration of African ancestors by [its] authentic relationship with divine reality. . . . the eminent assumption of the spiritual destiny which African ancestors seek to guarantee to their earthly descendants is obtainable through an indigenous Christian definition of the Holy Spirit.[15]

Therefore, the eschatological implications of membership in the Christian assembly could be deepened by African insights that conceive the Spirit as the enabler of unity among the members of the body of Christ across time and space, as the facilitator of ongoing communion with the "living dead," and as the Ancestor whose mission is the present and future spiritual welfare of the entire community.

Materiality: Preparing Bodies

In his body of work, Mitchell repeatedly invokes the principle that culture and the body are primary sites of liturgical experience.[16] We are born into a cultural milieu that bestows a symbolic framework upon individual bodies and upon the social body as a whole.

---

[15] Caleb Oluremi Oladipo, "The Development of the Doctrine of the Holy Spirit in the Yorube (African) Indigenous Christian Movement," American University Studies, Series 2, *Theology and Religion* 185 (Frankfurt: Peter Lang, 1996): 104, 107–8, in Kärkkäinen, ed., 412–13.

[16] See, e.g., Nathan D. Mitchell, "New Horizons," *Worship* 84, no. 2 (2010): 172; here he comments on the work of Catherine Bell.

Just as the Spirit erupts in the metaphoric speech of various cultures, its operations are also inscribed in bodies and even crucial to the formation of "bodies" from what would otherwise be disjointed parts that could not function effectively as a unit. Thus where there are bodies, the Spirit is never far from view. Through the power of the Spirit, for example, a body was prepared for the divine Word who became incarnate in the person of Jesus Christ. The Spirit likewise animates other facets of Christ's body, making the Christian assembly into the church comprised of people called by God, indwelling the eucharistic body of Christ whose consumption deepens the communion among members of Christ's ecclesial body, and establishing the "body" of a new social order in the world that transcends customary divisions through the radical newness of God's life pulsing through its collective veins.[17]

"From the beginning," Mitchell insists, "the body, a complex ensemble of signs, has been at the center of the church's self-understanding and hence at the center of its worship. . . . Body thus became the basis for personal integration and social cohesion, precisely because its final significance and eschatological destiny are revealed in the crucified and risen body of Christ."[18] As symbols, bodies bear the cultural system in which they inhere; as Louis-Marie Chauvet asserts, *every symbolic element brings with itself the entire socio-cultural system to which it belongs.*"[19] As the preeminent symbol bridging personal and corporate experience, Chauvet declares the living body "the arch-symbol of the whole symbolic

---

[17] For further treatment of the historical and theological relationship between the historical, ecclesial, and eucharistic bodies of Christ, see Nathan D. Mitchell, "Ecclesiae Dei sociari; Ecclesiae incorporari; in corpus Ecclesiae transire," *Worship* 84, no. 2 (2010): 350–51. The last two of these have both been described as the mystical body of Christ given the inseparability of the ecclesial and eucharistic bodies: "the Church is fed by Christ's body and blood and itself continually comes-to-be as Christ's body" (351).

[18] Nathan D. Mitchell, "Giotto's Joy," *Worship* 79, no. 3 (2005): 267.

[19] Louis-Marie Chauvet, *Symbol and Sacrament: A Sacramental Reinterpretation of Christian Existence,* trans. Patrick Madigan and Madeleine Beaumont (Collegeville, MN: Liturgical Press, 1995), 115 (italics in the original).

order."[20] As Mitchell observes, drawing again on Chauvet, it is therefore in the bodies of members of the Christian assembly, individually and collectively, that God's body is extended in the world—and this insight has profound consequences for how matter is viewed. "For the resurrection of Jesus and the gift of the Spirit specify *corporality* as the eschatological place of God. God wants to assume flesh, the flesh of the Christ, by the Spirit. For us, this is the theological import of an ethics lived as the prime place of a liturgy pleasing to God."[21]

Therefore, the full, conscious, and active participation of members of the liturgical assembly claiming their role as the proper subject of the liturgical action demands as a consequence that the "body" that is the church inhabit the world with an awareness of its larger cosmic dimensions and the ethical impingement of the ecclesial body upon other bodies encountered there. Mitchell treats the latter concern quite extensively in his insistence that the church's liturgy must be verified in the "liturgy of the neighbor"[22] that transpires primarily in the world outside the church's walls. What bodies found in the world might be moved to doxology if the Christian assembly provided a better witness to hospitality? What bodies are intentionally or inadvertently marginalized and not treated with the full dignity they deserve as persons and communities loved by God and made in God's image? Does the tendency toward exclusion which often prevails in the world creep like an infection into the Christian assembly gathered for worship? "If we are serious about recovering dignity and decorum in worship," Mitchell writes, "we should begin by finding ways to welcome the marginalized, to offer them the full, conscious, active participation that is theirs by baptismal right, not by ecclesiastical concession."[23] The imperative of the liturgical assembly to emulate

---

[20] Ibid., 151.

[21] Ibid., 264. Mitchell elaborates further on these principles in "Whose Liturgy?" *Worship* 76, no. 3 (2002): 268–77.

[22] Chauvet, 265.

[23] Nathan D. Mitchell, "'Plenty Good Room': The Dignity of the Assembly," *Worship* 70, no. 1 (1996): 68–69.

God who prodigally makes enough room for everybody without exception presents an ongoing challenge and call to conversion for the Christian assembly.

Beyond the liturgical and ethical experience of personal, human bodies, the full scope of the paschal mystery proclaims that, for Christians, materiality is inescapable. As Karl Rahner observed in a homily on the Ascension as the "festival of the future of the world" that Mitchell cited often in his teaching and writing, "The flesh is redeemed and glorified, for the Lord has risen for ever. We Christians are, therefore, the most sublime of materialists. We neither can nor should conceive of any ultimate fullness of the spirit and of reality without thinking too of matter enduring as well in a state of final perfection."[24] Thus dualism between body and soul is precluded. Furthermore, the material camaraderie embodied human persons share with the larger cosmos (some elements of which are taken up and transformed in a liturgical context) invites further reflection on how Christian bodies treat the non-human material world which is likewise a good creation of God with an eschatological future beyond short-term human utility.

Motion: Ministering to the World

Consideration of the Spirit's activity animating bodies in the world flows naturally into discussion of the Spirit's movement as a constitutive dimension of God's life. Mitchell reminds us that the life of the triune God "is a communion not of colliding egos, but of self-emptying persons who 'make room' for one another . . . God is a community of persons forever 'caught in the act' of surrendering, in love to each other and to us."[25] However, it is often easier to watch this process unfold as a partnership among the three persons enacted across time and space than to see the Spirit coming in the moment, so as to have a better chance to capture what it is about at

[24] Karl Rahner, "The Festival of the Future of the World," trans. David Bourke, in *Theological Investigations*, vol. 7 (New York: Seabury Press, 1977), 183.

[25] Mitchell, "Croodling," 166.

any particular instant. Somewhat resembling the theological ana-
logue of the Heisenberg uncertainty principle, the more one strains
to deduce *exactly* where and how the Spirit is acting at any given
point in time, the less its trajectory of motion can be detected.
Conversely, tracking its movements typically yields more insights
into where it has previously passed through than predictive ability
about where it will turn up next. Like pinning the wings of a
specimen, important insights are both gained and lost through
close observation. In the case of the Spirit, however, it seems safe to
conclude that the Spirit *acts* and people are changed. They may be
charged, compelled, chastened, or comforted, but they are not left
with the option of remaining the same.

Mitchell's concern for attending to the polyvalent dimensions of
ritual practice beyond its textual traces (which are most readily
preserved for posterity) suggests further ways to probe the Spirit's
movement in the liturgy. While ritual texts can provide clues to
what Christians through the ages *thought* about worship, members
of the assembly are formed as worshipers through engagement of
the body and its senses. They are first washed (baptism) and fed
(Eucharist). They are initiated into God's life through movement
directed toward their bodies. After sending the assembly out to
engage the world and minister to the needs of neighbors, the Spirit
regularly re-gathers the assembly for worship in silence that
"speaks" before any words are uttered. The Spirit is likewise detected when "God's Word breaks in—disrupts, interrupts—the
assembly's speech and silence."[26] The Spirit is similarly at work
through other sonic dimensions of the liturgy to retrain our vision
through listening so that we in turn might see the world differ-
ently. "When we *hear,* our body first does the thinking."[27] The body
also "thinks" through its gestures and postures, and Mitchell
insists that it is the *"emotional* quality of human word and gesture

---

[26] Nathan D. Mitchell, "Elected Silence," *Worship* 82, no. 6 (2008): 554.

[27] Nathan D. Mitchell, "Seeing Salvation," *Worship* 76, no. 2 (2002): 172.
Mitchell is inspired here by Bernard of Clairvaux.

that lets us have relationships, that enables us to connect and form communities."[28]

While various dimensions of the liturgy school us in the skills we need to "croodle," we are not meant to croodle as self-satisfied liturgical assemblies relishing our newfound comfort. As people who have been transformed by our encounter with God, we are called to participate with God in the transformation of the world. The Spirit sends us back out into the world, mumbling our inadequate metaphors, bearing our broken bodies to a similarly fractured world, and going through the motions that have been written into our bodies—motions that (ideally) have become so ingrained that they serve us well as our default ritual repertoire. Most of the time, we have only the barest inkling of what we are supposed to be doing. Yet we occupy a space opened for us by God, having been "inscribed into the Word as it returns in the Spirit to the Father."[29] We are compelled by the God who first gathered us to go out into the world to gather, to welcome, to invite, to greet, and so to embody the hospitality that our doxology has instilled in us. Sometimes we wander through the world as awed tourists, other times with the air of overly confident would-be professionals who need to be shaken up by the Spirit occasionally to remind ourselves that we are still far from getting God, ourselves, or the "others" who inspire, confound, and rankle us "right." Again and again, summoned by the Spirit, "We gather, not in our own name or on our own passport, but *in the name* and *as the body* of the One who calls us out of darkness into light. Driven by our indelible desire for the o/Other . . . we become a pilgrim people, ever seeking God and one another."[30]

---

[28] Mitchell, "Ritual as Ars Amatoria," 259.
[29] Nathan D. Mitchell, "Consuming Liturgy," *Worship* 79, no. 2 (2005): 174.
[30] Mitchell, "Croodling," 174.

"Croodling"[1]

Do you croodle? Croodling is what persons in the northern latitudes of the northern hemisphere do between late November and mid-March. They hunker down, drawing their bodies in against the darkness, sleet, and snow; they huddle, clinging to others for warmth and companionship. To croodle, it seems, is human. Or perhaps it is a natural and spontaneous instinct we share with other warm-blooded animals, for a 1788 Yorkshire glossary, quoted in the OED, defines cro(w)dle as the act of creeping "close together, as children round the fire, or chickens under the hen," while a Cheshire glossary of 1884 says the verb means "to snuggle, as a young animal snuggles against its mother, to crouch down." More revealing still is the word's early history, for croodle's ancestry takes us back to *cludder* and *clodder*, words already used by Chaucer and found, ca. 1400, in a devotional poem that speaks of Christ's appearance in his passion: "In clodders of blood his hair was clung." Croodling thus conjures complex images of crowding, crouching, clustering, clotting, heaping up, shedding blood.

Despite its long lineage, it is unlikely that "croodle" will appear any time soon in approved English versions of the Roman liturgical books. For while there is no evidence the church has ever condemned croodling, neither has it countenanced its presence in the liturgy. Or has it? Think of those fur-lined choir robes and night-shoes medieval monks wore in winter as they made their way in the middle of the night to sing nocturns in unheated churches. Surely such garments invited a bit of croodling. Or recall

[1] This essay originally appeared in "The Amen Corner," *Worship* 78, no. 2 (March 2004), 165–75.

how the tenth-century English monastic agreement known as *Regularis concordia* describes the furtive actions of a vested singer during the final responsory of Easter Vigils. Holding a lit lantern, the monk is directed to prowl stealthily through the choir, crouching low and peering about "as if in search of someone." Suddenly a sweet voice sings, "Whom do you seek?" "Jesus of Nazareth," the croodling seeker replies. "He is not here," the voice answers, "He is risen!" Then all the church bells peal, the *Te Deum* is sung, and the rest, as they say, is history.

God's Life: The Wellspring of Worship

My purpose in calling your attention to the history of an obscure, if colorful, English word is not antiquarian but pastoral. In my column for January, I asked the question, "Where do we go from here?" suggesting that the populist liturgy envisioned forty years ago by *Sacrosanctum Concilium* (SC) seeks to join, however imperfectly, community and transcendence. I concluded with Paul Woodruff's keen observation that when ceremony becomes too rigidly controlled, it fossilizes, losing "its power to express reverence."[2] Over the course of this year's columns, I hope to present to readers a twenty-first century version of Ronald Knox's old classic, *The Mass in Slow Motion*.[3] My intent is to examine the "principal parts of the Mass" not so much for their ritual structure but for what their shape tells us about the experience and theology of worship itself. Beginning with the rites of gathering and entrance, in this issue, I'll move on, in subsequent columns, to the Liturgy of the Word, the Preparation of Gifts, the Eucharistic Prayer, and the Communion Rite.

In our debates about how best to define worship, we sometimes forget that liturgy is always an act of hospitality and pastoral care, of making room and making welcome. To say this is not to reduce worship to cheap sentiment or fuzzy intimacy, but to root it in the

[2] Paul Woodruff, *Reverence: Renewing a Forgotten Virtue* (New York: Oxford University Press, 2001), 208.

[3] Ronald Knox, *The Mass in Slow Motion* (New York: Sheed & Ward, 1948).

very life of God. For God's life is a communion not of colliding egos, but of self-emptying persons who "make room" for one another. God, so to speak, is a village—or to put it more accurately, God is *a communion of persons forever in a condition of giving themselves away, freely, to each other.* The persons of the Trinity are not "personalities," nor are they "discrete, individuated centers of consciousness" (as we are). As Thomas Aquinas liked to say, the divine persons are "subsistent relations" whose very identity is constituted by giving (*donatio*)—by *kenosis*, self-emptying, mutual outpouring. God is a community of persons forever "caught in the act" of surrendering, in love to each other and to us. In God, "person" is neither ego nor celebrity, but *bestowal*, mutual *given-ness*. Thus, to be made "in the image and likeness of God" is to be created for community, for partnership, for life with others, for an existence that enacts and embodies itself as *self-surrender*, as life bestowed on behalf of others. Ours is a God who "makes room," opens up space for the stranger, welcomes the "other." In God's life, hospitality is doxology, and doxology is hospitality.

For this reason, the most Godlike thing humans can do is to create personal—i.e., interpersonal—community. The Hebrew poems in the first chapters of Genesis remind us that God created a world for humankind by creating a rich *diversity* of living things; God created community by creating *difference*. But to say "difference" is to say "desire," for difference introduces strangeness into familiarity and triggers our inextinguishable longing for "the other." God's creating Word thus gave birth to art, for art is the act of making the strange intelligible by first making it *stranger*.[4] "This dialectic of strangeness and familiarity," writes Avivah Gottlieb Zornberg, "is the gift of art" and, one might add, the gift of creation itself, because the "cycle of desire is present in all dimensions of life, intellectual, interpretive . . . emotional."[5] Because God sweetens the longing that brings us together, this mystery of strangeness and familiarity—of communion within difference and unity within

[4] See Avivah Gottlieb Zornberg, *The Beginning of Desire: Reflections on Genesis* (New York: Doubleday Image Books, 1995), xiv.

[5] Ibid.

diversity—encamps at the very heart of our sacramental symbols. "Be careful to assemble for *one* Eucharist," wrote Ignatius of Antioch to the Philadelphians, "for *one* is the flesh of our Lord Jesus Christ, *one* is the cup that unites us with his blood, *one* is the altar, and *one* is the bishop, serving with the presbyters and deacons." More than a millennium later, Thomas Aquinas affirmed the same principle, viz., that the goal of eucharistic activity (and the final purpose of eucharistic real presence) is *unio ecclesiastici corporis*, the unity of that Body which is the church.

At Vatican II, *Sacrosanctum Concilium* sounded similar themes: "The liturgy daily builds up those who are in the Church, making of them a holy temple of the Lord, a dwelling-place for God in the Spirit, to the mature measure of the fullness of Christ" (SC 2). So did *Lumen Gentium*, whose second chapter, "The People of God," insists, as SC 48 does, that by participating in the eucharistic sacrifice, the baptized faithful truly "offer the divine victim to God and themselves along with it," and thus, that "both in the offering and in Holy Communion" their action manifests "that unity of the People of God which this holy sacrament aptly signifies and admirably realizes" (LG 11). In this way, as Edward P. Hahnenberg has recently noted, Vatican II repeated the traditional view that baptism assimilates believers to the *one* priesthood of Christ.[6]

Here, however, a word of caution is also needed. When ancient baptismal liturgies called chrismated Christians priests, they were not making "priesthood" a metaphor for ministry. They meant to affirm *baptism* as the radical sacrament of sacerdotality in the church; they were not seeking to derive the "priesthood of the laity" from the "priesthood of the ordained." That is why we sometimes refer to the *ministerial* priesthood of the ordained, the implication being that the Christian's radical identity as "priest" has already been bestowed in baptism. Our failure to notice this during the council's immediate aftermath may have clouded our initial approach to lay liturgical ministries. As Hahnenberg puts it, "Early attempts to recover an active ministry for the nonordained in the liturgy per-

[6] Edward P. Hahnenberg, *Ministry: A Relational Approach* (New York: Crossroad Publishing Company, 2003), 175.

haps erred in this direction: they based their view of the common priesthood on the model of the ordained priesthood," seeking to extend the ordination franchise, as it were, by "granting the laity a 'priesthood' of their own."[7]

Aidan Kavanagh drew our attention to this point (and potential problem) more than a quarter-century ago. In his memorable essay, "Unfinished and Unbegun: The Rite of Christian Initiation of Adults," Kavanagh wrote:

> [T]he Church baptizes to priesthood: it ordains only to executive exercise of that priesthood in the major orders of ministry. . . . While every presbyter and bishop is therefore a sacerdotal person, not every sacerdotal person in the Church is a presbyter or bishop. Nor does sacerdotality come upon one for the first time, so to speak, at one's ordination. In constant genesis in the font, the Church is born there as a sacerdotal assembly by the Spirit of the Anointed One himself.[8]

This, of course, is precisely the theology of baptism embedded in both *Sacrosanctum Concilium* (SC 7, 14, 47–48) and the RCIA, and the conclusion, as Kavanagh noted, is inescapable: "[T]he foundation upon which the communication of sacerdotality rests is primarily *communion with Christ in his Church* rather than the sacramental acts of baptism or holy orders taken in themselves and abstracted apart from this same communion."[9]

In sum, God's own life as interpersonal communion summons and bestows our desire for that "holy living together" we call church, a united-but-diverse people called to priestly cult and pastoral care. As SC 7 says, "The liturgy is rightly seen as an exercise of the priestly office of Jesus Christ. . . . In it, full public worship is performed by the Body of Jesus Christ, head and members." To say this doesn't reduce Christian worship to a whirring blender

---

[7] Ibid.

[8] Aidan Kavanagh, "Unfinished and Unbegun: The Rite of Christian Initiation of Adults," *Worship* 53, no. 4 (1979): 335–36.

[9] Ibid., 338.

that dices differences and homogenizes the assembly. On the contrary, SC 28 notes that "in liturgical celebrations each person, minister, or layman who has an office to perform, should carry out *all* and *only* those parts which pertain to his office." (Note well: this proviso applies to both ordained clergy and non-ordained ministers!)

Thus, liturgy is the place par excellence where our hospitable God "makes room," opening a space where communion can flourish *in* and *as* difference and diversity. Our desire for the other in a world where strangeness and familiarity play side-by-side is the human root of our desire to come together as church. Our identity as church is thus as much a meeting of strangers as a meeting of familiars. That is why the responsibility to welcome the stranger lies at the heart of Christian hospitality, and why Vatican II called the church *sacramentum mundi*—a sacrament of the *world*, and not of the self-satisfied. For the church is not a self-congratulatory conventicle of righteous suburbanites who meet to commend one another for earning substantial incomes, driving superior SUVs, shopping at "better" stores, and sending their kids to "the right schools." We don't come together Sunday after Sunday to prove we have "got it right," but precisely because we *do not* have it right, and never will. It is why our liturgy begins with the improbable paradox of praise *and* repentance, confidence *and* self-accusation. For our grandeur, by God's grace, consists in this: that though we love to play in the mud, we are forever looking at the stars—and we can never decide whether we would rather croodle or conquer.

Meeting the Holy in the Homely

For all these reasons, the time and space where Christians gather for worship has become an important dimension of postconciliar architecture and liturgical theology. Gathering is not a merely utilitarian act; it's a theological principle. As the Canadian Catholic bishops note in their 1999 document, *Our Place of Worship*, "[T]he assembly of believers is the starting point for developing a house for the Church," precisely because the "full, conscious, active participation called for by the Council and demanded by the liturgical rites requires that liturgical space be developed to support this ideal."[10] Historically, the bishops observe, that is why churches "were often preceded by gathering places . . . open courtyard or spacious open porch," and why, in cities like Rome, the assembly often "gathered or 'collected'," first, at a designated church from which a procession then formed, wending its way toward the "basilica or house-church where the liturgy of the day was to be celebrated."[11] Similarly, the U.S. bishops' document *Built of Living Stones* (48) reminds us that

> [t]he church building houses the community of the baptized as it gathers to celebrate the sacred liturgy. . . . The primary concern in the building or renovation of a space for worship must be its suitability for the celebration of the Eucharist and other liturgical rites of the Church. Consequently, the fundamental prerequisite for those engaged in the building or renovation of a church is familiarity with the rites to be celebrated there.

When Western church architecture created gathering spaces for stations and processions, it was thus implicitly affirming the assembly's acts of gathering, greeting, and welcome as the living icon of the hospitable God who "makes room and makes welcome," who gathers people from age to age and unites them as a "holy nation, a royal priesthood." This, after all, is what liturgies and sacraments do: they open our eyes to see in human deeds—the washing of a body, the eating and drinking of a meal—the gracious arrival of One who is both strangely familiar and familiarly strange. We cannot forget that on the road to Emmaus, it was a *Stranger* whom the disciples "recognized in the breaking of the bread" (Luke 24:35).

My point here is not to urge restoration of the ancient stational liturgies that once characterized Christian worship in the city of

---

[10] Canadian Conference of Catholic Bishops, *Our Place of Worship* (Ottawa, ON: Publications Service CCCB, 1999), 17; 13. Cf. SC 124.

[11] Canadian Conference of Catholic Bishops, *Our Place of Worship*, 23.

Rome, but to remind readers that the modern Roman Rite is still punctuated by processions: during the entrance rite, at the proclamation of the Gospel, at the presentation and preparation of gifts (for the eucharistic table and for the poor), at communion. Much of the time, modern liturgical catechesis is content to explain processions as either *utilitarian* (getting the assembly and/or ministers from one place to another); *educative* (ritual choreography that teaches us about the feast or season); or *honorific* (e.g., the use of lights, incense, and movement to accompany proclamation of the Gospel). While I do not deny that utility, education, and honor play a role in liturgical processions, I suspect that Romano Guardini was nearer the truth when he wrote, forty years ago, that the deeper question is whether we can "relearn a forgotten way of doing things."[12] When we interpret processions as utilitarian, educative, or honorific, we implicitly privilege rational thought over ambiguous action. Our assumption is that a procession means what *we* say it means, that we are serenely, supremely, and self-consciously in charge of the proceedings. As Annie Dillard once wrote,

> The higher Christian churches . . . come at God with an unwarranted air of professionalism, with authority and pomp, as though they knew what they were doing, as though people in themselves were an appropriate set of creatures to have dealings with God. . . . In the high churches they saunter through the liturgy like Mohawks along a strand of scaffolding who have long since forgotten their danger. If God were to blast such a service to bits, the congregation would be, I believe, genuinely shocked.[13]

Dillard's point—and Guardini's too, I suspect—was that our proud professionalism blinds us to the very real danger of "walking in the presence of God" and welcoming the stranger into our midst. We imagine that our processions are "Sunday afternoons in

---

[12] "A Letter from Romano Guardini," *Herder Correspondence* 1, no. 1 (Special issue, 1964): 24–26; here, 24.

[13] Annie Dillard, *Holy the Firm* (New York: Bantam Books, 1979 [1977]), 60.

the park with George," forgetting that a symbol's depth is never plumbed when *we* say what it "means." On the contrary, as Guardini observed, our well-meant explanations may actually prevent our grasping "how the act of walking [itself] becomes a religious act, a retinue for the Lord progressing through his land, so that an 'epiphany' may take place."[14] The epiphany in question is not always a consoling one—and it may well defy every expectation. As Martha Graham once replied to a questioner who asked what her dances "meant": "Darling, if I knew what they meant, I wouldn't dance them." We are well advised, then, to let our symbols be roomy and our explanations spare.

Moreover, as Andrew Ciferni has observed, "All liturgical reform is based on some model of celebration which largely determines the details of revised rites."[15] A key clue to the model at work in the Missal of Paul VI can be found in the most recent version of the GIRM (*tertia editio typica*, 2002). GIRM 47 states:

> After the people have gathered, the Entrance chant begins as the priest enters with the deacon and ministers. The purpose of this chant is to open the celebration, foster the unity of those who have been gathered, introduce their thoughts to the mystery of the liturgical season or festivity, and accompany the procession of the priests and ministers.

Even a cursory glance at this text reveals that the purpose of the entrance rite and its music is not to herd the people inside the building or get the ministers into position with a minimum of misdirection and mayhem. The focus is not on "traffic flow" or the "presiding celebrity's" entrance, but on *the assembled people*, whose singing "opens . . . fosters . . . introduces . . . accompanies." Contrast the opening words of GIRM 47, "After the people have gathered" (*Populo congregato*)—with the Tridentine *Ritus servandus* ("Rite to be observed in the celebration of Mass"). Each of the first

---

[14] "A Letter from Romano Guardini," 25.

[15] Andrew D. Ciferni, "The Ceremonial of Bishops: Challenges and Opportunities," *Assembly* 17, no. 5 (September, 1991): 532.

three sections of the *Ritus* began with the word *"Sacerdos,"* while the remaining ten sections speak either of the "celebrant" (*Celebrans*) or something the celebrant has just said or done. Clearly, the *Ritus* expects lay people to remain passive during the eucharistic rite, and hence, almost nothing is said of their presence or role.[16]

In contrast, the Missal of 1970 represents a decisive "shift from Trent's priest-server model of eucharistic celebration to Vatican II's assembly-priest."[17] It cannot be said too often that this shift was not merely "ritual," but *theological*—and that the council's theology has been authoritatively reaffirmed in GIRM 2002 (112–113):

> In the local Church, first place should certainly be given, because of its significance, to the [stational] Mass at which the Bishop presides, surrounded by his presbyterate, deacons, and lay ministers, and in which the holy people of God participate fully and actively, for it is there that the preeminent expression of the Church is found. . . . Great importance should also be attached to a Mass celebrated with any community, but especially with the parish community, inasmuch as it represents the universal Church gathered at a given time and place. This is particularly true in the communal Sunday celebration.

GIRM 2002 thus leaves little doubt about which eucharistic celebrations constitute the "preeminent expression of the church." The first is what the *Ceremonial of Bishops* (119) calls a "stational" liturgy, when Mass is celebrated by the bishop "surrounded by his college of presbyters and by his ministers, and with the full, active participation of all God's holy people" (COB 119; GIRM 2002, 112),[18] the second is the "communal Sunday celebration" of Eucharist in

---

[16] Section VIII of the *Ritus servandus* explains that the priest is to show the consecrated bread and wine to the people; while section X outlines the rite for giving the people communion (the "minister," i.e., Mass server, having first said the Confiteor for them).

[17] Ciferni, "The Ceremonial of Bishops," 532.

[18] "Stational" is the term used by the *Ceremonial of Bishops* (119) for the Mass just described. "This Mass, which is called the stational Mass, shows forth the unity of the local church as well as the diversity of ministries exercised around the bishop and the holy eucharist" (COB, 119).

the local parish "inasmuch as it represents the universal Church gathered at a given time and place" (GIRM 113).

It seems obvious, then, that both SC and postconciliar documents such as the GIRM and COB see the assembly—its gathering, its word and song, its action, its offering—as the *subject* (proactive agent) of the liturgical action, and not merely as its object (reactive recipient). The action and space of gathering, the entrance procession and its music—all these exemplify what Andrew Ciferni calls "Vatican II ecclesiology made flesh."[19] Their significance is not merely pastoral, strategic, utilitarian, or logistical. Nor are "gathering spaces" and "entrance rites" cheap pretexts invented by postconciliar enthusiasts who seek to "exalt" the assembly at the expense of the ordained. Nor does the importance of the assembly's place for gathering somehow rival or reduce the significance of the "sanctuary" space. Although some traditionalists see the "sanctuary" as a strictly clerical preserve, the Canadian bishops wisely remind us that "The Rite of Dedication of a Church speaks of the whole assembly space as 'sanctuary,'" and that "[i]n the Roman tradition, placement of the eucharistic table in the midst of the assembly has ancient precedent."[20] Surely it goes without saying that the purpose of the sanctuary is to unite, not to divide.

For as Edward Hahnenberg suggests, the "fundamental model for church and ministry is not the dividing line but concentric circles."[21] Dividing lines drawn too rigidly lead precisely to that "unwarranted air of professionalism," that "authority and pomp" that can turn an entrance rite into a theater for self-display rather than an expectant opening, in joy, fear, and trembling, to the divine "epiphany." For at the end of the day, our rites of gathering, welcome, entrance, and greeting have to do with our deepest identity. We gather, not in our own name or on our own passport, but *in the name* and *as the body* of the One who calls us out of darkness into light. Driven by our indelible desire for the o/Other (a way, perhaps, to reformulate in categories of human experience what

<hr>

[19] Ciferni, "The Ceremonial of Bishops," 532.
[20] *Our Place of Worship*, 26.
[21] *Ministry: A Relational Approach*, 212.

theological tradition calls the sacramental "character" of baptism), we become a pilgrim people, ever seeking God and one another. To discover the divine in the daily; to meet the holy in the homely; to reach up by reaching out; to confess the Creator's transcendence by "croodling," is to perform our identity as human and Christian. *That* is why a generous and hospitable gathering space is so vital for the Sunday assembly. *That* is why our entrance rites are not logistical and utilitarian but ritual, symbolic, and epiphanic. *That* is why participation must be "full, active, and conscious" from the get-go. *That* is why Roman liturgical tradition is historically stational and processional. *That* is why, perhaps, Meister Eckhart once said that God is at home; it is *we* who are poor travelers in a far country.

Chapter Four: *Beauty*

Portals to Transcendence

Clare V. Johnson

At the heart of liturgy lies Beauty. From his first "Amen Corner" to his last, Nathan Mitchell never tired of exploring this notion in a quest to open for his readers portals to transcendence, glimpses of beauty mediated through poetry, music, art, and literature, specifically selected, expertly exegeted and mined for meaning to be applied not only to liturgy, but to life. As a liturgical theologian, Mitchell habitually ranges beyond the expected binary formula of *lex orandi, lex credendi*[1] to delve into the broader, more complex and challenging *lex agendi* (rule of action/behavior),[2] with the aim of prodding his readers to move out of comfort and complacency and into (at times) uncomfortable action "by introducing that subversive element of indeterminacy"[3] which destabilizes, de-centers, discomforts.[4]

The Berakah Award presented to Mitchell by the North American Academy of Liturgy in 1998 recognized that he is "sustained by poets, artists and theologians."[5] In his "Amen Corner,"

---

[1] This loosely translates as let the rule of prayer establish the rule of belief.

[2] Nathan D. Mitchell, *Meeting Mystery: Liturgy, Worship, and Sacraments* (Maryknoll, NY: Orbis Books, 2006), 39.

[3] Ibid.

[4] Ibid., 40.

[5] "The 1998 Berakah Award to Nathan D. Mitchell," *Proceedings of the North American Academy of Liturgy* (Evanston, IL: North American Academy of Liturgy, 1998), 16.

Mitchell used these sources of sustenance to introduce a banquet of cogent commentary on important contemporary and historic liturgical matters and demonstrated in the process not only that beauty provides glimpses of the divine, but also that studies of the beautiful can offer insight into matters of both liturgy and life. Understanding the alluring power of beauty, Mitchell never permits his readers simply to be entranced by its qualities of attraction or distraction, but always seeks to entice them through contemplation of beauty back into the world possessed of new insights.[6]

Having shared selections from a splendid array of poets[7] for over twenty years in his "Amen Corner," Mitchell's final essay fittingly took the form of a poetic construction of his own, inspired by and quoting from the work of his favorite poets. In "A Meditation on Eucharistic Praying,"[8] Mitchell chose for his starting point and recurrent refrain a quote from the Roman Canon[9] (1973 translation, adapted for inclusivity[10]): "We come to you, God, with praise and thanksgiving." Weaving together liturgy, theology, justice, life and beauty, Mitchell's commentary highlights the ineffectiveness yet inevitability of the many words with which we try to describe and praise and thank our God in worship. Fully cognizant of the irony of offering to the author of all beauty what can only ever be our flawed best efforts at reflecting that beauty, Mitchell's final "Amen Corner" concludes appropriately with an unresolved suspended

[6] See Nathan D. Mitchell, "The Amen Corner: Making the Connections," *Worship* 86, no. 3 (May 2012): 256–68. Graham Ward notes that in experiencing the beautiful, "we are not transported beyond this world into some pure and immediate relation to divinity. We are returned to the world more profoundly by the beautiful." "The Beauty of God," *Theological Perspectives on God and Beauty* (Harrisburg, PA: Trinity Press/Continuum, 2003), 57.

[7] See Gilbert Ostdiek, "Let the Poet Speak," *Ars Liturgiae: Worship Aesthetics and Praxis—Essays in Honour of Nathan D. Mitchell*, ed. Clare V. Johnson (Chicago: LTP, 2003), 115–33.

[8] Nathan D. Mitchell, "A Meditation on Eucharistic Praying," *Worship* 86, no. 6 (November 2012): 552–66.

[9] See Nathan D. Mitchell, "The Amen Corner: That Really Long Prayer," *Worship* 74, no. 5 (September 2000): 468–77.

[10] See Nathan D. Mitchell, "Sunday Morning," *Worship* 65, no. 6 (November 1991): 544–45.

seventh:[11] "so we come into God's presence with psalms and paper and paint, with color and art." The topic which so fascinates Mitchell—God's beauty—bears further scrutiny.

The Subversion of Beauty

The concept of "beauty" is slippery, ambiguous, and intrinsically possessed of a potential to slide into the realm of pure subjectivity if it lacks appropriate hermeneutic parameters to guide its interpretation and application within a given context. When "beauty" is considered in a Christian context, it is understood as transcendental, a property of Being itself, an aspect of God. Mitchell explains that for Thomas Aquinas, "being itself is derived from the beautiful: 'The beautiful which is God, is the goal, the summit and cause of everything that exists.' Indeed, 'from the Beauty, being flows forth to enliven all things.'"[12] Understanding beauty according to Christian theological categories entails making reference to Christ as "the distinct speaking and doing form of God's self-revelation . . . the one through whom we construct our understanding of God's beauty since he is the nexus of God's being, beauty and Christian living."[13] As the human face of God, Christ demonstrates through his actions, words, life, death and resurrection, the Christian manifestation of beauty, God made accessible within the limits of human comprehension,[14] but in a form of the "beautiful" that is not

[11] In music, a suspended chord holds over a note from the previous chord to create a moment of discord which if unresolved results in an unfinished feeling.

[12] Nathan D. Mitchell, "The Amen Corner: Being Good and Being Beautiful," *Worship* 74, no. 6 (November 2000): 551. Mitchell quotes and provides his own translation of St. Thomas Aquinas, *In librum beati Dionysii de divinis nominubus*, ed. C. Pera (Rome: Marietti, 1950), Caput IV lectio V, paragraphs 353 and 349, 114–15.

[13] Stephen M. Garrett, "God's Beauty-in-Act: An Artful Renewal of Human Imagining," *International Journal of Systematic Theology* 14, no. 1 (October 2012): 463.

[14] Graham Ward explains that "we cannot receive the beauty of God itself, being human. We can only receive the beauty of God in relation to the world He has created." "The Beauty of God," 57. See Col 1:15.

easily construed if considered within regular culturally-determined aesthetic categories.

A Christian understanding of what constitutes Beauty must be centered on the beauty encountered in Christ incarnate. Graham Ward explains that "incarnation does not divide form from content or medium from message or the signifier from the signified. The beauty makes manifest something of the truth of the thing that is perfected in the manifestation."[15] According to Hebrews 2:9, the glory of Christ, the beauty of God, is made manifest in the death of one who suffers for all. Stephen Garrett clarifies that "Christ's death and resurrection become necessary for discerning God's beauty."[16] The subversion of typical notions of beauty perceptible in Christ, solitary, suffering, silent, hanging in agony on the cross is not necessarily apparent to the uninitiated. One must *learn* to perceive the counterintuitive, countercultural depiction of beauty in the image of Christ on the cross if true Beauty is to be apprehended in what appears at first glance to be an image of such disturbing ugliness, horror and despair that no sane person would ever call it beautiful. Mitchell describes this image of Christ, the icon of God's beauty as one which "embodies the self-effacing, self-erasing, self-surrendering Servant (celebrated by the prophet Isaiah) who lets himself 'be disfigured,' lets himself be seen 'without beauty or comeliness,'". . . so that he might reveal "the ultimate glory of God in human disfigurement."[17] This Christ is the beauty of God made manifest, beauty accessible only through the eyes of faith. Once one's perception of true beauty aligns with the Beauty of God revealed in Christ crucified, perceiving the beauty, dignity, and worth of the lowliest among human society becomes possible, and having perceived true beauty in the helpless human person, the consequent Christian moral response of care, concern, and comfort can ensue. Comprehending the link between the beautiful and the moral in Christian theological thought ideally should result in

[15] Ward, 44.

[16] Garrett, 468.

[17] Nathan D. Mitchell, "The Amen Corner: Liturgy and Life—Lessons in Benedict," *Worship* 82, no. 2 (March 2008): 170.

application in real life of the countercultural hermeneutic enabled by perception of the beautiful in Christ.

In the Image and Likeness of God

Christian theological anthropology rests on the understanding that God, source of all beauty, creates a beautiful world which he blesses and deems to be good. Into this world of beauty God creates humankind "in his image, in the image of God he created them; male and female he created them" (Gen 1:27). Ward claims that "to be made in the image of God accentuates that human beings are creative fashioners of images also,"[18] as we are *homo symbolicus* because each is constituted as an image; each represents, incarnates, something of God."[19] This artistic aspect of humankind, this insatiable innate urge to create beauty, is attested to throughout history as, according to philosopher Nicholas Wolterstorff, there is no people or culture which does not express itself creatively through music, story, poetry, and art.[20] Ward explains this unassailable cultural fact in terms of theological anthropology, noting that "we represent because we are ourselves a representation, and so to represent is not only a human action, but a *divinely sanctioned* human action."[21] Because we are created in the image and likeness of God, therefore we have the capacity and the desire to be co-creators of beauty as an inherent aspect of our fundamental human beingness.

On this basis, moral theologian Patrick T. McCormick writes intriguingly of what he terms "a moral right to beauty," noting that "more than a luxury, the enjoyment and creation of beauty is a fundamental right of all peoples, as we are fashioned to be co-creators of beauty and we need some element of beauty to survive and flourish as persons and communities."[22] McCormick explains the

[18] Ward, 41.

[19] Ward, 42.

[20] Nicholas Wolterstorff, *Art in Action* (Grand Rapids, MI: Eerdmans, 1980), 4.

[21] Ward, 42.

[22] Patrick T. McCormick, *God's Beauty: A Call to Justice* (Collegeville, MN: Michael Glazier, 2012), xi.

"moral right to beauty" on the basis that the human person has "fundamental rights that flow from their nature as persons," rights which "flow from our nature as free and intelligent beings *and* from the fact that we are fashioned in the image and likeness of God."[23] McCormick quotes Pope John Paul II's position that persons have a right to develop "their openness to the transcendent,"[24] noting that "in order to become fully human, we must be allowed to realize our gifts and talents, to fulfill our vocation as cocreators of beauty. . . . And so the right to development and participation certainly imply a right to become cocreators of beauty, while a right to develop into creatures open to the transcendent would seem to imply a right to some small beauty in our souls."[25] McCormick references John O'Donohue's exploration of the etymology of "beauty" drawn from the Greek: *to kalon*, related to the word *kalein* and including within its definitional range the notion of "call."[26] O'Donohue explains that "when we experience beauty we feel called. The Beautiful stirs passion and urgency in us, and calls us forth from aloneness into the warmth and wonder of an eternal embrace."[27] The experience of beauty then, can provide a mode of connection, a portal to transcendence, an opportunity for divine encounter.

God, the source of all beauty, calls to us through the experience of beauty mediated via the created world (natural creation, artistic creation) and often our response to beauty's call is expressed in a desire to cooperate with God as co-creators of beauty. Elaine Scarry claims that the experience of beauty acts to "un-self" us, to "de-center" us from ourselves. She writes that in the presence of beauty "it is not that we cease to stand at the center of the world, for we never stood there. It is that we cease to stand even at the center of

[23] McCormick, 41–42.

[24] Pope John Paul II, Encyclical: "*Sollicitudo Rei Socialis*," (December 12, 1987), par. 32, http://www.vatican.va/holy_father/john_paul_ii/encyclicals/documents/hf_jp-ii_enc_30121987_sollicitudo-rei-socialis_en.html, accessed November 13, 2013.

[25] McCormick, 43.

[26] Ibid., 46.

[27] John O'Donohue, *Beauty: The Invisible Embrace* (New York: HarperCollins, 2004), 13.

our own world. We willingly cede our ground to the thing that stands before us."[28]

In order to be apprehended, beauty must be both comprehensible and mysterious, for lacking comprehensibility, beauty results in bafflement; lacking mystery, the beautiful is reduced merely to the "pretty." Beauty "oscillates between the sensible and the intellectual, the concrete and the universal," it "totters more precariously on the precipice between complete abstraction and total particularity."[29] That is part of its allure. We can never possess the beautiful, for "to experience the beautiful is not only to be satisfied but also to be frustrated satisfyingly; a desire to see more of what arrives . . . is always involved."[30]

Encountering Beauty in Liturgy

The experience and effect of beauty on the human being in general, such as has been described briefly above, is concentrated and magnified in the particular, privileged and unsurpassable encounter with Beauty which is available to the faithful in the liturgy. While beauty in general calls us and elicits a creative response from us, in the liturgy, the God who is Beauty calls us into his presence and we respond to that call creatively. While the experience of beauty in general "un-selfs" us and "de-centers" us so that we "willingly cede our ground to the thing that stands before us," the experience of God's beauty in the liturgy unselfs and decenters us so that we relinquish control of individual identity in order to participate in the common action of the worshiping assembly, to discern and become imbued with shared meaning in the presence of the one who calls us in order to express and strengthen our faith

---

[28] Elaine Scarry, *On Beauty and Being Just* (Princeton, NJ: Princeton University Press, 2001), 112.

[29] Daniel B. Gallagher, "The Analogy of Beauty and the Limits of Theological Aesthetics," *Theandros: An Online Journal of Orthodox Christian Theology and Philosophy* 3 (Spring/Summer 2006).

[30] John Millbank, "Beauty and the Soul," *Theological Perspectives on God and Beauty*, 1–2.

so that we might live lives inspired to moral action by the beauty we encounter. While the beautiful as both comprehensible and mysterious both satisfies and frustrates us with its allure, the God who is Beauty, encountered in liturgy as both comprehensible and mysterious,[31] both satisfies and frustrates us as we glimpse that which we cannot yet possess fully: perfect uninterrupted unity with the object of our desire, God.

Liturgical celebration ideally should provide access to an experience of beauty, an encounter with beauty and an opportunity to become co-creators of beauty in God's presence.[32] Canon law instructs that baptism incorporates one into the church of Christ and constitutes one a person in that church "with the duties and the rights which, in accordance with each one's status, are proper to Christians."[33] It mandates that one of the rights of Christ's faithful is "the right to worship God according to the provisions of their own rite approved by the lawful Pastors of the Church."[34] The right to worship according to the provisions of the approved rites, which when celebrated as designed *are* beautiful, promises access to an experience of, a privileged encounter with, and an opportunity to be co-creators of, beauty. This means that the faithful have a right to beautiful rites. Pope Benedict XVI puts it thus: "Beauty, then, is not mere decoration, but rather an essential element of the liturgical action, since it is an attribute of God himself and his reve-

---

[31] See Nathan D. Mitchell, "The Amen Corner: Ritual as Revelation," *Worship* 79, no. 4 (July 2005): 363.

[32] Pope Benedict XVI clarifies that the experience of Beauty in liturgy: "is no mere aestheticism, but the concrete way in which the truth of God's love in Christ encounters us, attracts us and delights us, enabling us to emerge from ourselves and drawing us towards our true vocation, which is love." Pope Benedict XVI, "*Sacramentum Caritatis*," Post-Synodal Apostolic Exhortation on the Eucharist as the Source and Summit of the Church's Life and Mission, (Feb. 22, 2007), par.35, http://www.vatican.va/holy_father/benedict_xvi/apost_exhortations/documents/hf_ben-xvi_exh_20070222_sacramentum-caritatis_en.html#Ars_celebrandi, accessed November 15, 2013.

[33] Catholic Church, *The Code of Canon Law in English Translation* (London: Collins, 1983), canon 96, p. 14.

[34] Ibid., canon 214, p. 35.

lation. These considerations should make us realize the care which is needed, if the liturgical action is to reflect its innate splendor."[35]

Ars Celebrandi

In 2007, Pope Benedict XVI focused on the need for attention to be paid to the *ars celebrandi* of liturgy, defined in *Sacramentum Caritatis* 38 as "the art of proper celebration." Benedict XVI writes that "proper" celebration entails "faithful adherence to the liturgical norms in all their richness" because "for two thousand years this way of celebrating has sustained the faith life of all believers."[36] Of course the Christian community's "way of celebrating" has changed greatly over the course of two thousand years and myriad cultural instantiations, but it is presumed that the pope intended the focus of this statement to be "faithful adherence to liturgical norms," as they are articulated and interpreted by the church in a given period of history. The key point made here by Benedict XVI is that "the primary way to foster the participation of the People of God in the sacred rite is the proper celebration of the rite itself. The *ars celebrandi* is the best way to ensure their *actuosa participatio*."[37]

Celebrating the liturgy properly enables the full, conscious, and active participation of the faithful in the liturgy, which sustains the faith life of the believer. This means that the manner of liturgical celebration is a matter of the most serious consequence. This principle was expressed simply and tellingly by the US Catholic Bishops' Committee on the Liturgy in its 1972 document "Music in Catholic Worship" which states: "Faith grows when it is expressed in celebration. Good celebrations foster and nourish faith. Poor celebrations may weaken and destroy it."[38] Determining precisely

[35] Pope Benedict XVI, "*Sacramentum Caritatis*," par. 35.

[36] Ibid., par. 38.

[37] Ibid. See also Catholic Church, "General Instruction of the Roman Missal," *The Roman Missal* (London: Catholic Truth Society, 2011), par. 18, p. 31.

[38] USCCB Bishops' Committee on the Liturgy, "Music in Catholic Worship," in *The Liturgy Documents: A Parish Resource*, 3rd ed., Elizabeth Hoffman, ed. (Chicago: LTP, 1991), par. 6, p. 277.

what makes a "good" celebration is difficult, but there are certain basic nonnegotiable aspects of the *ars celebrandi* which must be present for a liturgical celebration to be considered "good" and therefore "beautiful," if beauty is understood as "an essential element of the liturgical action."[39] *Sacramentum Caritatis* enumerates several of them: "faithful adherence to the liturgical norms in all their richness" (par. 38); fostering "a sense of the sacred and the use of outward signs which help to cultivate this sense, such as, for example, the harmony of the rite, the liturgical vestments, the furnishing and the sacred space" (par. 40); "making known the current liturgical texts and norms, making available the great riches found in the *General Instruction of the Roman Missal* and the *Order of Readings for Mass*" (par. 40); "attentiveness to the various kinds of language that the liturgy employs: words and music, gestures and silence, movement, the liturgical colors of the vestments" (par. 40); attentiveness to "every work of art placed at the service of the celebration . . . unity of the furnishings of the sanctuary . . . painting and sculpture, where religious iconography should be directed to sacramental mystagogy" (par. 41); "liturgical song" that is "well integrated into the overall celebration" and the "texts, music, execution" of which "correspond to the meaning of the mystery celebrated, the structure of the rite and the liturgical seasons" (par. 42).

If liturgy is beautiful because it is an encounter with Christ the expression of God's beauty, and if liturgy is the expression of faith of those created in the image and likeness of the Beautiful, an assembly of the beautiful (as Christ's body at worship), then it can be argued that the faithful have a right to beauty in worship, and a right to become co-creators of beauty in worship by participating in the work of God which is the liturgy. What is less-than-beautiful in the manner of celebrating the liturgy thus must be avoided at all costs. If what is at stake is the faith-life of believers, which poor celebrations risk weakening or destroying, then good celebrations, beautiful celebrations, are vital because the encounter with Christ's beauty in the liturgy is that which changes us/opens us up to

---

[39] Pope Benedict XVI, "*Sacramentum Caritatis*," par. 35.

desire the promotion of what we have experienced: exposure to God's beauty prompts us both to promote and emulate that beauty beyond the realm of the liturgical.

An attitude of ambivalence or indifference toward the proper celebration of the liturgy on the part of liturgical ministers neglects the intrinsic nature and requirements of the ritual itself to be performed properly, intentionally, beautifully, and to the best possible standard given situational restrictions. Such an attitude also neglects the right of those participating in the liturgy in non-ministerial roles (but who are powerlessly subject to the attitude of liturgical ministers), to "worship God according to the provisions of their own rite approved by the lawful pastors of the Church" (can. 214) which entails fostering the best possible opportunity for the assembly to encounter God's beauty within liturgical celebration. It is necessary to consider whether harm is being caused to the faith life of the assembly by failure to provide access to God's beauty through inspirational proclamation of Scripture, or carefully prepared presidential prayers rehearsed to facilitate aural comprehension, or the choice and quality performance of apt and beautiful ritual music, appropriate intentional silences, and beautiful art and environment.

Within a worship context, creative expressions, exercises in imagination, and demonstrations of giftedness on the part of faithful human beings are not for their own sake, but for God's sake. Aspiring to offer our best as co-creators of beauty in worship ought to be the regular mode of operation for an assembly that appreciates that exposure to beauty in worship is both a right and a duty of the faithful daring to enter into the presence of God to offer praise.

"Beauty Makes the Celebrated Faith Grow"

Fostering the beautiful in liturgy does not have as its *telos* the expression of beauty for its own sake, but rather the employment of beauty for facilitating: God's revelation; co-creative participation in God's beauty; re-identification and formation of the faithful as those made in the image and likeness of God; and growth in faith. In a papal message on the occasion of a joint performance by the

Synodal Choir of the Patriarchate of Moscow and the Sistine Chapel Choir, Pope Francis wrote of the profound nature of "a moment of spiritual elevation . . . through musical art," noting that

> In the Church in fact art in all its forms does not exist having only as its end a simple aesthetic fruition, but that through it, in every historical moment and in every culture, the Church is the interpreter of the Revelation to the People of God. Art exists in the Church essentially to evangelize and it is in this perspective that we can say with Dostoyevsky: "Beauty will save the world.". . . Music, painting, sculpture, architecture, in one word, beauty unites to make the celebrated faith grow, in prophetic hope, and in witnessed charity.[40]

Apprehension of beauty is something that can be learned indirectly, incidentally, experientially through the liturgy. In liturgical celebration our notions of Christian beauty are formed, and the eyes of faith are opened in the midst of God's beauty encountered in the presence of Christ. Liturgy celebrated well, celebrated beautifully, provides an encounter with Christ's beauty, which enables us to recalibrate our countercultural "beauty perceptors" so that we can perceive Christ's beauty in others. In this way the *ars liturgia* serves to foster the *ars moralis*. A consequence of perception of beauty, exposure to beauty, and the choice to allow it to change us, is that we can become more like the beauty in whose image and likeness we are made, that special kind of Christian beauty which begets itself in us so that we can both be and foster Christ's beauty in the world.[41]

---

[40] Pope Francis, "Papal Message to Russian Orthodox Choir That Sang in Rome," *Zenit*, November 5, 2013, http://www.zenit.org/en/articles/papal -message-to-russian-orthodox-choir-that-sang-in-rome, accessed November 9, 2013.

[41] See Nathan D. Mitchell, "The Amen Corner: Being Good and Being Beautiful," *Worship* 74, no. 6 (November 2000): 553.

"God at Every Gate"[1]

'Tis a dangerous moment for any one
    when the meaning goes out of things
    and Life stands straight—
    and punctual—
    and yet no signal comes.

Yet such moments are.
If we survive them they expand us,
if we do not,
    but that is Death, whose if is everlasting—
    the if of Deity—
    Avalanche or Avenue—
    Every Heart asks which . . .[2]

A couple of columns ago I called attention to Emily Dickinson as a poet who subverted conventional religious symbols with amazing concision and wit. With the merest handful of words, she could pull the plug on centuries of convoluted debate about God's being and human destiny. Dickinson had an astonishing talent for giving familiar biblical or theological phrases a sardonic twist—as this little quatrain reveals:

God is indeed a jealous God—
He cannot bear to see

---

[1] This essay originally appeared in "The Amen Corner," *Worship* 68, no. 3 (May 1994): 245–56.

[2] From an 1884 letter of Emily Dickinson, cited in J. Leyda, *The Years and Hours of Emily Dickinson* vol. 2 (New Haven, CT: Yale University Press, 1960), 424; here arranged in sense lines.

That we had rather not with Him
But with each other play.[3]

Here the sternly righteous, patriarchal God of Puritan piety is
lampooned as a petulant bully—wisely avoided by everyone else
on the playground! In another short poem, Dickinson gently
parodies the believer's blind confidence in the power of prayer:

At least—to pray—is left—is left—
Oh Jesus—in the Air—
I know not which thy chamber is—
I'm knocking—everywhere—
Thou settest Earthquake in the South—
And Maelstrom, in the Sea—
Say, Jesus Christ of Nazareth—
Hast thou no Arm for Me?[4]

So much for "leaning on the everlasting arms!" In still another
poem—ominous and almost hallucinatory in tone—God is a host
of frenzied pianists, fumbling "at your Soul / as Players at the
Keys," then hurling "One—imperial—Thunderbolt / That scalps
your naked soul."[5]

Dickinson was thus a woman who preferred the discomforts of
doubt to the cheap assurances of traditional theology: "Much
Gesture, from the Pulpit— / Strong Hallelujahs roll— / Narcotics
cannot still the Tooth / That nibbles at the soul—."[6] In the letter
cited at the beginning of this essay, she suggests that God is neither
a who nor a what, but an if. *Death, whose if is everlasting—the if of
Deity—Avalanche or Avenue . . .* " This is an astonishing insight, and
it shows how distant Dickinson was from the popular, pretentious
God of New England's pulpits. For "if" is a humble, mystery-laden
word whose origins and ends are hidden from us; a slippery word
that defies exact definition; an ambiguous word introducing condi-

---

[3] Poem 1719; in *The Complete Poems of Emily Dickinson*, ed. T.H. Johnson
(Boston: Little, Brown, 1960), 698.

[4] Poem 502; ed. Johnson, 243–244.

[5] Poem 315; ed. Johnson, 148.

[6] Poem 501; ed. Johnson, 243.

tions where every possibility of fulfillment or non-fulfillment is left open. The *if of Deity* . . . For Emily Dickinson, God is neither a personified task (watching, prodding, punishing) nor a compulsive parent (forever feeling your forehead, taking your temperature), but the troubling Presence of all possibilities. *Avalanche or Avenue— Every Heart asks which* . . .

This question vexed Dickinson throughout her life, for she realized that God is no Big Easy. Because God is an *if,* Deity meets us—alluringly, alarmingly—in every possibility, under every condition, at every gate. Eternity is not some unceasing, mellow numbness that awaits the godly, but an *"odd Fork in Being's Road"*— a choice, in other words, that leads through "the Forest of the Dead" to that place where one must either retreat, rebel or surrender:

> Our journey had advanced—
> Our feet were almost come
> To that odd Fork in Being's Road—
> Eternity—by Term—
> Our pace took sudden awe—
> Our feet—reluctant—led—
> Before—were Cities—but Between—
> The Forest of the Dead—
>
> Retreat—was out of Hope—
> Behind—a Sealed Route—
> Eternity's White Flag—Before—
> And God—at every Gate—[7]

Rebellion, retreat or surrender were not easy alternatives for a woman like Dickinson, who had chosen the rigorous path of doubting faith. While still a young student at Mount Holyoke, she prized her impenitence but paid the price: "I regret that last term," she wrote, "when that golden opportunity was mine, that I did not give up and become a Christian. It is not now too late . . . *but it is hard for me to give up the world."*[8]

---

[7] Poem 615; ed. Johnson, 303.

[8] Letter 23 to Abiah Root, 1848; in *The Letters of Emily Dickinson*, 3 vols. ed. T.H. Johnson (Cambridge: The Belknap Press, 1958), 1:67; emphasis added.

Hard to give up the world? A strange comment indeed from one whose life was so singularly reclusive and cloistered. What world did Dickinson fear losing to religion? Was it Thoreau's rapturous "poem of creation"—rural New England, with its whippoorwills and scarlet tanagers, its snow storms and rain storms? Was it the secure, tranquil world of family loyalties and private affections? Was it a secret world of sexual intrigue and passionate, unrequited love, as these lines suggest:

> Title divine—is mine!
> The Wife—without the Sign!
> Acute Degree—conferred on me—
> Empress of Calvary! . . .
> Born—Bridalled—Shrouded—
> In a Day—. . .[9]

No, I suspect the world Dickinson found "hard to give up" was neither nature, home, hearth, or sex, but the habitat created by her poems. For in that world she could walk in perfect freedom, unfettered by expectations about "how *proper* women must behave." In that world, love is unconditional and desire unrestricted: the "Empress of Calvary" is born, betrothed and buried in a single day! In that world, the rules respecting God-talk are relaxed, so that received religious "wisdom" can be questioned, even taunted:

> Of God we ask one favor,
> That we may be forgiven—
> For what, he is presumed to know—
> The Crime, from us, is hidden—. . .[10]

In these bitter lines, written toward the end of her life, Dickinson wonders aloud what kind of God would require us to repent simply for the "crime" of living! Does God begrudge even the smallest happiness we humans wrest from this harsh world? If so, is such a

[9] Poem 1072; ed. Johnson, 487.
[10] Poem 1601; ed. Johnson, 662.

God worth believing in, worth soliciting for mercy? Such irreverent questions could hardly be raised among nineteenth-century New England Puritans—but in the world of her poems, Dickinson could raise them, and did. To the end, she fearlessly maintained God's *if-ness*, acknowledging that the Deity might be avalanche or avenue—who knows which? ". . . *Is* there more?" she agonized in a letter of 1883, "More than Love and Death? Then tell me its name!"[11]

The world Emily Dickinson refused to forfeit to religion was thus the world of her poems. She understood, better than most, that poetry is a way of life, not a profession or a career. As Marvin Bell has written:

> A career means you solicit the powerful and the famous. A way of life means you live where you are with the people around you. A career means you become an authority. A way of life means you stay a student, even if you teach for a living. A career means your life increasingly comes from your art. A way of life means your art continues to arise from your life. Careerism feeds off the theoretical, the fancified, the complicated, the coded, and the overwrought: all forms of psychological cowardice. A way of life is nourished by the practical, the unadorned, the complex, and a direct approach to the mysterious . . . . For poetry to be a way of life in a referential world, it requires of us the courage of clarity—linear, syntactical, and referential— which in no way compromises the great wildness of experience and imagination.[12]

Dickinson had the courage of clarity, the courage to be complex without being complicated. Her poems were a field of dreams, common ground where all life's players could find room to negotiate their relations with self, others, God, and world. (That is why we read them still.) She knew that every poem is an *ars poetica*, an "essay" on the poet's art, the craft of catching the self in the act of turning—of turning toward the vast, low murmur of life unedited;

[11] Letter 873 to Mrs. J. G. Holland; ed. Johnson, III: 803.

[12] "Homage to the Runner: Bloody Brain Work," in *The Pushcart Prize XVIII* (Wainscott, NY: Pushcart Press, 1993), 297–98.

of turning toward "the great wildness of experience and imagination"; of turning toward the Mystery (avalanche or avenue, who knows which?) that looms at every fork in being's road, at every gate.

If every poem is an *ars poetica*, perhaps it can also be said that every act of public worship is an *ars liturgica*, an essay on the etiquette embodied and the energy aroused by the assembly, corporate and converting. For liturgy too is a field of dreams, where communities enact meanings and embody beliefs through ritual symbols, remembered traditions, and renegotiated patterns of power. Like a poem, worship invites participants to negotiate anew their relations with self, others, God, and world. For these reasons, indeed, I have often argued that liturgy is poetry and, hence, that its texts and utterances must be poetic. Poetry here should obviously not be equated with prettiness and rhetorical technique, nor with the presence of meter and metaphor. As a poem, worship is a way of life, not a career plied by professionals. As Marvin Bell noted, careerism is characterized by psychological cowardice; it "feeds off of the theoretical, the fancified, the complicated, the coded." But a way of life "is nourished by the practical, the unadorned, the complex . . . a direct approach to the mysterious." Every *ars liturgica* (like every *ars poetica*) must be, as well, an art of losing. As Elizabeth Bishop wrote in her poem "One Art":

> The art of losing isn't hard to master;
> so many things seem filled with the intent
> to be lost that their loss is no disaster.
>
> Lose something every day. Accept the fluster
> of lost door keys, the hour badly spent . . .
>
> Then practice losing farther, losing faster:
> places, and names, and where it was you meant
> to travel. None of these will bring disaster . . .[13]

---

[13] Elizabeth Bishop, *The Complete Poems, 1927–1979* (New York: Farrar, Straus, Giroux, 1983), 178.

Perhaps it sounds bizarre to say that the *ars liturgica* is an art of losing. But such is the case—in the Latin West, at any rate. As scholars like Christine Mohrmann never tired of noting, the classic language of the Roman Rite is characterized by the absence—the loss—of precisely those elements professionals rely on to make their living (the theoretical, the complicated). Mohrmann's inventories of liturgical Latin in its classic phase of development revealed a language that was lean and lapidary, austere and sober, sacral and hieratic. It was a deliberately stylized speech, characterized by quasi-juridical precision. Those who shaped the earliest Latin liturgy were poets who knew how to fast from language, how to lose words. They understood the difference between complexity and complication. (Beethoven's Archduke Trio is *complex*; the movie Ace Ventura: Pet Detective is *complicated*.) They understood (as Emily Dickinson did) that hype and hysteria cannot pass for passion, that filler cannot take the place of keen observation. Because it eschewed pious speeches and convoluted discussions of doctrine, the language of the Roman Rite could be broadly inclusive. It could accommodate participants with diverse points of view; it could embrace believers at many different stages of spiritual development.

These points need to be recalled especially today. The "genius" of the Roman Rite lay in its clear understanding that *doctrine arises from doxology, not vice versa*. The earliest shapers of our tradition did not set out to score doctrinal points. (Indeed, when such attempts were made—in certain prefaces of the Verona and Old Gelasian sacramentaries, for example—they fell flat and failed to survive in the subsequent tradition.) As any high school Latin student knows, a phrase like *"accipiens et hunc praeclarum calicem in sanctas ac venerabiles manus suas"* in the old Roman Canon reflects rhetorical motives, not Christological or eucharistic ones. Rhythm and balance in Latin prayer texts (whether pagan/classical or Christian) required this kind of periphrastic construction when stylistic elegance and hieratic effect were being sought after. In modern English, such periphrasis would be considered "overwriting," ineffectual embellishment. Thus Elizabeth Bishop's admonition that the poet must not be afraid of *losing*—for loss creates the space where *another*'s meaning can take possession of us. That is why poetry favors the "soft focus" over the hard sell, the plurisignificant over the univocal. And that is also why *ars liturgica* (like *ars poetica*) is an exercise in multiple meanings rather than "clear and distinct ideas."

Take, for example, the ancient collect assigned for the third Mass of Christmas in the Missal of 1970 (and quoted partially in the private prayer said at the preparation of the chalice). The Latin reads, in part, *"Da, quaesumus, nobis eius divinitatis esse consortes, qui humanitatis nostrae fieri dignatus est particeps"* (literally, "Grant that we may be sharers in the divinity of him who deigned to become a partaker in our humanity"). Rhetorically, this prayer is a huge success. The rhythm and balance of the parallel cola (*"Da . . . consortes / qui . . . particeps"*) are beautiful. There is a level, however, at which this prayer is hyperbolic (and theologically inaccurate!) nonsense. After all, classical theology holds that the "hypostatic union" of the divine and human natures in the one person of Christ is unique. There is no way that *our* share in *divinity* could be exactly identical with *Christ's* share in our *humanity*. Yet this is precisely what the prayer suggests. It breaks the bonds of theological propriety and exposes us to a greater (and far more dangerous) mystery—the possibility that God's lot has somehow become our own! It does no good to try squirming out of such implications by pointing to the use of different words—*"consortes"* (for us) and *"particeps"* (for Christ). For in early Christian Latin, the word *consortes* was used precisely to describe the union of Christ and the Spirit with the Divine substance.[14]

Doctrine is derived from doxology, not vice versa. The ancient authors of the Roman Rite understood this instinctively. They knew the difference between rhetorical device and theological gambit. They recognized the need for softly focused texts that distinguish *ars liturgica* from *ars theologica*. They admitted their indebtedness to juridically precise secular/pagan models of prayer (as witnessed by such clauses in the old Roman Canon as *"Quam oblationem, tu,*

---

[14] See Tertullian, *Adversus Praxean*, 3.

Deus . . . benedictam, adscriptam, ratam, rationabilem, acceptabilemque facere digneris . . ."). They would have rejoiced in the courageous wisdom of Emily Dickinson, who realized that even if you are wearing ruby slippers, the way to the emerald city lies through Death's everlasting if—"the if of Deity."

"A Meditation on Eucharistic Praying"[1]

This is my last "Amen Corner." More than twenty years have gone by since the first. Yet, it seems like yesterday. My heartfelt thanks go to Kevin Seasoltz and to all of you readers. I hope you do not mind that for the occasion I leave you with some poetic thoughts and reflections. *Maranâ' thâ'!*

"We come to you, God, with praise and thanksgiving"

We come to you, God, with praise and thanksgiving . . .
- *We come to you with praise—with speech and utterance, language and word;*
We come from every corner of the world,
our eyes wakeful, watching God,[2]
our dusky souls deep as rivers.[3]
We come weaving silky webs of word and image, art and song.
We come with cymbal and tambourine, pipe and drum,
We come in torrents of driving dentals, lilting labials, hissing sibilants.
We come into your holy presence, tongue lifting against palate,
spittle and mucus parting like the Red Sea;
We come echoing your *own* voice—"resounding on the waters,
flashing flames of fire, shaking the wilderness,
rending the oak tree, and stripping the forest bare."[4]
We come as orphans seeking shelter in a storm
our breath like tides pushing toward the shore,
our blood surging like breakers beating against rock,
our hearts drifting like smoke in a swirl of sacrifice.

---

[1] This essay originally appeared in "The Amen Corner," *Worship* 86, no. 6 (November 2012): 552–66.

[2] Source of the image: Zora Neale Hurston.

[3] Source of the image: Langston Hughes.

[4] Cf. Ps 29:3-9.

We come to you, God, with praise and thanksgiving,
"Giver of Breath and Bread, World's strand, Sway of the sea,
Lord of the living and the dead"[5]

- *We come to you with words that crack, breaking words, broken words.*
  We come to you, knowing
  that every word we utter is weight and wound and wonder;
  We come burdened and weary, wrestling with a welter of words
  that wriggle and rebel, that refuse to stay put,
  that balk whenever we try to tell our story.
  We come, praying,
  "Teach us to care and not to care—teach us to sit still,
  Even among these rocks,
  Our peace in [God's] will."[6]
  We come stammering, stuttering—beginning, stopping, beginning
  again, repeating the same words in the same rhythm:
  Lord have mercy, Lord have mercy, lord have mercy;
  Lord, I am not worthy to receive you,
  but only say the word and I shall be healed.
  We come to you, God, with praise and thanksgiving . . .
- *We come to you in a riotous company of colors*
  —The midnight blue of Christmas, the white heat of Easter, the red
  flame of Pentecost—for

> "Red is the body's own deep song,
> the color of lips, of our busy
> organs, heart and stomach and lungs,
>
> . . .
>
> the color of tongues and the flag of our blood.
> Red is the loudest color
> and the most secret
>
> . . .
>
> . . . red coils in the wineglass
>
> . . .
>
> . . . rises like a perfumed ghost
> inside the chambers of your nose."[7]

[5] An allusion to "The Wreck of the Deutschland," by Gerard M. Hopkins.
[6] From "Ash Wednesday," by T. S. Eliot.
[7] Marge Piercy, "The Wine," in *The Art of Blessing the Day* (New York: Knopf, 1999), 57.

So, God, we come to you *red*—red as love and fire and surrender, red as wine poured out. For

> In the mouth wine opens
> its hundred petals like a damask rose
> and then subsides, swallowed to afterglow.
> . . .
> the heat of our love ferments
> our roundness into the midnight red
> flowering in the wine
> . . . into feast, that can celebrate
> and sing through the wine of the body[8]

We come, rejoicing—bringing in the sheaves, "hurrahing in harvest."[9]
We come with the "barbarous beauty of summer," lifting heart and
     eyes, scanning "all that glory in heaven to glean our Saviour."[10]
We come with "[w]ords plain as pancakes syruped with endearment."[11]
We come with faces "simple as potatoes, homely as cottage cheese. /
Wet as onions, dry as salt. / Slow as honey, fast as seltzer."[12]
We come singing to Christ our Savior, "O!

> "[M]y raisin, my sultana, my apricot love
> my artichoke, furry one, my pineapple
> I love you daily as milk,
> I love you nightly as a romantic port.
> . . .
> When we are alone we make love in deeds.
> And then in words. And then in food."[13]

We come to you, God, with praise and thanksgiving . . .
- *We come to you as words of the Word made flesh—*
We come as members of his Body who lived and died and rose to
     shed his joyful light on all humankind.
We come, knowing that Christ's body is now our own and only
     language—the sensible sign that sweetens our longing for one
     another,

---

[8] Ibid., 58.
[9] Title of a poem by Gerard M. Hopkins.
[10] Image drawn from the poetry of Hopkins.
[11] Marge Piercy, "House Built of Breath," in *The Art of Blessing the Day*, 59.
[12] Ibid.
[13] Ibid.

our desire for companions at table,
our hunger for stews that spoons won't sink in,
our passion for pasta in a thousand varieties.
We come, knowing that you have
Gardens to give away, cities to spare, history that hasn't
even been used yet.
We come, knowing that the last of all your mercies is your merry
heart,
that shows us, even in Christ's passion, the divine mirth,
promises us that even in our cities of exile,
you call us to catch the glory, to offer the world whose
service still shapes the City of God.[14]
We come, acknowledging that ours is the most precious of all priest-
hoods—the priesthood of Eve and Adam.
We stand as priests, knowing that our real work is to look at the things
of the world and to love them for what they are. For that is what
you do, and we were not made in your image for nothing.[15]
We stand in our ancient priesthood, acknowledging that every person
we meet has a history which threatens or promises involvement
in our own history; for we know that every thing, every place,
every time, is a mysterious . . . sign to be interpreted.[16]
We stand as priests who make towns and join clubs, who paint and
whittle, who write novels, poems and fugues.
We stand as priests who, from our cribs, from the first delicious stirring
of speech, have never ceased to love making sounds that rock,
roll, rhyme, and rattle.
We stand as priests of creation—offerers, intercessors, agents of its
shape and history.
We stand, knowing that culture and civilization are simply the sum of
our priestly successes, the fulfillment of our priestly vocation.
For we recognize that the life of Eve and Adam is parks and
plazas, porches and playgrounds—places that *invite* and *cherish*
the human, houses *worthy* of our priesthood.
We stand, then, in our ancient priesthood, struggling to shape creation
into a city for God, a city *of* God—a new Jerusalem coming

[14] Images in this and the preceding section drawn from Robert Farrar
Capon, *An Offering of Uncles* (New York: Sheed & Ward, 1967), 158.
[15] Based on Robert Farrar Capon, *The Supper of the Lamb* (New York:
Doubleday, 1969), 19.
[16] Ibid., 26.

down out of heaven, Bride of the Lamb, new heavens and new earth where there is no more mourning or death or wailing or pain, where every tear is wiped away.[17]

We come to you, God, with praise and thanksgiving . . .
- *We come gladly, aglow with gratitude and prayer.*

We come early each morning;

> "When the night slides under with the last dimming star
> and the red sky lightens between the trees,
> and the heron glides tipping heavy wings in the river,
> when crows stir and cry out their harsh joy,
> and swift creatures of the night run toward their burrows,
> and the deer raises her head and sniffs the freshening air,
> and the shadows grow more distinct and then shorten,
>
> then we rise into the day still clean as new snow . . .
>
> Every day we find a new sky and a new earth
> with which we are trusted like a perfect toy.
> We are given the salty river of our blood
> > winding through us, to remember the sea and our
> > kindred under the waves, . . .
>
> > We are given the wind within us, the breath
> > to shape into words that steal time, that touch
> > like hands and pierce like bullets, that waken
> > truth and deceit, sorrow and pity and joy, . . .
>
> > We are given the body, that momentary kibbutz
> > of elements that have belonged to frog and polar
> > bear, corn and oak tree, volcano and glacier. . . .
>
> > We are given fire to see against the dark,
> > to think, to read, to study how we are to live,
> > to bank in ourselves against defeat and despair . . ."[18]

Yes, Lord, we come with joy and gladness crowning our days because you are the God who is new each morning.
Fill us, then:

---

[17] Images in this and the preceding four paragraphs are based on Capon, *An Offering of Uncles*, 26–28.

[18] Marge Piercy, "Nishmat," in *The Art of Blessing the Day*, 129–30.

"Fill us as the rushing water overflows the pitcher.
Fill us as light fills a room with its dancing.
Let the little quarrels of the bones and the snarling
of the lesser appetites and the whining of the ego cease.
Let silence still us so you may show us your shining
and we can out of that stillness rise and praise."[19]
We come to you, God, with praise and thanksgiving . . .

• *We come to the Supper of the Lamb—*
We come with hands smelling of basil and thyme; rosemary, marjoram,
and mint; garlic and sage; chives and summer savory.
We come into the presence of your holiness, the tips of our gnarled
fingers long acquainted with moist loam and lily, sweetpea and
ginger root.
We come, acknowledging our love of meringue and lemon custard;
of leeks and linguine and lasagne; of pies so thick with fruit the
juices ooze through the flaky crust, leaving fragrant, steaming
lakes.
We come—our fingers finely tuned to the smooth ebony of oboe or
clarinet, the taut catgut of violin, violincello, and viola.
We come, our cheeks brightened by the feel of fresh laundry—linen
and cotton, silk and wool;
We come—our knuckles sore from stirring, sifting, gripping lids and
ladels and rolling pins; we come with palms warmed by the
smooth, floury surface of dough, egg-yellow, rich, rolled out and
cut into thin strips for noodles that will stick to our ribs.
We come—arms loaded and hands filled, grown weighty and wise
after seventy or eighty years of kneading dough and shaping
loaves and brushing butter on baking bread.
We come, lifting hands that have given life to lasses and lads, to lands
and larks and lambs; hands ridged and veined, solemn and wise
from smoothing a thousand troubled brows, from cradling
countless grieving heads. Yes, Lord, yes. We come to the Supper
of the Lamb.
We come with our foggy modern eyes and our great white latter-day
vanity;
We come anxious and desperate, dimmed by melancholy, disarmed
and defeated by a hundred forms of *angst* and *ennui*;

---

[19] Marge Pierce, "Nishmat," 131.

We come limping, on the lam, looking for love or luck;
We come springing fresh from the house of mirth—yet fearful of a
    spookier house, darkened by dread and death.
We come to make Eucharist; but we make it not from bread and wine
    alone; we make it of our own water, blood, breath, bone and
    body; we make it of our salt, sweat and tears, our syrup and
    semen, our eggs and meat.
We come to make Eucharist from "our desire for June and evening," [20]
    from our cancer and chemotherapy, from our despair and hope-
    lessness, from our falling hair and fading strength.
We priests of Eve and Adam come to make Eucharist even when the
    "snow is frozen moonlight on the marshes," [21] even when our
    lungs ache, and our knees knock, and our eyes weep.
Yes, we make Eucharist from whatever is at hand—from emeralds
    singing in the grasses, the May moon, a summer storm, a chorus
    of crickets and katydids, the flowering plum, a cry of terror or
    remorse, the long shadow of the cross.
We come, a flock of loud, thieving magpies—prodigals amazed and
    jubilant at God's bounty; children who suddenly discover a
    peck of peaches at a bend in the road, for
        "From laden boughs, from hands,
        from sweet fellowship in the bins,
        comes nectar at the roadside, succulent
        peaches we devour, dusty skin and all, . . .

        O, to take what we love inside,
        to carry within us an orchard, to eat
        not only the skin, but the shade,
        not only the sugar, but the days, to hold
        the fruit in our hands, adore it, then bite into
        the round jubilance of peach.

        There are days we live
        as if death were nowhere
        in the background; from joy
        to joy to joy, from wing to wing,

<hr />

[20] This phrase is taken from "Sunday Morning," by Wallace Stevens.
    [21] This phrase is from Marge Piercy, "The Hunger Moon," in *The Art of Bless-
ing the Day*, 124.

from blossom to blossom to

impossible blossom, to sweet impossible blossom."[22]

Yes, we come to the Supper of the Lamb, to make Eucharist from
whatever lies at hand.

We come in the harsh and dreadful knowledge born of Easter.

We come, knowing that

"Instinct will end us.

The force that measles the peach tree

will divest and undo us.

The power that kicks on

the cells in the lilac bush

Will tumble us down and down."[23]

We come to the Lamb's Supper,

knowing that on the table lie Christ's body and ours, bread and
wine, life and death and surrender.

We come, knowing that the "definer of all things / cannot be spoken
of."[24]

We come to you, God, with praise and thanksgiving . . .

- *We come to you with images, with painted prayers—*

We come in the company of alphabets dancing across parchment and
paper;

We come lifting hide-bound books aloft,

holding high gospels that are greeted with perfume,

clothed in gold and gems, encircled by fire and light.

We come into your presence with art—drawn on paper,

inscribed in books, and carved on bone.

And we paint the air itself with the movement of our bodies—

For we know that the spaces where we worship are built

from the spaciousness of our own bodies.

We know we experience buildings with bodies, with outstretched
arms and pacing feet, with the roving glance and the ear, and
above all else, with our breathing.

[22] Li-Young Lee, "Blossoms," in *Sixty Years of American Poetry* (New York:
Harry Abrams, 1996), 262.

[23] Charles Wright, "Easter 1989," in *Chickamauga* (New York: Farrar, Straus &
Giroux, 1995), 10.

[24] Ibid., 11.

We know that our body's space forces itself outward to meet the
building's skin, which lies so close to a dancing people.[25]
We come, our faces lit by the holy fire burning in ancient icons, for we
know, with all the holy saints of Russia, that the spires, the
"onion domes" of churches, are neither domes nor onions, but
flames, spiraling tongues of fire, flames.
Yes, Lord, earth is afire and our cities are seas of flame.
We come to you, God, with praise and thanksgiving . . .

- *We come in worship, bearing in our hands work and worry and prayer—*
for the tools of our daily tasks and trades are to be treated,
as your holy monk Benedict once said, like the very vessels of
the altar.
We come, knowing that human work is the way you know and see
the world through the eyes of your creatures.
Yes, we bring our labor, our own bodies as our first response to you,
our answer to a world received as gift and recognized as your
dwelling.
In your honor, on behalf of our bodies, we build huts and houses;
we create hearths for heat and comfort;
we design kettles to sing at tea-time;
we fashion spinning wheels and looms for weaving wool and
flax into fabulous fabric, extending our own skins into climates
hot and cold;
we stretch our feet to the stars, building rockets that hurl us to the
moon—the moon which is so "empty and vain, a glittering
dune, . . . a useless beauty in a pit" of empty space.[26]
We offer you, then, O Lord, our brother the body: Use it to craft creation, to build a habitat for humanity, a habitat for the kingdom
of heaven.
We offer you, O Lord, our hands: Use them to lift the slumbering
image from the silent block of marble; use them to release the
song from hollow wood; use them to strike the stretched mem-
brane of a drum.

[25] Images in this and the preceding paragraph drawn from Rudolf Schwarz,
The Church Incarnate, trans. Cynthia Harris (Chicago: Henry Regnery Company, 1958), 27.

[26] The phrase in quotation marks from Delmore Schwarz, "The starlight's
intuition pierced the twelve," in Jacob Trapp, *Modern Religious Poems* (New
York: Harper & Row, 1964), 94.

We come to pray, knowing what your holy friar John of the Cross
taught us: "*Come empty; do nothing.*"
We come, knowing that creation begins when God calls us and names
us.
We answer your call "with our existence, our bodies, our work . . . all
taken up in to your loving freedom; for we know it is your holy
habit to be moved by our human pleas."[27]
We come to you, God, with praise and thanksgiving . . .

- *We come to the table, feasting with family and friends—feasting even with
foes.*
We come in the company of a cloud of witnesses, saints and sinners,
poets and prophets;
We come in the company of

". . . people thronging 47th Street in Chicago and Lenox Avenue in
New York and Rampart Street in New Orleans, lost disinherited dis-
possessed and happy people filling the cabarets and taverns and other
people's pockets needing bread and milk and shoes and land and
money and something—something all their own;

". . . [we come in the company of] people walking blindly spreading
joy, losing time being lazy, sleeping when hungry, shouting when burdened, drinking when hopeless, tied and shackled and tangled among
ourselves by the unseen creatures who tower over us omnisciently
and laugh;

". . . [we come in the company of] people standing staring trying to
fashion a better way from confusion, from hypocrisy and misunderstanding, trying to fashion a world that will hold all the people, all the
faces, all the adams and eves and their countless generations . . ."[28]

We come praying:

Let a new earth rise. Let another world be born. Let a bloody peace be
written in the sky. Let a second generation full of courage issue forth;
let a people loving freedom come to growth. Let a beauty full of healing and a strength of final clenching be the pulsing in our spirits and

[27] Based on Rudolf Schwarz, 32.
[28] Margaret Walker, "For My People," in Jacob Trapp, *Modern Religious
Poems: A Contemporary Anthology,* 155–56.

our blood. Let the martial songs be written, let the dirges disappear. . . ."[29]

We come, then, not only in the company of our families, friends and familiars, but in the company of strangers.

We come not only happy and hopeful, but hospitable; for being hospitable means making room—making room for the presence of those we do not know and, perhaps, cannot love (though we know you do).

We come, certain that at the table of God's kingdom, there is always room for one more—always room for the shy stranger, always room for the have-nots and the has-beens, always room for the ramshackle and the miserable and marginalized, always room for those who have been shut up and shut out.

We come singing: *Let a new earth arise. Let another world be born. . . . Let a beauty full of healing and a strength of final clenching be the pulsing in our spirits and our blood.*

We come to table, loving and welcoming strangers, for *we* were once strangers—strangers in a strange land, strangers in Egypt, strangers and pilgrims called to follow the footsteps of Christ, who bore our sins in his body on the tree and healed us by his wounds. (See 1 Peter 2:11; 21-24)

We come to table, where every one of us has a place because we are all *Forgiven*—rescued like straying sheep and redeemed by the "shepherd and guardian of our souls." (See 1 Peter 2:25)

We come to you, God, with praise and thanksgiving . . .

• *We come, then, forever free and forgiven, praising the great God of our life.*

We come, making our own the words of another:

"Great God of our life, we will praise you on the three shores of your one light.

We will plunge with our song into the sea of your glory: with rejoicing into the waves of your power.

Golden God of the stars, loud God of the storms, flaming God of the fire-spewing mountains,

God of the streams and of the seas, God of all beasts, God of all the cornfields and wild roses,

We thank you for having awakened us;

Lord, we thank you to the choirs of your angels.

[29] Margaret Walker, "For My People," 156.

Be praised for all that lives.
God of Jesus, great God of eternal compassion, great God
of erring humanity,
God of all who suffer, God of all who die,
sisterly God on our dark spoor;
We thank you that you have delivered us . . .
Be praised for our blessedness!
God of your own Spirit, flooding in your depths from love
to love,
Seething down into my soul,
Rushing through all the chambers, bringing fire to every
heart,
Holy Creator of your new earth:
We thank you for making it possible to thank you; we
thank you to the choirs of your angels;
God of our psalms, God of our harps, God of our organs
and of our mighty music,
We will sing your praises on the three shores of your one
light.
We will plunge with our song into the sea of your glory:
with shouts of joy into the waves of your power."[30]

We come to you, God, with praise and thanksgiving . . . through Jesus
Christ our Lord. For through him, with him, in him, in the unity
of the Holy Spirit, all glory and honor is yours, almighty Father,
for ever and ever.

• *We come to you, God, in a state of supreme attention—*
We come taking notice, taking notes, naming names to render the
highest possible justice to the visible universe[31]

To enter the holy presence with praise and thanksgiving is to
greet God with *art*—with fingers that know the smooth rush of wet
clay spinning on the potter's wheel, fingers that turn finely textured
vellum into painted worlds—people and pastures and pleasures.

[30] Gertrud von Le Fort, *Hymns to the Church*, trans. Margaret Chanler (New York: Sheed & Ward, 1953), 51–52; text altered.

[31] Flannery O'Connor, "The Nature and Aim of Fiction," in *Mystery and Manners: Occasional Prose*, selected, ed. Sally and Robert Fitzgerald (New York: Farrar, Straus, Giroux, 1969), 63–86.

It is surely no accident that over the centuries Benedictine life has produced so much art, so many artists. Artists of word and image like Hildegard, Gertrude, Mechtilde; artists like Diarmaid, the monk of St. Gall who produced a sumptuous purple-vellum psalter as a wedding gift for Emperor Otto's son—one of the most famous and exquisite manuscripts of the Carolingian renaissance. If you are a fan (as I am) of Ellis Peters' "Brother Cadfael" mysteries, you may have read her description of this precious painted psalter toward the end of her novel *The Heretic's Apprentice*: The purple vellum of the [book's] binding [Ms. Peters tells us], was stretched over thin boards, and the first gathering of the book, and the last . . . were also of gold on purple. The rest of the leaves were of very fine, smooth finish and almost pure white. There was a frontispiece painting of the psalmist playing and singing, enthroned like an emperor and surrounded by musicians earthly and heavenly. The vibrant colors sprang ringing from the page, as brilliantly as the sounds the royal minstrel was plucking from his strings. Here was no powerful, massive, Byzantine block coloring, classic and monumental, but sinuous, delicate, graceful shapes, as pliant

. . .

. . . page after page . . . numerals and initials flowered in exquisite colors, laced and bordered with all manner of meadow flowers, climbing roses, little herbers no bigger than a thumbnail, where birds sang in branches hardly thicker than a hair, and shy animals leaned out from the cover of blossoming bushes. Tiny, perfect women sat reading on turfed seats under bowers of eglantine, golden fountains played into ivory basins, swans sailed on crystal rivers, minute ships ventured oceans the size of a tear.

. . . [T]he final exultant psalms were again inscribed in gold, and the psalter ended with a painted page in which an empyrean of hovering angels, a paradise of haloed saints, and a transfigured earth of redeemed souls all together obeyed the psalmist, and praised God in the firmament of [God's] power, with every instrument of music known to man [and woman]. And all the quivering wings, all the haloes, all the trumpets and psalteries and harps, the stringed instruments and organs, the timbrels, and the loud cymbals were of burnished gold, and the denizens of heaven and paradise and earth alike were as sinuous and ethereal as the tendrils of rose and honeysuckle and vine that intertwined with them, and the sky above them as blue as the irises and periwinkles under their feet, until the tips of the angels' wings melted into a zenith of blinding gold, in which the ultimate mystery vanished from sight.[32] So we come into God's presence with psalms and paper and paint, with color and art.

[32] Ellis Peters, *The Heretic's Apprentice* (New York: The Mysterious Press, 1990), 244–46.

Chapter Five: *Justice*

Linking Cult to Care: Social Transformation and the Liturgical Movement

Katharine E. Harmon

In September of 1935, Virgil Michel, OSB, addressed a group of lay Roman Catholics gathered in Mankato, Minnesota, for the thirty-seventh annual meeting of the Minnesota branch of the Central Verein: "What has the liturgy to do with social reconstruction or the social question?" Michel asked. "Can the liturgy help to give jobs or raise wages? Can there be any connection between the liturgy and the social problem?"[1] Michel's address, which appeared in *Orate Fratres* (now *Worship*) a few months later, drew a sharp distinction between the isolated, private prayer which Roman Catholics commonly experienced during Mass, and the social, transformative experience of worship inherent within the liturgical ritual. For Michel, and for so many others, liturgy was not defined by the recital of rosaries during a correct rubrical performance on the part of ministers,[2] but by the manner in which the liturgy continued to be performed by all members of Christ's body in the context of the world. As Michel explained:

[1] Virgil Michel, "The Liturgy the Basis for Social Regeneration," *Orate Fratres* 9, vol. 12 (1935): 536.

[2] See *The Liturgical Movement*, Popular Liturgical Library, 4th ser., no. 3 (Collegeville, MN: Liturgical Press, 1930).

By becoming members of the Mystical Body of Christ through Baptism, we no longer belong to ourselves alone but above all to Christ and His cause. . . . Similarly the liturgy of the Church not only makes and keeps us members of this fellowship, but it always puts the idea of fellowship in Christ into full practice. . . . This is why the liturgy is so truly the primary and indispensable source of the true Christian spirit: it not only teaches us what this spirit is but also has us live this spirit in all its enactments. In the liturgy the teaching is inseparable from the putting into practice.[3]

If Christians could interpret the unity taught by the ritual experience of communal, liturgical celebration, Christians could bring unity, care, and justice to their particular human communities. In contrast, reliance on isolated, passive worship offered no pattern for combatting a complacent indifference toward the acute needs of society.

In more recent years, inheritors of the liturgical movement's[4] hopes and dreams continue to question the dangerous disconnect between liturgical celebration and social justice. As my teacher, Nathan Mitchell, wrote some sixty-one years following Michel's words:

What does it mean when we wrap our assemblies in miasmas of incense while two blocks away a drug deal is going down and another child is lost to gunfire? What does it mean to declare that the Church's worship is "immune from" or "above" public policy and politics when the safety net protecting the weakest, poorest, most vulnerable members of our society, is being shredded like yesterday's newspaper? Have we become a Church of liturgical isolationists, afraid of the consequences of linking cult to care?[5]

[3] Michel, "The Liturgy the Basis for Social Regeneration," 541–42.
[4] Hereafter, the term "liturgical movement" will refer to the mid-twentieth century.
[5] Nathan D. Mitchell, "The Violent Bear it Away," *Worship* 70, no. 4 (July 1996): 337.

Far from liturgical isolationists, liturgical movement advocates of the past and present have sought to shift the center of Catholic devotional gravity from self-absorption and drive-by communions to interactive and cohesive ritual experiences, attending to cultural particularity[6] and responding to specific social needs. The liturgy, and especially the Eucharist, cannot be ignorant of life. Nathan has continually stressed the absurdity of objectifying the Eucharist (the divine prisoner in the tabernacle) while ignoring the Eucharistic subjects who truly are prisoners of violence, oppression, and need. As he described in 2012, "the greatest threat to Christian Eucharist is precisely that moral numbness that prevents our seeing God's presence in the least and the littlest, that prevents our seeing the Risen One among the most vulnerable citizens of our chaotic world."[7] The Eucharist is not to be watched; the Eucharist prepares us to watch and to wait upon the world around us.

This present essay revisits the great hopes for social transformation which lie at the heart of the twentieth-century liturgical movement by illustrating how an attentiveness to *social contexts* was central to liturgical renewal for modern (and postmodern) Roman Catholics. To do so, this essay will describe three realms in which liturgical pioneers explored the socially-transformative potential of liturgical worship to address pointed sociological concerns of the day: 1) racism; 2) poverty; and 3) the role of women. As Nathan has modeled, attention to social questions disturbs a tendency to trace the liturgical movement along reports from well-known clerics alone. While detailing the work of religious and clerics is historically crucial, attending to questions of social marginalization requires retrieving historically marginalized witnesses, particularly lay, non-religious women and men.[8]

---

[6] See Aidan Kavanagh, "Liturgical Inculturation: Looking to the Future," *Studia Liturgica* 20, no. 1 (1990): 95–106; and Nathan D. Mitchell, "The Coming Revolution in Ritual Studies," *Worship* 67, no. 1 (1993): 74–81.

[7] Nathan D. Mitchell, "Making the Connections," *Worship* 86, no. 3 (May 2012): 260.

[8] Nathan D. Mitchell, "A Mansion for the Rat," *Worship* 68, no. 1 (January 1994): 68.

I. Racism and Justice

Understanding the liturgy as a social force was a continual refrain for *Orate Fratres*. It drew its inspiration from the theological concept, the Mystical Body of Christ.[9] By the 1940s, relying on the Mystical Body motif for social justice was further buoyed by Pius XII's encyclical, *Mystici Corporis* (1943). With papal approval, liturgical movement advocates could describe how the solidarity afforded by communal liturgy foiled the isolationism of individualized spirituality and an indifference to social injustices. Yet, while the idea of unification in prayer might be inspiring, what of the reality of deeply divided social structures along lines of race? At the 1941 Liturgical Week meeting held in St. Paul, Minnesota, Fr. Paul Hanly Furfey, professor of sociology at The Catholic University of America in Washington, DC, called those gathered to discuss the liturgy to confront the sin of racism:

> [C]onsider the social problem of race relations in the United States. About a tenth of our population is Negro. These Negroes are our brothers in Christ, fellow members of the Mystical Body. . . . Cold, hard statistics prove the following facts: We have denied equal economic opportunity to our colored fellow citizens. We have often excluded them from our schools—even Catholic schools. We have made a mockery of the sound American principle of equal justice before the law. We have denied civil and political rights to Negroes on a large scale. We have made it difficult for them to share the benefits of medical service on the same scale as whites. We have— this is most humiliating to say; but we have even dragged our nasty prejudices into the presence of Christ in the Tabernacle. Think of it! We Catholics have dared to prate of charity and then insult our fellow Catholics by diverse discriminations in the very presence of the Incarnate God.[10]

---

[9] For a brief history of theology of the Mystical Body, see Keith F. Pecklers, *The Unread Vision: The Liturgical Movement in the United States of America, 1926–1955* (Collegeville, MN: Liturgical Press, 1998), 29–34.

[10] Paul Hanly Furfey, "Liturgy and the Social Problem," *1941 Liturgical Week Proceedings* (Newark: Benedictine Liturgical Conference, 1942), 182. Here, and throughout, the non-inclusive language of the original will be retained.

Furfey's words prompted listener Alice Summers, an undergraduate at St. Benedict's College in St. Joseph, Minnesota, to recount her own experience in confronting racism. Summers described how, in the late 1930s, two young African American women were admitted to St. Benedict's, despite serious protests from alumnae. Summers and her classmates worked to welcome the two young women, introduced them to activities of the school, and even made it "their business to see that the girls were taken to all of the school proms." As Summers concluded, "We are now very confident that our future alumnae will realize their responsibility as Christians and will not make a protest against such a step again."[11] Summers understood her taking part in racial inclusion as an application of her formation in the liturgy. Similarly, at another women's college in Minnesota in the latter 1930s, the College of St. Catherine's, undergraduate Genevieve M. Casey described in *Orate Fratres* how her liturgical study club had proved instrumental in introducing the women of the campus to racial tolerance. The girls met every Sunday through the winter of 1936–37 to discuss articles on the liturgy and its social implications, drawing from *Orate Fratres*, *Liturgy and Sociology*, and the *Catholic Worker*. The group of about twenty included several African American girls. Casey reported:

> We talked of how an effective faith in the mystical body of Christ could solve the present problems of society; of how social Catholicism, generally practiced, could overcome such evils as war, class hatred, unequal distribution of wealth, interracial prejudice, the totalitarian state. We talked about the obstacles in our own small sphere, and as we talked, racial prejudice was forgotten. Increasingly, as we found ourselves in the divine life, we also discovered the negroes—as other Christs, as more than brothers.[12]

[11] Miss Alice Summers, "Discussion," *1941 Liturgical Week Proceedings* (Newark: Benedictine Liturgical Conference, 1942), 189.

[12] Genevieve M. Casey, "The Liturgy as the Solution of the Negro Problem," in "The Apostolate," *Orate Fratres* 11, no. 8 (1937): 370–71.

Again, the Body of Christ provided a powerful motif for early efforts at breaking down racial boundaries.

As the United States continued to grapple with questions of integration and racial violence in the 1950s, overcoming racial prejudice remained a topic amongst liturgical movement pioneers. In 1955, Bishop Vincent S. Waters of Raleigh, North Carolina, spoke about interracial conflict during the National Liturgical Week annual meeting. Waters, who had recently integrated two parishes in his diocese, believed that "individualism" fed the sin of racism, as it led to a selfishness which destroyed the rights of other individuals.[13] Likewise, individualism defied the nature of worship, and thus the call of God for unity and love. As Waters claimed, "Catholics are united in a Christian social body by the greatest possible bond in the universe, the Mystical Body of Christ." Such a bond was "the greatest reality of the universe revealed by our Catholic faith," forged in baptism and increased through participation in the other sacraments.[14] As Waters concluded, "The Mass means union of those who are brethren with Christ who offers the Mass and, therefore, union of his brethren among themselves."[15] On the campus and in the parish, realizing the Mystical Body of Christ demanded that barriers of prejudice be broken.

II. Poverty and Care

Forgetting poverty was impossible for the early liturgical movement advocates, as the movement's first few years coincided with the disastrous economic situation of the 1930s and the dangerous specter of social upheaval cast by Communism. In response, liturgical pioneers explored the liturgy as a counterforce to the disordered and disheartened through multiple venues of the liturgical movement. As Fr. Paul Bussard observed, writing in the spring of 1936 from Washington, DC, a "peculiar correlation [exists] between

---

[13] Vincent S. Waters, "Discussion," *1955 Liturgical Week Proceedings* (Elsberry, MO: The Liturgical Conference, 1956), 159.

[14] Waters, 160.

[15] Waters, 161.

those in the Church who are active in helping the poor and those who are interested in the liturgical movement." In his experience, "no one who understands and lives the liturgy" could neglect caring for those in economic distress. Noting the recent appearance of the (short-lived) journal, *Liturgy and Sociology*, as well as the more durable Catholic Worker organization, Bussard explained that "Catholics who are really helping the poor . . . are universally not so much interested in the liturgy as in living the liturgy."[16]

To that end, a young Franciscan priest from Michigan, Fr. Edwin Schick, wrote a letter to Virgil Michel in February of 1938, describing a new Catholic Worker which had been founded in the city of Detroit. As was common for Catholic Workers, this new House of Hospitality was also a gathering place for theological (and liturgical) discussion. Schick related to Michel:

> Only two days ago a series of weekly instructions and discussions was begun on the Liturgy, and special emphasis placed on the manner in which the Liturgy should be the source whence comes the spiritual power for such work. The beginning was small, some eight or nine persons in attendance . . . but we must remember the parable of the mustard seed.[17]

As the director of the study group, Schick chose Michel's pamphlet, *The Liturgy of the Church*, as the basis for the talks and discussion.[18] Michel was committed to keeping the liturgical movement connected with social justice initiatives, a connection which was reflected by the content of *Orate Fratres* especially before Michel's death in November of 1938. For example, a two-part article by Fr. Francis Ketter of St. John's University, appearing in 1932, suggested that ritual participation and prayer could become the inspiration for economic change. Ketter described how processions, in

---

[16] Paul Bussard, "The Source of Christian Spirit," *Orate Fratres* 10, no. 7 (1936): 325.

[17] Edwin Schick to Virgil Michel, February 4, 1938, Z 27: 4 "S," SJAA.

[18] Schick to Michel, February 4, 1938, Z 27: 4 "S," SJAA. Schick refers to Virgil Michel, *The Liturgy of the Church According to the Roman Rite* (New York: Macmillan Company, 1937).

which people could band together in the public square, caused people "to take notice and more readily grant petition," reminding his readers of a recent "pilgrimage" of the unemployed to Washington, DC, led by Fr. James Renshaw Cox.[19] Ketter discussed a series of liturgical processions included in the Roman Missal which might afford Catholics the same, liturgical way of focusing on solidarity and drawing attention to social needs. For example, a "Procession in Time of Famine," included a recital of Psalm 23. Ketter explained how the text of the psalm could inspire those gathered for the ritual:

> Taking the first part of the psalm, portraying the shepherd guiding aright, and applying it to a famine in our day, we have a good setting. In our modern economic system the captains of industry are largely responsible when hunger afflicts the masses. . . . What we can ask for, then, is to have God send us good rulers who will help us stabilize industry, establish peaceful relations between capital and labor, assure the farmer a sufficient return on the products of the soil, and provide employment for all.[20]

Ritual motion, paired with psalmody, the Litany of the Saints, and the Our Father might serve to acknowledge the acute and particular needs of those participating in the ritual, and, on the other hand, heighten participants' awareness of poverty around them through a social experience of liturgical activity.

Questions surrounding poverty and economic stress also became discussion points for National Liturgical Weeks. In 1943, Dom Lambert Dunne described how a Christian approach to labor had to be informed by an attention to both the dignity of the individual, anointed in baptism, and the cohesiveness of the "greater social whole."[21] Dunne drew a parallel between the power of social

[19] Francis Ketter, "The Use of Psalms in Liturgical Processions," *Orate Fratres* 6, no. 11 (1932): 503.

[20] Francis Ketter, "The Use of Psalms in Liturgical Processions," 549.

[21] Lambert Dunne, "The Spirit of Sacrifice in Christian Society: The Labor Problem," *1943 Liturgical Week Proceedings* (Ferdinand, IN: The Liturgical Conference, 1944): 133.

liturgy and the power of collective bargaining in the economic sphere:

> If all men were prompted by the spirit of sacrifice in the Mystical Body, a different picture might be presented. . . . In the spirit of the Mystical Body, certain rights and duties come to man through the medium of collective bargaining. . . . Unionism appears to be the formal means of making economic and social life meet the purpose God intended for it.[22]

Liturgical movement pioneers routinely stressed the call to fair labor practices and care for those in economic stress; likewise, Catholics exploring practical methods for solving problems of economic justice and labor relations found ready theological support in the liturgical movement.[23] Avenues for discussion took place in print materials, such as the journal *Work*, edited by Edward Marciniak; in organizations such as the National Catholic Rural Life Conference; in degree programs in sociology, such as the Institute of Catholic Social Studies at The Catholic University of America; and in weekend institutes, such as the Institute for Social Study at St. John's University. Though their spheres of influence may have been somewhat limited, such organizations and programs provided forums for discussing practical implications of the spirit of Christian renewal.

III. The Role of Women and the Volition of the Laity

As women's social and political freedom began to expand, particularly in the United States and in Western European contexts of the early twentieth century, women's roles became a subject of much discussion by both women and men. With respect to the liturgical movement, the role of women paired closely with increased attention on the role of the family and the volition of lay Catholics. In the United States, Virgil Michel, Joseph Kreuter, OSB,

---

[22] Dunne, 136. See also, David J. O'Brien, *American Catholics and Labor: The New Deal Years* (New York: Oxford University Press, 1968), 97–119.

[23] See O'Brien, *American Catholics and Social Reform*, 189–93.

and the monks of Conception Abbey who published *Altar and Home,* all considered how venues traditionally controlled by lay women (the home, caring for children) might also become venues for introducing liturgical renewal, citing the importance of the family as the first social sphere in which the Mystical Body of Christ might be realized.[24]

However, the best efforts of the liturgical movement pioneers often skirted the danger of remaining in the abstract, and relied on patterns of society where women's roles were defined by the home, roles which were increasingly questioned or contradicted. With the introduction of lay women authors, lecturers, and writers, the liturgical movement gained a practical and practiced voice for bringing spheres usually assigned to women more clearly in concert with the liturgical movement. For example, Dr. Therese Mueller, a sociologist with particular interest in the family, stressed the importance of parental roles in teaching children about faith, and described the home as a legitimate location for liturgical theology. Drawing upon her experience in the German liturgical movement, Mueller wrote and spoke about practices that American families might adopt in order to incorporate liturgical traditions into the home, thus challenging the assumption that private and domestic practices were not properly "liturgical."[25] Perhaps her most successful introduction was the "Advent wreath," the hands-on symbol which brought the liturgical season to life at the family dinner table. As Mueller explained during her presentation at the 1941 Liturgical Week:

> There is hardly any liturgical season so easily explained and celebrated within the family and so easily grasped by little children as the Advent season. Let the liturgy teach us to contemplate in the Advent season not only our Lord's first coming in Bethlehem,

---

[24] For example, Virgil Michel, "The Liturgy and Catholic Women," *Orate Fratres* 3, no. 9 (1929): 274–75; Joseph Kreuter, "The Christian Family and the Eucharistic Sacrifice," *Orate Fratres* 9, no. 12 (1935): 546–50; and "The Purpose of Our Paper," *Altar and Home* 1, no. 1 (February 1934), 4.

[25] See Teresa Berger, *Gender Differences and the Making of Liturgical History: Lifting a Veil on Liturgy's Past* (Farnham: Ashgate, 2011), 10–11.

but also the growth of His Kingdom and His final coming in glory; and we shall avoid the error which sees in Christmas only a sentimentalized and commercialized holiday.[26]

Thus domestic liturgical leadership could counter rosy metallic trees and department store Santas. Bringing her own voice of experience in witnessing to the possibilities of family-based liturgical life, Mueller illustrated both the importance of women's perspective in advancing the liturgical movement and the importance of lay volition in adopting active participation and liturgical practice to transform the social unit of the Christian family.

Other liturgical movement advocates, such as writer, editor, and lecturer Mary Perkins Ryan, translated traditional "women's work" into the sacramental realm, drawing connections between daily life and work in the Christian home and the pattern of Christian living as experienced in the Mass. For example, Perkins Ryan described the Mass as following the "basic plan" of a "family meal."[27] Therefore, family meals could (aspire to) resemble that hope of unity expressed by the Mystical Body of Christ in the sacramental celebration of the Eucharist. Unity, care, and social justice might be expressed through the practice of family meals by employing ingredients of nutritional value from sustainable sources, incorporating multiple members of the family in food preparation, and enjoying food paired with charitable conversation amongst family members. Such a meal, Perkins Ryan suggested, stood in stark contrast to a meal framed by priorities of greed, efficiency, and self-absorption:

> [I]magine a meal which the father earned by a piece of "sharp business" in which he did somebody out of the price of a day's food; a meal consisting of food which the mother obtained by pushing ahead of ten other people for a bargain at the supermarket; which she

[26] Mrs. Franz Mueller, "The Christian Family and the Liturgy," *1941 Liturgical Week Proceedings* (Newark: Benedictine Liturgical Conference, 1942), 169.

[27] Mary Perkins Ryan, "Home Training in Christian Living," *Worship* 26, no. 10 (1952): 461.

prepared in a temper and shoved onto an untidy and not-too-clean table; food which itself all looked like something else and contained practically no real nourishment; a meal to which the children come completely unwashed, knocking each other over in their hurry; a meal eaten in uncharitable silence, or to the accompaniment of mother's complaints about the neighbors.[28]

While a woman's work of the family meal would likely not be as coordinated as the celebration of the Mass, treating the media of domestic life—income, groceries, table conversation, children's manners—as signs with sacramental resonance had the potential to reinforce the presence of Christ in all things.

Finally, the American Grail Movement became an important center for young Roman Catholic women to consider their responsibilities as lay women in the Church and to experience social, liturgical prayer in the 1940s and 1950s. The Grail Movement offered week-long or summer-long sessions at "Grailville," in Loveland, Ohio, inviting women to experience communal prayer and living, and to take social experiences of liturgy to their own social realms of family, school, and community.[29] Through the leadership and activity of these women and many others, the liturgical movement discovered practical methods to ground liturgical activity in the family, invited liturgical reflection on uncharted frontiers (such as the kitchen table), and found new liturgical and spiritual ambassadors to teach and lead the liturgical life.

V. Conclusion

As we are human, we are both powerfully drawn in—and mightily distracted—by the *form* of our liturgical worship. Along with other Christian denominations, Roman Catholics have

---

[28] Perkins Ryan, 461–62.

[29] See Janet Kalven and Grail Members, "Living the Liturgy: Keystone of the Grail Vision," *U.S. Catholic Historian* 11, no. 4 (1993): 29–38; and Alden V. Brown, *The Grail Movement and American Catholicism, 1940–1975* (Notre Dame, IN: University of Notre Dame Press, 1989).

struggled with niggling concerns regarding aesthetics, conservative-progressive "liturgy wars,"[30] and, most recently, the retranslation of the Roman Missal in English. Yet to be distracted into anchored, obstinate minds and hardened, unbending hearts dares to undo that eschatological hope of union to which the liturgy steadily calls us. The liturgical movement did devote a significant amount of energy toward advocating for improved aesthetic experiences of the liturgy, but the vision of the liturgical movement never ended in its media, be it worship aids, missals, microphones, or vernacular translations. The liturgical movement was a social movement, seeking to bring the faithful to a deeper realization of their role in the great Mystical Body of Christ, both within the act of worship and as faithful members of the baptismal priesthood in the world.[31] In responding to racial intolerance, providing care and support to those in economic stress, and in championing women's insights for liturgical theology and practice, proponents of mid-century liturgical renewal insisted that the "liturgical movement" did not end in wafts of incense or satisfied isolationism. Their insistence provides a powerful witness to the hope to which participation in the People of God calls us in the present: being the Body of Christ at worship and in the world, a Body which is not afraid of linking cult to care.

[30] See Nathan D. Mitchell, "Culture Wars: Connecting Cult and Culture, Some Proposals," *Worship* 71, no. 2 (March 1997): 168–78.

[31] Keith Pecklers also makes this argument in, among other places, *Worship*, New Century Theology Series (New York: Continuum, 2003), 91–116.

"A Mansion for the Rat"[1]

> . . . And so I came home a woman starving
>   for images
> to say my hunger is so old
> so fundamental, that all the lost
>   crumbled burnt smashed shattered defaced
> overpainted concealed and falsely named
> faces of every past we have searched together
>   in all the ages
> could rise reassemble re-collect re-member
> themselves as I recollected myself in that presence
>   as every night close to your body
> in the pain of the city, turning
> I am remembered by you, remember you
>   even as we are remembered
> on the cinema screens, the white expensive walls
> of collectors, the newsrags blowing the streets
>   —and it would not be enough.
> This is the war of the images.
> We are the thorn-leaf guarding the purple-tongued flower
>   each to each.[2]

In this powerful poem, Adrienne Rich feels the pulse of women victimized by the images others have of them. She speaks passionately of the power that even language and art possess to *conceal*

---

[1] This essay originally appeared in "The Amen Corner," *Worship* 68, no. 1 (January 1994): 64–72.

[2] Adrienne Rich, "The Images," in *A Wild Patience Has Taken Me This Far: Poems 1978–1982* (New York: Norton, 1981), 5.

women's pain beneath a romanticized veneer of "beaten gold worm-worn Pietas." She lashes out angrily: "When did we ever choose / to see our bodies strung / in bondage and crucifixion across the exhausted air?"

Rich's potent words kept coming back to me as I began to organize my thoughts for this essay on women and worship. *This is the war of . . . images.* For quite some time, many of us male academics have tried to defuse the challenge that feminist liturgical scholarship poses by imagining it as either an "ordination movement" (thorny; best left to church authorities) or a call for "inclusive language" (harmless as long as it doesn't touch our God-talk). *"I can never romanticize language again / never deny its power for disguise for mystification. . . ."* In point of fact, the question of women's relation to worship has moved well beyond those two issues during the past decade. While linguistic inclusivity and access to ordained ministry remain part of an unfinished agenda, other more urgent concerns have come to the fore.

Marjorie Procter-Smith, for example, has written perceptively about "the intersection between liturgy and domestic violence."[3] She notes that when we speak about "patriarchalism" in the liturgy we are not simply noting the "male rule of women" but "a structure of interlocking patterns of dominance and submission in which not only gender but also age, class, race and status become important factors."[4] And because the primary victims of violence and abuse in our culture are precisely the marginalized and the invisible (children, women, the poor and elderly), corporate worship may unintentionally support structures of victimization by hallowing traditions of male control and authoritarianism. For liturgy, Procter-Smith notes, shares with language the ability to lie: "Christian liturgy, like any other 'form created,' can disguise and mystify domestic violence and its roots, making the abuse seem not only acceptable, but even divinely sanctioned. And because liturgy (again, like language) shapes us gradually and in tiny increments,

---

[3] See her "Reorganizing Victimization," in *Perkins Journal* 40, no. 4 (October 1987): 17–27.

[4] Ibid., 18.

words and gestures which are used regularly and repeatedly, although appearing small, have a powerful effect."[5]

Moreover, if liturgy is the "work of the people"—and if a majority of people in our pews are women—then "the experiences of women and their struggles for survival and dignity must take a central place as the locus out of which the primary theology which is the liturgy grows."[6] For as Aidan Kavanagh has often argued, liturgical theology takes shape not as concept and proposition, but "on the edge of chaos":[7]

> Mrs. Murphy and her pastor are primary theologians whose discourse in faith is carried on not by concepts and propositions nearly so much as in the vastly complex vocabulary of experiences had, prayers said, sights seen, smells smelled, words said and heard and responded to, emotions controlled and released, sins committed and repented, children born and loved ones buried . . . Their critical and reflective discourse is not merely *about* faith. *It is the very way faith works itself out in the intricacies of human life both individually and in common.* Its vocabulary is not precise, concise, or scientific. It is symbolic, aesthetic, ascetical, and sapiential.[8]

The point here is simply that the "feminist liturgical movement" is not about "ordination" nor even about "inclusive language." It is about recognizing the struggles of women for survival and dignity, about giving those struggles voice and visibility in our public worship. It is about turning aside from those styles and structures of liturgical prayer that encourage destructive dominance (by males) and passive acceptance (by women). It is about refusing to cave in to that "symbolic reductionism" which, as Mary Collins has wisely written, would "equate the historical church with the reign of God," would confuse "Jesus Christ with the one who presides in Jesus' name," and would make "maintaining or dethroning

---

[5] Ibid.
[6] Procter-Smith, 24.
[7] *On Liturgical Theology* (New York: Pueblo, 1984), 73.
[8] Ibid., 146–47; emphasis added.

gender-marked pretensions of spiritual power the only operative meaning in eucharistic liturgy."[9]

In what follows I hope to sketch some of the factors that have contributed to the androcentric portrayal of Christian worship and its history, and to suggest how women's wisdom might turn us in another direction.

Androcentric History

To date, the history of the modern liturgical movement has been written primarily as *history for, by, and about men.* This androcentrism is evident among most researchers who chronicle the movement's progress in both Europe and the United States, in both Roman Catholic and Protestant communities. Contributions by women are routinely ignored or relegated to a position of secondary importance. As Teresa Berger has pointed out, for example, the history of the liturgical movement in twentieth-century Europe has been portrayed almost exclusively as the work of specific *men* (or men's communities), e.g., the monks of Maria Laach (especially Abbot Ildefons Herwegen and Dom Odo Casel); Romano Guardini (who had been active in the German youth movement); Pius Parsch (the Austrian Augustinian whose work on the liturgical year is familiar to many through the English translation published by the monks of St John's Abbey, Collegeville); Josef Jungmann (whose monumental *Missarum Solemnia* remains in print after nearly half a century); and Ludwig Wolker (who was leader of the Catholic Young Men's Association in Germany).[10]

Nineteenth-century pioneers have also been portrayed primarily as *men* whose agendas were linked to the larger social, political, and ecclesiastical struggles of their day. Prosper Guéranger (1805–1875), abbot of Solesmes, is probably the most renowned Roman Catholic example. Although he has often been dismissed as a howling ultramontane reactionary, recent studies are more sympa-

[9] See "Is the Eucharist Still a Source of Meaning for Women?" *Origins* 21, no. 14 (September 12, 1991): 228.

[10] See Teresa Berger, "The Classical Liturgical Movement in Germany and Austria: Moved by Women?" *Worship* 66, no. 3 (1992): 231–51.

thetic. They have shown that Guéranger's deeper interests lay not so much in extolling papal power as in recovering common ritual symbols that could serve as a basis for renewing social life in a fragmented Europe.[11] Historical accounts of nineteenth-century Protestant liturgical reforms are also limited, for the most part, to reviewing the work done by *men*. This is true of both the German Reformed (Mercersburg) and Lutheran (Wilhelm Loehe, Matthias Loy) movements in nineteenth-century North America. Matthias Loy, for instance, sought to establish set forms of liturgical prayer for American Lutherans that would steer a middle course between Roman excess and Reformed austerity. To this end, he insisted on a recovery of the principles that (in his judgment) had inspired the Lutheran liturgical reformers of the sixteenth century: the centrality of Sunday as the "festival of the Lord's resurrection"; weekly Eucharist; attention to sacred art and architecture; the need for distinctive ministerial vesture; and a love for the altar as the "symbolic representation of the place where the Lord dwells."[12]

But neither Loy nor Loehe (nor John Nevin and Philip Schaff at Mercersburg) ever allude to the experience of women in the Church as a pastoral or theological source in their deliberations about reforming mainline Protestant worship. And historians of this period have maintained a similar silence.

New Directions

The reasons for such androcentric portrayals of the liturgical movement are not, of course, difficult to discover. Until quite recently, women were almost entirely locked out of the academic arenas where "advanced" historical and theological studies of worship took place. (Professor James F. White has estimated that the first PhD in *liturgical studies* was not awarded to a woman until well past the middle of this century.) In many churches, women

[11] See, for example, R. W. Franklin, "Guéranger: A View on the Centenary of His Death," *Worship* 49, no. 6 (1975): 318–36.

[12] See Loy's 1853 essay, "The Lutheran Cultus," in T. G. Tappert, ed., *Lutheran Confessional Theology in America, 1840–1880* (New York: Oxford University Press, 1972), 301–21.

have also been excluded from those positions of ordained ministry that might have given them some pastoral voice in the shaping of reform. As has often been noted, history is usually written by the "winners," i.e., by those who dominate the discussions, establish the rules, and promulgate the decisions. In the case of the liturgical movement and its history (especially among Roman Catholics), those "winners" have almost always been males.

This does not mean, of course, that women have failed, factually, to make any contribution to worship studies and pastoral praxis in the twentieth century—only that their contributions have been neglected or, more commonly, sought for in the wrong places. In the past decade particularly, this neglect has begun to be addressed. One cannot accurately speak of the influential work of Odo Casel, for instance, without also noting the efforts of women scholars from the Benedictine Abbey of the Holy Cross in Herstelle. It was Herstelle's Agape Kiesgen, as Teresa Berger notes, who did most of the early work on the index to *Jahrbuch für Liturgiewissenschaft*, the influential liturgical journal which Casel edited for nearly two decades.[13] And some of the most moving—and historically accurate—meditations on the liturgy for Sundays and solemnities were being written in the 1930s by Aemiliana Löhr (also a nun of Herstelle), as the following example shows:

> With marvelous insight, [the early church] chose the Paschal Night for her great baptismal solemnities. Together with the newly baptized she celebrated a true and holy Passover from the . . . night of sin . . . unto the Promised Land of grace, the bright Day of Christ. Her children, washed in the holy waters of baptism, were now sprinkled with the blood of the true Lamb; and their lips (which St. Ambrose calls *doorposts* and *portals* for the entry of the divine *Logos*) empurpled with the eucharistic wine of Christ's blood. Emerging from the purifying stream, they found both new life and the wondrous food by which it is sustained and nourished; the pure flesh of the Lamb, sacred unleavened bread of the Eucharist.[14]

[13] Berger, 234.

[14] *The Year of Our Lord;* translated by a monk of St. Benedict (New York: P. J. Kenedy & Sons 1937), 159.

In the United States, too, as Kathleen Hughes has demonstrated in her book *How Firm a Foundation: Voices of the Early Liturgical Movement*,[15] women were already active contributors in the preconciliar period. Hughes cites, for example, a passage from Dorothy Day's 1963 book *Loaves and Fishes*, where night prayer ("compline") at the Catholic Worker house is described (pp. 80–81):

> Some sing *basso profundo* and some sing *recto tono*, and if there is an Irish tenor he complicates the sound still more. It does not help matters that two or three older women who are tone deaf delight in singing too. But they enjoy themselves and it is the night prayer of the church, and God hears. The agnostic sings with the Catholic, because it is a communal act and he loves his brother. Our singing prepares us for another day. Early tomorrow morning the work will start again, and so our life, which St. Teresa of Avila described as a night spent in an uncomfortable inn, resumes. It will continue. The surroundings may be harsh, but where love is, God is.

This passage is remarkable for its grasp of the meaning of communal prayer, for its radical inclusivity (the agnostic singing with the believer), and for its understanding of God's presence in ritual celebration. It shows that the "mothers" of the modern liturgical movement were every bit as capable as the "fathers" of providing astute insights into the theology of worship.

The difference, of course, is that our liturgical foremothers often made their contributions in ways—and in places—not always linked with the traditional (and male-dominated) centers of academic and ecclesiastical life. Because they published in papers like the *Catholic Worker* or celebrated the liturgy of the hours in soup kitchens, the work, experience, and insight of these women has been discounted, marginalized, and devalued. As a result, Day's astonishingly good theology of worship is neglected (by male academics, especially) because it is perceived as insufficiently systematic and scholarly, as lacking seriousness, or as "too far out on the fringes." Women's contributions to our understanding of ritual

---

[15] Kathleen Hughes, *How Firm a Foundation: Voices of the Early Liturgical Movement* (Chicago: Liturgy Training Publications, 1990).

have thus been victimized by what Catherine Bell calls a "cognitive apartheid" which urges us, first, to differentiate sharply between thought and action, and then to subordinate act to thought, theory to practice.[16] The further assumption is that thinking and theory are gender-specific—the special talent of *males*—and so should be controlled by them.

As an illustration of what I mean, consider the career of evangelist and healer Aimee Semple McPherson, founder of the Church of the Foursquare Gospel. With her Sunday evening "illustrated sermons" at Angelus Temple in Los Angeles during the 1920s, she almost singlehandedly invented what we would today call "interactive multi-media performance art." Her famous "Attar of Roses" sermon, preached in the spring of 1931 on texts from the Song of Songs, was a boldly imaginative theater piece that celebrated "the erotic dimension of the spiritual life," the "passionate love for Christ's body, the Rose of Sharon."[17] With a poet's skill, Aimee used the erotic impulse to trigger larger questions about pain and violence, suffering and humiliation. The sermon concluded with a whispered account of Jesus' crucifixion so convincing that all present could acknowledge in it their own history of agonized brokenness. Liturgy "professionals" of today might accuse her of manipulative sensationalism, but it is clear McPherson understood instinctively that public worship "is symbolic, aesthetic, ascetical, and sapiential . . . a sinuous discourse" by which "innumerable millions . . . work out . . . what it really means when God is poured out into humanity, into the world as a member of our race."[18] Few have understood as well as Sister Aimee how to exploit the innovative potential of ritual action. But because McPherson did her work in ways and in places that many (male) religionists disdain as outlandish, heretical, and disgusting, her creative contributions as preacher and liturgist are neglected.

[16] See "Discourse and Dichotomies: The Structure of Ritual Theory," *Religion* 17 (1987): 95–118; here 112–15.

[17] Daniel Epstein, *Sister Aimee* (New York: Harcourt Brace Jovanovich, 1993), 357.

[18] Aidan Kavanagh, *On Liturgical Theology*, 147; slightly altered.

The Seduction of Symbols

The contributions of women to worship must be looked for, then, in unexpected sources—and these do not always fit comfortably within the rarified groves of academe. At the beginning of this essay I appealed to a poem that critiques the power of art and language to mask reality and disfigure women's experience. Such a perception is deeply embedded in the history of poetry by American women. Perhaps the most striking example flows from the work of Emily Dickinson—a "liturgical theologian" if ever there was one—whose "genteel" poems constitute a scalding attack on the religious symbol systems of both Puritan and Transcendentalist New England. (Her critique extended, as well, to the church's liturgy, from which she eventually withdrew.) In "The Soul Selects Her Own Society," one of Dickinson's most famous and widely anthologized poems, the poet cleverly borrows the symbolic language of Puritanism to critique both Puritans and Transcendentalists:

> The Soul selects her own Society—
> Then—shuts the Door—
> To her divine Majority—
> Present no more—
> Unmoved—she notes the Chariots—pausing—
> At her low Gate—
> Unmoved—an Emperor be kneeling
> Upon her Mat—
> I've known her—from an ample nation—
> Choose One—
> Then—close the Valves of her attention—
> Like Stone—[19]

This little poem is *not* an "optimistic rhapsody on the soul"; rather, it is an acerbic commentary on the "essentially egotistical and elitist" program of the Puritans and the equally cliquish

[19] Emily Dickinson, "The Soul Selects Her Own Society," *The Complete Poems of Emily Dickinson;* ed. T. H. Johnson (Boston: Little, Brown and Company, 1960), 143.

attitudes of the Transcendentalists.[20] Pushed to their logical conclusion, Dickinson suggests, both these religious systems produce a "majority of one"—an antisocial self-seeker who haughtily usurps God's authority and reduces the real, living cosmos to the narrow dimensions of the ego. Puritanism, the poem hints, begets self-worship, and self-worship begets death. (Note how the final stanza concludes with the chilling image of the heart's valves clanging closed like stone, a certain figure of death.)

Dickinson thus denounced any religious schema that would make the individual soul "its own sainted self-creator."[21] She also rejected (with lyrical sarcasm!) any theology that promoted submissiveness to tyrannical power:

> Papa above!
> Regard a Mouse
> O'erpowered by the Cat!
> Reserve within thy kingdom
> A "Mansion" for the Rat!
>
> Snug in seraphic Cupboards
> To nibble all the day,
> While unsuspecting Cycles
> Wheel solemnly away![22]

With painful clarity, Dickinson understood the persistence of the human passion to *possess* things, to confuse *partial* visions with true perceptions of cosmic unity. "The desire to make 'Mine'—like Adam, to name and thereby endow with symbolic significance the elements of the creation and thus to possess them—is ultimately [Dickinson knew] what fragments and fractures the universe."[23] Like her spiritual daughter, Adrienne Rich, Dickinson perceived,

---

[20] See E. Miller Budick, "When the Soul Selects: Emily Dickinson's Attack on New England Symbolism," *American Literature* 51 (1979–1980): 349–63; here, 353.

[21] See Budick, 356.

[22] *The Complete Poems*, 32.

[23] Budick, 363.

sadly, that while symbols *should expand* our vision, they may in fact become reductive and limiting. They may not only "fail to embody truth, they may limit and destroy it."[24]

Against the arrogant half-blindness of religious symbols, against those "Soft—Cherubic Creatures" who shrink in horror from "freckled Human Nature" and are "Of Deity ashamed" (poem 401), Dickinson proposed a radically new theology that includes "A 'Mansion' for the Rat!" We lesser mortals of the late twentieth century are still trying to catch up with her!

[24] Budick, 363.

"Making the Connections"[1]

The reason why I have chosen this title is because I want to explore the relationship between eucharistic celebration, ethical action, and the aesthetics of Christian worship. I will argue that celebrating the Lord's Supper, acting for justice, and finding beauty in ourselves and others form one single ethical imperative.

The Ethical Challenge

I begin by calling attention to a recently published book entitled *The Life You Can Save: Acting Now to End World Poverty*. Permit me to quote a passage from page 149 of this book:

> The problem is that we are living in the midst of an emergency in which 27,000 children die from avoidable causes every day. That's more than one thousand every hour. [*Incidentally, that translates to about 9,855,000 children per year.*] And millions of women are living with repairable fistulas, and millions of people are blind who could see again. *We can do something about these things.* That critical fact ought to affect the choices we make. To buy good stereo equipment in order to further my worthwhile goal, or life-enhancing experience, of listening to music is to place more value on these enhancements to my life than on whether others live or die. Can it be ethical to live that way? Doesn't it make a mockery of any claim to believe in the equal value of human life? For the same reason, philanthropy for the arts or for cultural activities is, in a world like this one, morally dubious. In 2004, New York's Metropolitan Museum of Art paid a sum said to be in excess of $45 million for a small Madonna

[1] This essay originally appeared in "The Amen Corner," *Worship* 86, no. 3 (May 2012): 256–68.

and Child painted by the medieval Italian master Duccio. In buying this painting, the museum has added to the abundance of master-pieces that those fortunate enough to be able to visit it can see. But if it only costs $50 to perform a cataract operation in a developing country, that means there are 900,000 people who can't see anything at all, let alone a painting, whose sight could have been restored by the amount of money that painting cost.[2]

The author of these words is the controversial Australian-born ethicist Peter Singer. Singer's views on population control, family planning, and euthanasia have raised hackles all around the Pacific Rim and on both sides of the Atlantic (particularly among Roman Catholics). For many, Peter Singer has become *the* ethicist "people of faith" love to hate. Yet as I like to point out (to myself, first of all), just because you do not like the messenger is no reason to ignore his message. Biblical history is full of discomfiting prophets whose words and deeds people loved to hate (consider Amos and Jeremiah). Christian history, too, is replete with messengers—some humble, some uppity—whose pronouncements have regularly rattled the cages of the powers that be (consider Francis of Assisi, Catherine of Siena, Blessed John XXIII, Mother Teresa). Yet here again, as the feisty old Dominican theologian Herbert McCabe once observed, just because the Church is a train wreck is no reason to leave it.

Here I am not asking you to consider Peter Singer's opinions on family planning or population control. But I would like to call attention instead to his less controversial (though no less challenging) views about world poverty and hunger. On 5 September 1999, Singer published a short essay in *The New York Times Magazine* that became the nucleus of his book, *The Life You Can Save*. In that essay, Singer explained why our taste for *foie gras* and three-thousand-dollar Armani suits may be causing children to starve.[3] The fact of

---

[2] Peter Singer, *The Life You Can Save* (New York: Random House, 2009), 149–50.

[3] Peter Singer, "The Singer Solution to World Poverty," *The New York Times Magazine* (5 September 1999), 60–63.

the matter is that in today's world, *ethical* problems are—more often than not—*economic* problems. Yet ethics, as Singer points out, is often confused with "morality" or "moralism"—and that confusion has given birth to forms of talk radio and political evangelism that pontificate on everything from a dying woman's feeding tube to suggestions that embarrassed AIG executives commit hari-kari in public. We need to clear the air, Singer writes, by first remembering that *ethics* is emphatically *not* the same thing as moralism: As Singer wrote in an earlier book entitled *Practical Ethics* (1993):

> [t]raditional moralists claim to be the defenders of morality in general, but they are really defending a particular moral code. They have been allowed to preempt the field to such an extent that when a newspaper headline reads BISHOP ATTACKS DECLINING MORAL STANDARDS, we expect to read yet again about promiscuity, homosexuality, pornography, and so on, and not about the puny amounts we give as overseas aid to poorer nations, or our reckless indifference to the natural environment of our planet. So the first thing to say about ethics is that is it not a set of prohibitions particularly concerned with sex. Even in the era of AIDS, sex raises no unique moral issues at all. Decisions about sex may involve considerations of honesty, concern for others, prudence, and so on, but there is nothing special about sex in this respect, for the same could be said of decisions about driving a car. (In fact, the moral issues raised by driving a car, both from an environmental and from a safety point of view, are much more serious than those raised by sex.) Accordingly [writes Singer in the second edition of *Practical Ethics*], this book contains no discussion of sexual morality. There are more important ethical issues to be considered.[4]

Priorities, in other words, are the mother's milk of ethics! If we are to believe the gospels, Jesus believed that as well: *ethics* (and for that matter, *morality*) is about *priorities*. And the priorities (if not the problems) that we humans meet in daily life are fairly simple: God first, others second—and the self? Well, the self is discovered

---

[4] Peter Singer, *Practical Ethics*, 2nd ed. (New York: Cambridge University Press, 1993), 1–2.

only—*only*—if one surrenders to the first two. And if you never find your self, well, do not worry; God will find it for you. Indeed, since God can be *seen* only in and as one's neighbor, Jesus insisted that God's love must have a human face, that the "two commandments" in fact constitute one single imperative. For Jesus, there is ultimately one sacrament, and one alone: God's love known, named, met, and embodied in love of neighbor. Love is less a feeling than a choice, a *verb*—and so is God. To love is to act justly and mercifully on others' behalf, without counting the cost—*and* without seeing or controlling the results. As Rabbi Hillel said, *"That's the whole law; the rest is commentary."*[5] Perhaps that is why Jesus occasionally became so exasperated. "You have eyes," he hollered, *"use* them. You have ears, *open* them." *Of course* a child's hunger has priority over corporate welfare, executive bonuses, or cuts in the capital gains tax. *That's the whole law; the rest is commentary. Of course* a widow's mite means more than any temple or any liturgy or any rich man's gift. *That's the whole law; the rest is commentary. Of course* mercy is superior to sacrifice. *That's the whole law; the rest is commentary. Of course* the future of the planet is more important than the future of Viagra. *That's the whole law; the rest is commentary.*

In a book titled *Living High and Letting Die: Our Illusion of Innocence*, an ethicist-colleague of Singer's by the name of Peter Unger suggests two simple but pointed cases that demonstrate the deadly consequences that follow a failure to act. The first case Unger calls "The Shallow Pond." Here it is:

> The path from the library at your university to the humanities lecture hall passes a shallow ornamental pond. On your way to give a lecture, you notice that a small child has fallen in and is in danger of drowning. If you wade in and pull the child out, it will mean getting your clothes muddy and either cancelling your lecture or delaying it until you can find something clean and dry to wear. If you pass by

[5] See D. Harrington, commentary on Mark in R. Brown et al., eds., *The New Jerome Biblical Commentary* (Englewood Cliffs, NJ: Prentice Hall, 1990), 41:79, p. 622.

the child, then, while you'll give your lecture on time, the child will die straightaway. You pass by and, as expected, the child dies.[6]

Almost everyone who hears this case reacts the same way: your conduct is morally abominable. Case closed. Now listen to the *second* case:

> In your mailbox, there's something from (the U.S. Committee for) UNICEF. After reading it through, you correctly believe that, unless you soon send in a check for $100, then, instead of each living many more years, over thirty more children will die soon. But, you throw the material in your trash basket, including the convenient return envelope provided, you send nothing, and instead of living many years, over thirty more children soon die than would have had you sent in the requested $100.[7]

Once again, our reaction to this case is virtually unanimous: our conduct is not morally reprehensible; in fact, there is nothing wrong about it at all. The poor, we know, will always be with us, and so many appeals are sent from so many worthwhile agencies that we can't possibly respond to them all. So our decision (we tell ourselves) is based on the reasonable conclusion that we are neither messiahs nor Wall Street moguls with unlimited bonus money to spend on the less fortunate.

This reaction is precisely what Peter Unger calls "the *illusion* of innocence." After all, you are not being asked to respond to all appeals; the UNICEF envelope merely invites you to respond to *one*. You are not being asked to make yourself destitute; you are merely being asked to surrender some of your abundance, to place a higher priority on a child's life than on a new gas-guzzling SUV or a $2000 chasuble when the ten green ones you already have in the sacristy will very likely last another year or ten. *The illusion of innocence*. What was it Rabbi Hillel said? *That's the whole law;*

---

[6] Peter Unger, *Living High and Letting Die: Our Illusion of Innocence* (New York: Oxford University Press, 1996), 9.
[7] Ibid.

the rest is commentary. Incidentally, after reading, if you would like to contribute to UNICEF or to OXFAM, you can go online to oxfamamerica.org, or to UnicefUsa.org.

In light of the challenges posed by Peter Singer and Peter Unger, I would like to suggest a simple question that I think every Christian eucharistic community must face: *What if "charity" isn't optional? What if we have no moral right to ignore the envelope?* What if "doing" Eucharist is contingent upon what we "do" with the envelope? As I said, we are living in an age when, more often than not, *ethical questions are economic ones.* We do not think, very often, about the economics of Eucharist. And that is too bad, because we really *should.* The greatest threat to Christian Eucharist today is not deficient theology or lousy liturgies (though both of these abound). Nor is the threat from progressive pastors and church architects who decline to reserve the Blessed Sacrament on the center of the altar. Nor does the threat come (God help us) from those who agitate for perpetual adoration in order to comfort the divine prisoner in the tabernacle. The ethical emptiness, the moral absurdity, of most modern discussions about the Eucharist are chilling. Yet I do believe that the greatest threat to Christian Eucharist is precisely that moral numbness that prevents our seeing God's presence in the least and the littlest, that prevents our seeing the Risen One among the most vulnerable citizens of our chaotic world. The greatest threat to Eucharist is world hunger. (It's not for nothing that the great Indian teacher of nonviolence, Mohandas K. Ghandi, once said that "if Christ ever comes to India, he'd better come as bread.") When a starving child dies, a member of Christ's body dies. Literally, not metaphorically. Paul did not say "you are the body of Christ because you are some homogenized lump;" he said "you are the body of Christ *member for member." That's the whole law; the rest is commentary.*

My point in saying these things is to make us all feel guilty. (I am sure you know the old joke: *"Guilt is the Catholic gift that keeps on giving.")* I recognize, too, that there are other issues in this world besides pain, poverty and hunger—issues worthy of moral consideration, issues like love and art and, yes, even cooking. As Susan Wolf wrote in an essay on "Moral Saints" more than thirty years ago, there is "no plausible argument [that] can justify the use of human resources involved in producing a *paté de canard en croute* against possible alternative beneficent ends to which these resources might be put."[8] Paté—like truffles or rack of lamb or *crème caramel*—are by definition unnecessary, unreasonable, lavish, excessive, useless, not to say fattening. Yet they do *exist*, and people (even "good people") continue to eat them. Their durability suggests that even when they are hungry, human beings in virtually all cultures *prize* gourmet cuisine—and thus, that this cuisine survives not because of any moral necessity, but rather because we have decided that *some* choices, *some* human activities, will be exempt from "morally beneficial alternatives." (That is, in fact, the point Susan Wolf was trying to make in the essay I just cited.)

Cooking, of course, isn't the only human activity we tend to exempt from moral judgment. Art, music, reading, ritual, even (perhaps) amateur athletics—all are understood to be "laudable pursuits," even though they do little to relieve the world's hunger (except, perhaps, its deep hunger for meaning). After all, "if the moral saint is devoting all his time to feeding the hungry or healing the sick or raising money for Oxfam, then [of necessity] . . . he is *not* reading Victorian novels, playing the oboe, or improving his backhand."[9] And that, of course, raises a related point. What is the point of saving the poor and starving only to cast them into a dismally barren, colorless world—a world bereft of music, art, literature, sports, even good old-fashioned romance? Something deep within us rebels against such a world. What is the point of a world without Mozart? For you surely know that in heaven, Bach sits at God's right; Beethoven, at God's left; and Mozart sits on God's lap, laughing. Something in us *wants* a little night music, Easter bunnies, a little Christmas; something in us *wants* chestnuts roasting on an open fire; *wants* carriage rides beneath the stars in Central Park, *wants* the fireworks, glitter, and glam of a summer Olympic games opening in London soon. Something in us *resents* the single-minded

[8] Susan Wolf, "Moral Saints," *The Journal of Philosophy* 79, no. 8 (1982): 419–39; here 422.

[9] Wolf, "Moral Saints," 421; emphasis added.

altruism of St. Francis or even (dare I say it?) Mother Teresa; we *prefer* the mischievous irony of G. K. Chesterton's Father Brown. Something in us *resents* the righteousness of Dr. Laura and prefers the breathy lasciviousness of Mae West's invitation to "come up and see me sometime." (It was our mother among the saints, Mae West, who once said, "When confronted with a choice between two evils, I like to pick the one I never tried before!")

Thus, there truly does seem to be "a limit to [just] how much morality we can stand."[10] *Virtus*—virtue—is, after all, a "power," an *ability*, a *competence* to do something worthy, something good. In human life as we know it, we recognize *virtues* that may not be exactly ethical or moral, yet they make life *bearable*: The beauty and talent of Julia Fischer, or Meryl Streep; the speed and competitiveness of Michael Phelps; the little six-year-old kid who is convinced it is finally time to order a Big Mac instead of a Happy Meal; the Irish women's soccer team competing for a national championship; the "*et incarnatus est*" of Mozart's great Mass in c-minor, or Beethoven's *Missa Solemnis*; a grandmother's hand that bears the print of every head she's ever cradled and comforted; the unearthly beginning of Handel's coronation anthem "Zadok the Priest." All these exist because they make life *bearable*.

So where does that leave us? It leaves us torn between radicalism and compromise, between ethics and aesthetics, between a rock and a hard place. *Our affluence has no defense in the face of famine; and our innocence is illusion.* At best, we are moral midgets, criminals clinging to life while others starve. As Peter Singer puts it in his 1999 piece in *The New York Times Magazine*:

> In the world as it is now, I can see no escape from the conclusion that each one of us with wealth surplus to his or her essential needs should be giving most of it to help people suffering from poverty so dire as to be life-threatening. That's right: I'm saying that you shouldn't buy that new car, take that cruise, redecorate the house or get that pricey new suit. . . . An American household with an income of $50,000 spends around $30,000 annually on necessities,

---

[10] Ibid., 423.

according to the Conference Board, a nonprofit economic research organization. Therefore, for a household bringing in $50,000 a year, donations to help the world's poor should be as close as possible to $20,000. . . . [T]he formula is simple: whatever money you're spending on luxuries, not necessities, should be given away. . . .[11]

That's the whole law; the rest is commentary. And did not someone we know say "Go, sell everything you have, give to the poor, and come follow me." Today, *all of us* are faced with Sophie's Choice; *all of us* are forced to *choose* between the lives of innocent children and the things we hold dear. That is the kind of world we live in. Of course, evolutionary psychologists will often tell us that "human nature just is not sufficiently altruistic to . . . sacrifice so much for strangers. On the facts of human nature, they [may] be right, but they would be wrong [Singer says] to draw a moral conclusion from those facts."[12] There *are* better things we can do with our money (whether it be personal income or government surplus). If this kind of world makes "living a morally decent life extremely arduous, well, then that is the way things are. If we do not do it, then we should at least know that we are failing to live a morally decent life—not because it is good to wallow in guilt but because knowing where we should be going is the first step toward . . . [getting there]."[13]

Affluence has no defense in the face of famine—yet we *do* keep on buying, we *do* keep on cooking, we *do* keep on watching Meryl Streep win her Oscar; we do keep sending those squealing porkers out to search for truffles in the dark, moist earth. It is strange. The Vatican spends its time trying to teach us American Catholics "good liturgical English"; it wants to lift the excommunication of a schismatic "bishop" who denies the Holocaust; it wants to deny Communion to politicians who do not toe the line on abortion or stem-cell research; it wants to force the government to

---

[11] "The Singer Solution to World Poverty," *The New York Times Magazine*; here 63.

[12] "The Singer Solution to World Poverty," 63.

[13] Ibid.

eliminate the entire contraception mandate thus denying (and silencing) the fact that many (98%) Catholic women have other ideas when it comes to using methods of contraception other than natural family planning; but as far as I know, it hasn't yet slapped an interdict on the American church for failing to feed the hungry. Speaking for myself, I know I am a long, long way from meeting Peter Singer's challenge to sacrifice what I do not need so somebody else can live. I am not the stuff saints are made of; but I am willing to start growing along spiritual lines—and perhaps you are, too. If enough of us get to thinking and acting that way, maybe—just maybe—we will crack open what "real presence" in the Eucharist intends to signify. *Real presence* is, above all, gift. A gift is not "possession" we may control and manipulate. In Eucharist, *the gift, the giver, and the act of giving* are gift. In giving us his body and blood in the Eucharist, Christ gives us both *him*self and *our*selves. The body of Christ on the table feeds the body of Christ that is at the table. That is why paragraph 1396 of the *Catechism of the Catholic Church* tells us, "The Eucharist makes the Church. . . . Because there is one bread, we who are many are one body, for we all partake of the one bread [see 1 Cor 10:16-17]." And that is why paragraph 1397 of the *Catechism* says, "The Eucharist commits us to the poor. To receive in truth the Body and Blood of Christ given up for us, we must recognize Christ in the poorest, his [brothers and sisters]."

Real presence is thus not only the gift of Eucharist but the goal and work of Eucharist. Real presence means our God giving life to the world in the body and blood of Jesus Christ—giving life, giving it abundantly, lavishly, promiscuously, to those who are grateful and to those who are not, to those (as the paschal homily of St. John Chrysostom puts it) who kept the fast and to those who did not. Jesus, after all, is the one who tells us our place at the table will always be there. Jesus is the One who—like every mother crooning to the child at her breast—tells us to "Take, eat, this is my body *for you*." Jesus the *bread-breaker* becomes Jesus the *bread broken*. And if we who share that broken bread do not ourselves become bread-breakers, then (as Paul warned us) we eat and drink judgment to ourselves. *That's the whole law; the rest is commentary.*

The Aesthetic Challenge

And that brings us to the "aesthetic challenge," i.e., the link between "being just" and "being beautiful" as these shape our experience of the Church's eucharistic liturgy. Perhaps only a few of you can remember when Peter, Paul, and Mary released their hit version of the folk anthem, "If I had a hammer." And most likely even fewer of you would recall that many of us thought that song was exactly the right music for those informal, "coffee-table Masses" we flocked to during the mid-1960s. Today, such memories are pretty embarrassing; not even geriatric nostalgia can breathe new life into the "60's folk idiom." We are especially chagrined that we sang such things at Mass! All this is understandable—and I am certainly not recommending a return to "If I had a hammer" or "Michael, row your boat ashore" or any other 1960's "folk anthem" as suitable music at Masses which focus on "social justice." Yet our newfound liturgical sophistication (Renaissance motets instead of Peter, Paul, and Mary) may also miss the point. The folk music of the last century was, after all, legitimate art—not "high art," perhaps, not art to be memorialized in museums (not even Cleveland's Rock-and-Roll Hall of Fame), certainly not art to be imitated by composers of church music today, but *art* nonetheless. One of the strange things about beauty is its inexhaustibility, its plenitude, its surprising capacity to survive. The beautiful is astonishingly agile, plastic, elastic, nimble, capable of continuing to "carry greetings from other worlds" even after those worlds have long vanished.[14] So, as Harvard English professor Elaine Scarry notes, "[t]he temptation to scorn the innocent object for ceasing to be beautiful might be called the temptation against plenitude; it puts at risk not the repudiated object but the capaciousness of the cognitive act."[15] The temptation against plenitude; the refusal to let our minds and imaginations remain "capacious," large-hearted, roomy. Those are serious flaws. After all, when we repudiate something formerly experienced as beautiful, it is *we*—and not those

[14] Elaine Scarry, *On Beauty and Being Just* (Princeton, NJ: Princeton University Press, 1999), 47.

[15] Ibid., 49–50.

objects—who are diminished. So the question we need to ask is: If the face or the figure or the tune we found ravishing for two years seems, in the third, boring, bland, and unappealing—who changed?

Who changed? That is the question. Beauty not only confronts us with unprecedented joy and pleasure; it also convicts us of error and fickleness. And that brings me back to my theme of ethics and Eucharist, justice and the liturgy. At the end of Book One in her bestselling novel *Death in Holy Orders*, P. D. James summarizes a homily given at St Anselm's theological college by Archdeacon Crampton (who is later murdered). The archdeacon's theme was Christian discipleship in the modern world, and his message was unambiguous:

> Modern discipleship [Crampton urged] was not a matter of indulgence in archaic if beautiful language, in which words more often obscured than affirmed the reality of faith. There was a temptation to over-value intelligence and intellectual achievement so that theology became a philosophical exercise in justifying skepticism. Equally seductive was an over-emphasis on ceremony, vestments and disputed points of procedure, an obsession with competitive musical excellence, which too often transformed a church service into a public performance. The Church was not a social organization with which the comfortable middle class could satisfy its craving for beauty, order, nostalgia and the illusion of spirituality. Only by a return to the truth of the Gospel could the Church hope to meet the needs of the modern world.[16]

Sound familiar? James's fictional archdeacon has a point, I think. It is very easy to confuse our desire for decorum and "beauty in worship" with nostalgia, with self-indulgence, with snobbish appeals to "artistic excellence," with the costly amusements of the rich and privileged, with pandering to wealthy "art patrons," and, most fatally, with the assumption that God loves the poor but hates their art. I am not trying to make a manifesto here for the inclusion

---

[16] P. D. James, *Death in Holy Orders* (New York: Alfred A. Knopf, 2001), 146.

of inferior art in Catholic worship. On the contrary, we must work with all the talent and energy we can muster to see that what the Sunday assembly says, does, and sings is *good* ritual, *good* art, and *good* music. That is why, for example, I would reject the use of Mozart and Haydn Masses in modern Catholic worship—they are good art, indeed great art, but they are not "good ritual music." By the same token, some of the chant settings in the present Roman Missal (as well as some contemporary settings of the eucharistic prayer) strike me as neither great art nor good ritual music. They are clumsy, insipid, and difficult for presiders and congregations to sing. In a word, there is plenty of room for improvement all around.

But what does all this have to do with our theme of "justice and beauty?" Well, *everything*. I love to repeat that line from Rainer Maria Rilke's famous sonnet on the ancient torso of Apollo (the sculpture known as the Apollo Belvedere): "*You must change your life.*" Rilke understood that every human encounter with great art is a summons to conversion. Or as Elaine Scarry might say, our experience of beauty reveals *our capacity for error, for being wrong.* At this stage in the evolution of the Roman Catholic postconciliar liturgical renewal, maybe it is time for some conversion, for repentance. For establishing some new priorities. Perhaps that sounds odd—but to be honest, I think it is our only way forward. In one of his very first "Amen Corner" columns, Father Robert Hovda (a priest devoted to the work of social justice and good liturgy, and who died early in 1992) wrote these prophetic words:

> There is a devil abroad whose ascendancy is especially tempting, and whose masquerade obstructs and diminishes certain essential aspects of church reform and renewal in many of the quarters where serious efforts are happily occurring. It is a devil that pretends to be the friend of the poor and oppressed, but identifies the faith community's need of festivity's "excess," of beauty and artistry in the environments and other elements of celebration, as the enemy of social justice.[17]

[17] "Scripture Has It, Not on Bread Alone Shall Human Creatures Live," in John Baldovin, ed., *Robert Hovda: The Amen Corner* (Collegeville, MN: Liturgical Press, 1994), 161.

In other words, "concern for the poor" does not excuse the slovenly, inattentive, and downright ugly things priests and people sometimes do at Sunday Mass. Hovda went on to explain that the poor themselves have a much better sense of what "festivity" and "excess" are all about than jaded rich people from the suburbs do. Wrote Hovda:

> Oppressed and dispossessed people seem to understand the human need for festivity's "conscious excess" better than affluent or comfortable ones. A party, a festivity, a celebration, a liturgy has, for people who live daily with the aching pain of want, a psychological and social function whose healing power those who do not so live can scarcely imagine. Glimpses of this truth are everywhere, if we open our eyes. When, for example, a committee was planning an ethnic day for black people (many of them poor and all of them oppressed) before the Philadelphia Eucharistic Congress several years ago, a black representative to the committee laughed uproariously at their middle-class concern that the vesture of the participating bishops should not be, in any way, excessive. The black priest, who had lived with American racist oppression every day of his life, thought their concern very, very funny, and said, "If any one of those bishops were felt by the people to be *our own*, really with us and belonging to us, the more excessive the festivity and the more impressive the vesture, the better! Without that feeling, even their presence is an affront."[18]

Hovda went on to comment that it is not our "commitment to the gospel that has made us contemptuous of beauty, art, and that reverence for things, materials, forms, that open us to the language of being. It is rather the diminishment of a culture which has domesticated our gospel and robbed us of our power to serve it."[19] The solution to poverty, Hovda argued, is not ugly art and sappy music in our worship. On the contrary, "the more striking [the] beauty and integrity and careful celebration"[20] of the Sunday liturgy, the more deeply "Rilke's rule" should sink in: *you must change your life.*

[18] Hovda, 168.
[19] Ibid., 168–69.
[20] Hovda, 169.

Church of the Second Chance: Reconciliation Among the Saint Maybes

Melanie Ross

Introduction

The year is 1965, and life has been good to young Ian Bedloe, titular character of Anne Tyler's novel, *Saint Maybe*. The Bedloes are a Baltimore version of the "ideal, apple-pie household: two amiable parents, three good looking children, a dog, a cat, a scattering of goldfish." The family is taken aback when Ian's older brother Danny decides to marry Lucy, a divorcée with two small children, after only a two-week courtship. Upon hearing the news, the Bedloes swallow hard, put on a good front, and welcome Lucy and her children with open arms. Soon after the wedding—too soon, Ian suspects—Lucy gives birth to a baby girl. When Ian voices his suspicions about Lucy's fidelity to his brother, Danny commits suicide. A few months later, Lucy dies from an overdose of sleeping pills. Ian goes off to college wracked by guilt and grief.

Home from school and wandering the streets of Baltimore one dismal January night, Ian hears singing and is drawn into a storefront church. He finds himself stammering out a confession in front of a small, sincere congregation: "I used to be good," he confides. "Or I used to be not bad, at least. Not evil. I just assumed I wasn't evil, but lately, I don't know what happened. Everything I touch goes wrong. . . . Pray for me to be good again," he asks them. "Pray for me to be forgiven." After the service ends, Ian spills out his story in more detail to the congregation's leader, Reverend Emmett, and asks for confirmation that his prayer worked: "Don't you think I'm forgiven?" The pastor's response startles both Ian and the reader:

> "Goodness, no," Reverend Emmett said briskly. Ian's mouth fell open. He wondered if he'd misunderstood. He said, "I'm not forgiven?" "Oh, no." "But . . . I thought that was kind of the point," Ian said. "I thought God forgives everything." "He does," Reverend Emmett said. "But you can't just say, 'I'm sorry, God.' Why, anyone could do that much! You have to offer reparation—concrete, practical reparation, according to the rules of our church."

As Ian well knows, reparation is not always possible. There are some things that cannot be fixed, which is why Reverend Emmett introduces the "itchy word: Jesus." "Jesus remembers how difficult life on earth can be . . . He helps with what you can't undo. But only after you've *tried* to undo it." Reverend Emmett suggests that God is presenting Ian with a test: in order to show how far he'll go to undo the harm he's caused, nineteen-year-old Ian must drop out of college and raise Lucy's three young children. "But that's crazy! I'd have to be crazy! . . . What kind of a cockeyed religion *is* this?" Ian exclaims. "It's the religion of atonement and complete forgiveness," Reverend Emmett replies with a smile. "It's the religion of the Second Chance." Ian thought he had never seen anyone so absolutely at peace.[1]

Ian and Reverend Emmett represent two sides of a classic tension in Christian theology. Ian stresses the objective nature of forgiveness: human reconciliation with God through Christ is a *fait accompli* that lies outside the realm of any individual's experience or feelings. ("I thought God forgives everything.") For Reverend Emmett, forgiveness is subjective: it is located in the present and only really "happens" for a person when they embrace it in some manner. Of course, there are many reasons why Reverend Emmett's theology—long on works and short on grace—should give us

---

[1] Anne Tyler, *Saint Maybe* (New York: Knopf, 1991), 121–23.

pause. At the same time, there is something profoundly correct about the insistence that forgiveness and salvation must include a human response in the here and now. Herein lies the theological conundrum. Too much emphasis on salvation as a past event risks making our present experience the appendix to an already completed act. Too much emphasis on our present experience risks turning salvation into a simple matter of human feelings. A robust theology of reconciliation must allow for a shifting balance between the two poles.

Nathan balances this tension beautifully in his column, "Gathering as an Act of Reconciliation." As a better theologian than Reverend Emmett, Nathan knows that when we, a church in recovery, press Ian's question—"Are we forgiven?"—the response must be a swift and unequivocal "YES!" The only way out of human powerlessness, hostility, and estrangement was for "*God* to act, for *God* to do for us what we cannot (and could not) do for ourselves." The accomplishment of Jesus' crucifixion and resurrection is objectively fixed: "God refuses any longer to cook the books, to keep records, or to settle scores. The debit and credit game of winners and losers is over. Over. All are winners."[2] This is why when the church assembles for worship, "we always gather in *someone else's name*"—in the "name of the Father, and of the Son, and of the Holy Spirit." We "commence our journey forward traveling on somebody else's passport, using somebody else's visa."[3] Thanks be to God . . . amen, and amen!

But thus assured of our forgiveness, Nathan is not afraid to press Reverend Emmett's question: how far are we willing to live into this forgiveness by attempting to right our wrongs? While reconciliation is a divinely initiated and accomplished act, it "also has to be *human* and *historical*," involving our very breath, blood, and bone. From now on, it is up to the church to become "what God created us to be in the cross of Christ: a people living in righteousness, justice, and reconciliation." With the ethical force of a Hebrew

[2] Nathan Mitchell, "Gathering as an Act of Reconciliation," *Worship* 85, no. 6 (November 2011): 546.

[3] Ibid., 553.

prophet, Nathan calls us to be a "church of insomniacs": the people of God who own up to our individual and collective mistakes, who throw open our doors in radical welcome, who publicly rage against the activities of hate groups, who work so that not one more child in the world dies of starvation or curable disease. Thanks be to God . . . amen, and amen!

The problem, as we all know, is that there is often a pronounced gap between our intentions and our actions. We smile in recognition when James K.A. Smith confesses to reading Wendell Berry in the food court at Costco. Why is it, Smith muses, that "I *believe* Michael Pollan but still pull into the drive-through at McDonald's?"[4] Indeed. And why is it that we, as a Church, *believe* the reconciliatory Gospel message that there is neither Jew nor Gentile, slave nor free, male nor female, but still worship as though our internal divisions were insurmountable? Perhaps in this sense, we are all Ian Bedloe—"saint maybes" who know the good we ought to do, but struggle to enact it in the church and in the world (James 4:17).

My essay explores this tension by picking up at the place where Nathan's "Amen Corner" leaves off: with the claim that "every Christian gathering is always, inevitably, an act of reconciliation."[5] It is true that reconciliation is God's already-accomplished gift to the church; accordingly, Scripture enjoins us "to maintain the unity of the Spirit in the bonds of peace" (Ephesians 4:3). However, reconciliation is also a call: Scripture not only affirms the essential unity of Christ's body, but repeatedly admonishes Christians to *be* what they *are*. Jesus instructed his disciples to be a community of visible love (John 13:12-17) and prayed that they "may all be one" in order "that the world may believe that the Father has sent me" (John 17:21). Seen from one perspective, Christian gatherings are grace-filled sites of reconciliation. Seen from another, they are fraught reiterations of the world's political and economic divisions. In what follows, I will probe these divisions and press the question of how far we are willing to go to make amends.

---

[4] James K.A. Smith, *Imagining the Kingdom* (Grand Rapids, MI: Baker Academic, 2013), 9.

[5] Mitchell, 553.

Political Divisions

One of the most important advances in late twentieth-century liturgical theology was insistence (always implied but newly articulated) that *lex orandi* (the rule of prayer) and *lex credendi* (the rule of belief) must be verified by *lex agendi* (the rule of action or behavior).[6] But while there is ecumenical unanimity that action gives power to prayer and illumination to belief, Christians frequently clash over the practical forms their ethical service should take. Margaret Farley has identified the "difficulties in forming any corporate conscience in the church whereby it might 'take its stand' against evil and for good on the specific issues of the day—issues of welfare reform, corporate investment, women's rights, affirmative action, abortion, capital punishment, full employment, disarmament, and so on. These disagreements are not trivial. They spring from different worldviews—despite the fact that persons within the church seemingly share a fundamental religious worldview." Farley worries that "until we find a way to either form a corporate conscience (that is nonetheless free) or to understand and live with integrity the very pluralism that marks the social ethics of the church," the life of worship will be muted and faltering.[7]

The relationship of ethics to worship is a live issue in both Catholic and Protestant theological contexts. Catholic social commitments, shaped by clearly defined official church teachings, have long promoted a consistent "ethic of life." However, in 2006 Pope Benedict XVI remarked, "I see ever more clearly that in our age morality is, as it were, split in two." One morality focuses on "the great topics of peace, non-violence, justice for all, concern for the poor and respect for creation." The other part of morality concerns "commitment to life from conception to death," including defense

---

[6] See Kevin Irwin, *Context and Text: Method in Liturgical Theology* (Collegeville, MN: Pueblo, 1994), 55–56; Don Saliers, *Worship as Theology: Foretaste of Glory Divine* (Nashville, TN: Abingdon, 1994), 6–8. More recently, see Nathan Mitchell, *Meeting Mystery: Liturgy, Worship, and Sacraments* (Maryknoll, NY: Orbis Books, 2006), 38–40, 223–25.

[7] Margaret Farley, "Beyond the Formal Principle: A Reply to Ramsey and Saliers," *Journal of Religious Ethics* 7 (1979): 198.

against abortion and euthanasia.[8] Relatedly, scholars note an American tendency toward a selective "cafeteria Catholicism" on both the left and right, with "leaders and laity alike becoming vulnerable to single- or narrow-issue politics and the distortion that ensues."[9] Progressive Catholics praise the church's position on war and peace, its preferential option for the poor, and its strong opposition to the death penalty, while downplaying its teachings on sexuality. Conservative Catholics defend the Church's sexual teachings and are actively prolife, but tend to downplay its social teachings. Although "justice" and "life" issues are clearly non-dichotomous in official teaching, this unity is difficult for many Christians to sustain in practice.

The Protestant situation is equally vexed. In his book, *Evangelical vs. Liberal*, James Wellman reports that evangelicals and liberals espouse two opposing models of family life, each construed on different norms and based on a powerful moral worldview judged to be sacrosanct and absolute. The evangelicals in Wellman's study were more concerned with overcoming personal sin than confronting structural injustices or economic inequalities. Social change that is not preceded by repentance and a relationship with Jesus Christ was seen as inauthentic, even useless. Because evangelicals understand the traditional family as the heart of what God wants for humans, heterosexual marriage and family values are central planks in their moral worldview. Liberal Protestants counter that Jesus was at best ambivalent about the family—even his own. Jesus preferred sinners and was sometimes labeled as such himself: all are welcome at his table regardless of class, race, or gender. Accordingly, the liberal Protestants of Wellman's study understood

---

[8] Benedict XVI, "Conclusion of the Meeting of the Holy Father with the Bishops of Switzerland," November 9, 2006, http://www.vatican.va/holy_father/benedict_xvi/speeches/2006/november/documents/hf_ben-xvi_spe_20061109_concl-swiss-bishops_en.html, accessed March 14, 2014.

[9] Kristin Heyer, Mark Rozel and Michael A. Genovese, eds., *Catholics and Politics: The Dynamic Tension between Faith and Power* (Washington, DC: Georgetown University Press, 2008), 3.

supporting gay and lesbian individuals and couples as central to what the gospel calls them to do.

Christian worship reflects these political divisions. In their magisterial study, *American Grace: How Religion Divides and Unites Us*, sociologists Robert Putnam and David Campbell report:

> People sort themselves—whether consciously or not—into congregations with politically simpático members, through a self-reinforcing process. The more one kind of person predominates within a given congregation, the more that others who perceive themselves as similar will feel comfortable there (and those who see themselves as different will feel uncomfortable, to the point of leaving) . . . All this sorting makes many religious social networks into political echo chambers.[10]

Can we worship next to those with whom we vehemently disagree? Will reconciliation as Nathan describes it—a making *different*, a making *otherwise*, an at/one/ment, which results in a new relationship that changes both progressives and conservatives—be possible? This is the question of our age.

Theologian Ada María Isasi-Díaz suggests a way forward by emphasizing that our differences are more related to relationships than to distinctions. She writes, "Unless we embrace differences and diversity as constituents of relationships instead of seeing them as separating and opposing elements, we will not be able to heal what divides us."[11] Political divisions among believers may run deep, but they do not go "all the way down."[12] Christians are united by the sense that Jesus Christ has something important to say to them, and the conviction that he has chosen to speak through Word and Sacrament.

---

[10] Robert D. Putnam and David E. Campbell, *American Grace: How Religion Divides and Unites Us* (New York: Simon & Schuster, 2010), 442.

[11] Ada María Isasi-Díaz, *La Lucha Continues: Mujerista Theology* (Maryknoll, NY: Orbis Books, 2004), 223.

[12] Mark Douglas, "On Agreeing to Disagree," *Journal for Preachers* 23, no. 4 (2000): 36.

Furthermore, Christians on opposing sides of moral issues are united by their common appeal to Scripture: "while we may disagree with the way other people are using the Bible, we cannot deny that they are using it."[13] Scripture itself continually subverts our expectations. As Ellen Davis astutely notes, "Whenever we pick up the Bible, read it, put it down, and say 'That's just what I thought,' we are probably in trouble."[14] Furthermore, this potential for subversion is always present in worship. Whether we place ourselves on the left wing or right wing of an increasingly polarized Christianity, we err if we expect the liturgy to provide an unqualified affirmation of our entrenched theological positions. In the famous words of Urban Holmes, good liturgy leads its practitioners "to the edge of chaos, and out of that experience will come a theology different from any previous theology."[15]

Economic Divisions

Of course, the final intention of a liturgical rite is not to produce theological "meanings" (be they "conservative," "liberal," or something in between), but to produce a ritually inscribed body that knows how, liturgically, to "do" a redeemed world.[16] Ritual is not so much a way of thinking or speaking as it is an embodied skill that redefines the person who uses it. Thus we become hospitable, not by analyzing hospitality but by greeting guests, offering them the kiss of peace, and washing their feet. Following Michel Foucault, Nathan stresses that ritual is "a knowing that 'does *not* know,' a seeing that does *not* see, a grasp that neither seizes nor controls."[17]

[13] Ibid., 35.

[14] Ellen Davis, "Teaching the Bible Confessionally in the Church," in Ellen F. Davis and Richard B. Hays, eds., *The Art of Reading Scripture* (Grand Rapids, MI: Wm. B. Eerdmans, 2003), 16.

[15] Urban T. Holmes, "Theology and Religious Renewal," *Anglican Theological Review* 62, no.1 (1980): 18.

[16] Nathan Mitchell, "Liturgical Theology: Ritual as Reading," in Joanne M. Pierce and Michael Downey, eds., *Source and Summit: Commemorating Josef Jungmann* (Collegeville, MN: Liturgical Press, 1999), 178.

[17] Nathan Mitchell, "New Horizons," *Worship* 84, no. 2 (March 2010): 175–76.

This is good news for the unity of the church: liturgy's inexhaustible surplus of meaning cannot be contained by any one individual, congregation, or strand of the Christian tradition. But there is troubling news as well. Liturgy cannot be separated from its sociocultural context. Each of us is blind to his or her own class-based assumptions, and this is precisely the point where ritual as "a knowing that does not know" becomes sticky.

French theorist Pierre Bourdieu has noted that from the moment of birth, individuals begin to acquire a habitus: a particular way of thinking, feeling, and acting that is shared by all members of a group of people. Habitus encompasses both our cultural inheritances and our personal experiences: it is the sum of our conversational style, gestures, cultural tastes, and notions of beauty and justice. We learn it informally, unconsciously, and through our bodies. Members of the same class have feelings of affinity for one another based on similar lifestyles and preferences. Bourdieu suggests they also feel hostile toward, ridicule, or reject the cultural choices of those unlike themselves. Ultimately, this classism leads to the reproduction of the social order: the ruling class "inducts its young into certain dispositions, primarily aesthetic, that subsequently reinforce their status and distinguish them from other, lower classes."[18]

A similar classism is at work in worship. Nathan has shown that it can be subtle: "Secretly, many of us believe that God loves the poor, but hates their art. Surely, we suspect, God prefers Mozart to Randy Travis. A certain degree of elitist snobbery surrounds our rhetoric about 'excellence,' as applied to art that serves the Christian community."[19] It can also be overt. Sociological studies over the past fifty years show that American worshippers consistently segregate themselves by class. Generally speaking, individuals in higher ranked socio-economic brackets worship in theologically

[18] Luke Bretherton, "Sharing Peace: Class, Hierarchy & Christian Social Order," in Stanley Hauerwas and Samuel Wells, eds., *Blackwell Companion to Christian Ethics* (Oxford: Wiley-Blackwell, 2011), 337.

[19] Nathan Mitchell, "Glory to God in the Lowest," *Worship* 70, no. 3 (May 1996): 258.

liberal denominations with hierarchical church organizations and formal liturgical styles. Individuals on the lower end of the socio-economic spectrum tend to worship in theologically conservative denominations with congregational polity and more emotive and ecstatic worship styles.[20]

Sociologist and photographer Camilo José Vergara set out to explore the latter in his poignant and visually arresting book, *How the Other Half Worships.* Vergara traveled across the United States in search of "places where the homeless, the drug addicted, and those recently released from prison go for food, shelter, and clothing, and get those things plus religion."[21] Many of the "storefront" and "ghetto" churches he photographs have colorful names: "America Come Back to God Evangelistic Church," "Stop Suffering Universal Church of the Kingdom of God," "Heavenly Rainbow Baptist Church," and "Going Up Yonder Church of God in Christ." Some meet in traditional-looking church buildings with fortified exteriors: bars over the windows, metal doors installed, and signs placed prominently to indicate alarm systems. Others repurpose existing architectural structures by adding steeples and crosses to buildings that formerly housed Woolworth's, hardware stores, fast food restaurants, movie theaters, or car dealerships.

None of the churches stand above reproach. Vergara implicitly criticizes clergy who lure their congregations with false promises of success into contributing so much money that they "may not have enough left over to pay rent or utility bills or to buy food."[22] But neither does he dismiss outright stories of pastors who are magically healed by Jesus or who themselves heal stalled cars by the laying on of hands. Vergara reports "fire in my bones," and is "overwhelmed by an intense feeling of the sacred" when the congregation of a West Indian Baptist church in Brooklyn speaks in

---

[20] See Smith and Faris, "Socioeconomic Inequality in the American Religious System: An Update and Assessment," *Journal for the Scientific Study of Religion* 44, no. 1 (2005): 102.

[21] Camilo José Vergara, *How the Other Half Worships* (New Brunswick, NJ: Rutgers University Press, 2005), 281.

[22] Ibid., 154.

tongues. On another occasion, "words from Genesis . . . made my imagination spin wildly, giving me a taste of grandeur and eternity."[23] One can imagine the twinkle in Vergara's eye as he reflects back over the course of his research: "If I had wanted to write a book that was logical, consistent, and politically correct from beginning to end, I would have chosen a different topic!"[24]

Sociological efforts to explain the affinity between class and worship have been similarly vexed. Generally speaking, scholars have tended to frame the beliefs and worship practices of "the other half" as deviations from the norm of middle class belief and behavior. Stating the issue more colloquially: Why do "those people" worship "that way"? Sean McCloud's eye-opening book, *Divine Hierarchies*, chronicles how twentieth-century scholarship on race and class connected certain religious groups with everything from biological inferiority to social and economic deprivations. For example, not long ago scholars explained religious differences in terms of genetically inherited human character traits: inherently "depraved religions" attract inherently "depraved people." Particularly troubling is the fact that respected eugenicists, sociologists, and psychologists of the time all reached "nearly identical conclusions about which religious communities were the most depraved, degenerate, or unevolved"—namely, Roman Catholic, Fundamentalist, and Pentecostal Christians.[25]

If it is true that religious habitus is never separate from the larger social structures and hierarchies of culture in which it is situated, this raises an uncomfortable question: Where does theology end and social class begin? Worship practices may derive from Biblical texts, prophetic revelations, church traditions or whatever sources of authority are normative for a group. However, when these practices are performed, they take on social significance. Consider the practice of speaking in tongues: it is derived from Pentecostal theology and tradition, but "has taken on an additional

---

[23] Ibid., 23.

[24] Ibid., 281.

[25] Sean McCloud, *Divine Hierarchies: Class in American Religion and Religious Studies* (Chapel Hill, NC: University of North Carolina Press, 2007), 35.

meaning that locates its practitioners in social space, both for those who esteem it and for those who disdain it."[26] Luke Bretherton notes that "how we sit, talk, dress, and comport ourselves, as well as what and where we sing, read, and speak in worship, can express and reproduce class, not covenantal relations."[27] Liturgy then—at least on this side of the eschaton—not only "does" the world the way God meant it to be done in Christ: it also reinscribes the world's sinful divisions into the Church's body.

Will reconciliation as Nathan describes it—a making *different*, a making *otherwise*, an at/one/ment, which results in new relationships that change Christians across the socio-economic spectrum—be possible? This too is the question of our age. T.S. Eliot beautifully captures this tension in his final quartet: "From wrong to wrong the exasperated spirit/ Proceeds, unless restored by that refining fire/ Where you must move in measure, like a dancer." We assemble around the eucharistic table week after week for precisely this reason: to be restored "by that refining fire." Ultimately, however, our gatherings can only be understood as acts of reconciliation insofar as we allow the light and heat of the liturgy to burn away our comfortable pretenses. Consider Siobhán Garrigan's bracing challenge:

> What are we confessing/expressing contrition for? That we told three fibs this week and drank too much on Friday night, or that we are part of a desperate situation that leads us to normatively and indignantly view our neighbors with thinly-masked contempt? What are we being assured/absolved of? That God has always already forgiven us so we are free to get on with habitual righteous sectarian hatred or that God's forgiveness is useless if we are not open to its radical—for all people—presence in the world?[28]

[26] Timothy J. Nelson, "At Ease With Our Own Kind: Worship Practices and Class Segregation in American Religion," in Sean McCloud and William A. Mirola, eds., *Religion and Class in America: Culture, History, and Politics* (Leiden: Brill, 2008), 54.

[27] Bretherton, 337.

[28] Siobhán Garrigan, *The Real Peace Process: Worship, Politics, and the End of Sectarianism* (London: Equinox, 2010), 60.

Like a dancer, the church must move in measure between the "already" of what God has accomplished through Christ by the power of the Spirit, and the "not-yet" of unjust inequalities and ongoing divisions. The steps of reconciliation are complicated, and the company of saint maybes is prone to stumble. Thanks be to God for prophets like Nathan who lead the way, singing the truth and reminding us that Christianity is a cockeyed religion of atonement, complete forgiveness, and second chances. Amen and amen!

"Gathering as an Act of Reconciliation"[1]

Some time ago I had the pleasure of reading *Lying Awake*, a novel by the young American writer Mark Salzman. It is the story of a cloistered Carmelite nun, Sister John of the Cross, who, after many years of plodding, dry-as-dust service in her community, begins to experience dazzling visions. The visions are accompanied by unbearable headaches which, a CAT scan reveals, are possibly linked to an epileptic disorder that sometimes produces compelling (though false) visions—a condition ancient doctors called "holy madness." Further tests reveal that Sister John's seizures are actually the result of a raisin-sized meningioma which she agrees to let a surgeon remove. Of course, when the seizures end, so, most likely, will the "visions." Alone, recovering in the infirmary, Sister John reflects: "I'm too young to feel finished, too old to start over, and too worn out to see coherence in all this. How many times can a person fail before losing heart? Forgive me, Lord."[2] She reflects on a poem framed and hanging above the infirmary door.

What makes Salzman's spare, lyrical novel so gripping is the intense moral and psychological drama that was being played out in Sister John's life. Against her will, she is forced to face harrowing change; she has to choose whether or not to "make things different," to "make things otherwise," even at the risk of losing her unexpected gift, the gift of visions that had finally brought beauty and meaning into her lonely life. To use Paul's language, Sister John of the Cross was faced with a crisis of reconciliation. Because

[1] This essay originally appeared in "The Amen Corner," *Worship* 85, no. 6 (November 2011): 542–53.
[2] Mark Salzman, *Lying Awake* (New York: Knopf, 2000), 171.

that is exactly what the New Testament words for "reconciliation" (in Greek, καταλλαγή, καταλλάσσω) means when Paul uses them. They mean "making something other" they mean changing or altering something, making it *different*, making it *otherwise*. In Paul's perspective, reconciliation is always relational; it results in a new relationship which changes *both* parties. If only *one* party changes, what you have is obedience or submission—but not reconciliation. As we will see, when God reconciles the world in Christ, the result is a revolution not only in the world, but in God.

Those of you familiar with the practice of story-telling know that when recovering persons tell their story, they usually do three things: they tell us (1) *what it was like*; (2) *what happened*; and (3) *what it is like now*. Using Paul's theology of reconciliation in his Second Letter to the Corinthians as a lens, I would like to use this three-part structure of story-telling as a framework.

What Life Was Like

One of the most penetrating analyses of the human condition ever made was offered by Paul in the first chapters of his Letter to the Romans. Paul looks at the global situation of Jews and Gentiles, believers and unbelievers, and he comes up with a one-line conclusion that is pretty hard to resist in Romans 3:23: "Everybody has sinned and fallen short of the glory of God." *Everybody*—Jews, Greeks, observant Israelites who are learned in the Law, Gentiles trying to find and follow the law in their hearts, young, old, the sick and the healthy, women and men, gays and straights (they're in there too). *Everybody*. Everybody—everybody has sinned (literally, "has missed the mark") and fallen short of the glory of God. As far as Paul is concerned there are no exceptions: every human being who lives and breathes is a day late and a dollar short. No exceptions. That is what *our life was like*—that is what life is like, apart from the revelation of God, who reconciles the world in Christ.

So, in Paul's view, we humans are creatures who need changing, and what needs to be "changed" above all, what needs to be "made other than it is" are those pervasive conditions of hostility, rage, resentment, fear, and estrangement, that separate us from God and from one another. Those are conditions, Paul seems to feel, that start the moment we are born—the moment we flail our fists to protest that first sharp intake of breath with a loud cry—and it continues, and worsens, every time we try to justify ourselves, every time we try to create our own "righteousness" (or impose it on someone else). In short, *estrangement and hostility are what happen when God and humankind become "problems" for one another—when I become a "problem" for God and God becomes a "problem" for me.* And any attempt at self-justification, Paul warns, is bound to be deadly.

This catastrophic hostility is not limited, moreover, to human beings; the whole universe, the cosmos, is similarly sick, twisted, estranged, infected, hostile, at odds with itself and its Creator, out of joint, disordered, held in thrall by powerful, inhuman intelligences that Paul calls "principalities and powers." In sum, we are a mess, and so is the whole universe! That is *"what it was like,"* that is the situation, as Paul sees it—and it is a situation that only God's gracious initiative can change. We too were *done*; in Paul's view, we were trapped in a vicious cycle of rebellion, regret, remorse, and retaliation—*about which we could do nothing.* We were powerless; un*able* to change, un*willing* to change. That leads me to Section Two in this story of recovery:

What Happened?

As Paul sees it, humanity was stuck, stuck in the mud, stuck in a hopeless system of denial and death. Paul called that system *hamartia,* "missing the mark," "missing the point," *sin.* "Everybody, all have sinned and fallen short of the glory of God." The only way out of this swamp—the only way out of powerlessness, hostility, estrangement and the death these bring to human hearts and bodies—is for *God* to act, for *God* to do for us what we cannot (and could not) do for ourselves.

But there is a catch. The solution (what Paul will eventually call καταλλαγή, "reconciliation") has to be *divine*, but it also has to be *human* and *historical*. Reconciliation has to involve our own breath, blood, and bone; it has to involve our bread, marrow, and gristle, our wine and our bodily fluids, our milk, tears, salt and semen. And that means not only that *we* must change (or be changed) but that *God* must change. God too must become "some*thing* other, some*one* other." That is the throbbing scandal of Christian faith. *God too* must change, does change, becomes someone other.

For most of us, such an assertion sounds downright heretical. We were taught to think of God as an omnipotent, self-contained, perfect, limitless, independent, spiritual "He" (even though we might admit that God's "masculinity" had nothing to do with testosterone or other gender-related characteristics). It may thus shock us to hear that for Paul, this kind of a God—utterly transcendent, omnipotent, self-contained, limited, independent, spiritual, strong, silent and masculine—could not do what needed to be done, could not reconcile people, or creatures, or the cosmos. For Paul, reconciliation cannot happen if God stays on the outside looking in, if God merely "meddles" or dabbles in our history (but ultimately stays aloof and squeaky clean). If the mess was going to be changed, then *God would have to get down and dirty, would have to become part of the mess.* That, in a nutshell, is Paul's amazing argument. Paul puts it bluntly in his second letter to the Corinthians: God was in Christ—*in Christ* (not "near Christ," not "hanging out around Christ," not "close to Christ but holding the divine nose against the stench of humanity"). "God was in Christ, reconciling the world to Godself." That is exactly what the Greek text of Paul's letter says: "in Christ, God was reconciling the world to himself" (2 Cor 5:19). And if you back up a couple of verses, the astonishing claim that Paul makes:

> If anyone is in Christ, there is a new creation: everything old has passed away; see, everything has become new! All this is from God, who reconciled us to himself through Christ, and has given us the ministry of reconciliation; that is, in Christ God was reconciling the world to himself, not counting their trespasses against them, and entrusting the message of reconciliation to us. So we are ambassadors for Christ, since God is making his appeal through us; we entreat you on behalf of Christ, be reconciled to God. For our sake he made him to be sin who knew no sin, so that in him we might become the righteousness of God. (2 Cor 5:17-21)

If we were to look in the New Testament for "the gospel according to Paul," those four verses of 2 Corinthians 5 would certainly qualify! Paul's gospel assumes three basic things: First, it assumes that we human beings were powerless, that our lives had become unmanageable, undurable, unbearable, unlivable—that anger, rage, hostility, and despair were literally killing us. Second, Paul's gospel says that *God* decided to do something about that, God decided to do for us what we could not do for ourselves. Third, and how and what God decided to do for us is so outrageous, so preposterous, it makes your hair stand on end. Because what God chooses to do, first, is to scrap everything that has happened since the Big Bang and to start over again. This is God making nothing less than a new creation: *"Everything old has come to an end; behold, new things have come to be."*

In other words, God decides to trash the human past—with its sick, sorry history of hatred, violence, and destruction—and to create something utterly new between us and God, between us and one other. A new creation that takes flesh as a reconciled—and reconciling—community. But that is not all. *How* God chooses to do this is what really boggles the mind. Here is how Paul puts it: "[God] made him to be sin who knew no sin, so that in him we might become the righteousness of God" (2 Cor 5:21). God makes Jesus the Sinless One *to be sin*, so that *we* can become the righteousness of God! God decides to look for us in the place you would least expect—in the kingdom of death as it takes possession of a condemned man's body; God looks for us in the place where dead men are walking.

In sum, God pursues us all the way to the cross of Christ, to the place where *sin* itself was crucified. Crucifixion, I am afraid, is not the sanitized method of capital punishment practiced by today's state-sponsored executioners, who prefer easier, softer exits like "lethal injection." Crucifixion is slow death by suffocation, death by agonizing inches, each successive breath drug out of the body harder than the one before. Paul says that God made the One who knew no sin, to die, suffocating on the cross, the weight of his body slowly shutting off the supply of air to his lungs. Have you ever been unable to get your breath? Have you ever felt the panic and horror when you inhale and nothing happens? It is like being buried alive.

That, Paul says, is how God *reconciled* the world, how God made things different. In the cross of Jesus, God became a fool so we could become wise, agents of a new creation, ambassadors of reconciliation. And that means nothing—and no one—can ever be the same again. Not us—and not God. "God has discarded all the arithmetic that has to do with humanity's sins."[3] God refuses any longer to cook the books, to keep records, or to settle scores. The debit and credit game of winners and losers is over. Over. All are winners. And winning, I am here to tell you, is a far more difficult fate to accept than losing. From now on it is up to us to be, to become, what God created us to be in the cross of Christ: a people living in righteousness, justice, and reconciliation, a people who know how to make a difference to the rest of scabrous, suffering humanity.

And that leads to the third part of our story, *"What it is like now."* What does it mean for us to live as a gathered, reconciled—and *reconciling*—church? Who do we have to be, in order to become such a church—and *how*, and *why*?

What It Is Like Now:
Living a Reconciled Life as Church

Let me begin by suggesting what we can*not* be, if we hope to serve as God's reconcilers in the world. First, we can*not* be a community of the smug, the self-congratulatory, the self-satisfied; we cannot be a community of the becalmed affluent, numb to every virtue except prosperity. For example, in a book entitled *The Virtue of Prosperity*, the well-known Catholic conservative Dinesh D'Souza crows that the United States has at last succeded in creating "the first mass affluent class in world history" that "poverty is no longer a significant problem in America since the poor here are so much better off than the poor everywhere else in the world, and are also better off than average Americans were fifty years ago (evidence:

[3] Frederick W. Daner, *II Corinthians*, Augsburg Commentary on the New Testament (Minneapolis, MN: Augsburg, 1989), 82.

ninety eight percent of the poor have refrigerators)."[4] Most parents, D'Souza asserts, would rather have their children grow up to be like Bill Gates. While not perfect, D'Souza blithely concludes, in a paroxysm of jingoist euphoria, the prosperous United States culture of a decade ago is "probably the best society that now exists or has ever existed." I guess that is a cheerful conclusion you have no trouble accepting if you belong to D'Souza's "mass affluent class." But hey, as it turns out, to belong to that class you have to make more than $500,000 a year—and that amounts to about six million or so households in the United States, roughly five percent of our population. Since when did five percent become a "mass affluent class?" I do not know about you, but I do not belong to the "mass affluent class" and do not expect to any time soon, especially in the present economic crisis we are all experiencing. Statistics show that poverty continues alarmingly to plague even prosperous American society—especially its children and its elderly. Besides, how can Christians who claim that the Bread of Life is the "source and summit of their lives" allow even one more child in Somalia and the rest of the world to die of starvation and curable diseases? How can we do that and sleep at night? *If we're not a church of insomniacs, we're probably not doing our job.* As long as our *world* is hungry—as long as any*one* in our world is hungry—we are *not* fully doing the work of real presence, we are not fully *doing* Eucharist, we are not fully *being* Eucharist.

Second, we cannot be a church of reconcilers if we are more concerned with shutting people out than with letting them in, if our primary purpose is *ex*clusion rather than *in*clusion. How can the church *be* "the good news of reconciliation" to women if, through the use of specious scriptural arguments, it steadfastly and systematically refuses them any real or meaningful power-sharing? In our church, priesthood is power—*maybe* it should not be that way, *probably* it should not be that way, but it *is*. To exclude someone from priesthood is to bar that person from full, active, and conscious participation in power, pure and simple. The very fact that

[4] See the review by Rob Walker in *The New York Times Book Review* for Sunday, January 7, 2001.

we are still talking about this in 2011, the third millennium, witnesses to the depth and pervasiveness of our sin. For yes, Virginia, sexism (and discriminations based on sexual orientation) is as surely a sin as racism is. As long as its *power* is giving to *need* (whether compassionately or not), *nothing* has changed; no reconciliation has taken place.

Thirdly, we cannot be a church of reconcilers if we keep on claiming that we are always the victims and never the victimizers, if we keep on trying to "apologize" without ever repenting. That is why, for example, our church's relations with the Jewish community have become such a tar baby. Instead of repenting for the twenty centuries of anti-Semitic rhetoric and behavior that led directly to the unspeakable carnage of the Holocaust, we keep pretending that *we* (as much as the Jewish people) were actually innocent victims of Nazi oppression. But I suspect you may find it difficult to name one person who was killed by the Nazis simply because he or she was a Catholic. Edith Stein was not killed for being a cloistered Carmelite; she was killed because the blood of Israel flowed in her veins. Apologies are cheap; repentance calls for restitution, and restitution requires, according to the OED, *"reparation for loss or injury previously inflicted."* Then why can we not understand the bitterness of Jews when told that papal apologies—coming (as they did) more than half a century after the chimneys of Auschwitz stopped smoking—has "taken care of" our obligation to make restitution for the church's terrible silence during World War II? To say nothing of the more recent "cosmetic" revisions to the Good Friday prayer for the Conversion of Jews in the 1962 Roman Missal which undoubtedly represent a major departure from previous ecclesial teachings as well as numerous authoritative Catholic documents, including *Nostra Aetate*. And of course, to discuss the Catholic Church's handling of recent child abuse cases in the United States and Europe would require another time and space.

Four, we cannot be a church of reconcilers if we condone—by either passive acquiescence or active cooperation—the existence and activities of hate groups. When thirteen years ago Matthew Shepard, tied to a fence and left to die on a lonely road in Wyoming, did you hear any thundering condemnations coming out of the

NCCB, or EWTN, or, for that matter, out of the myriad websites that advertise themselves as "Catholic"? I suspect you did not. And yet, as Thomas More reminded his accusers at his trial, *qui tacet consentire*—silence bespeaks consent. We no longer live in a time or a place or a world that permits the luxury of a merely private outrage. Indeed, the Internet has all but obliterated the very distinction between "private" and "public." If, as the Right-to-Life movement insists, abortion is a hate crime, why is not capital punishment (are we not told to forgive, to turn the other cheek and say with Jesus "Father, forgive them; for they do not know what they are doing"?) or gay-bashing or the torching of synagogues and Jewish day-care centers or the killing of doctors who legally do their duty? Surely no Catholic would want to argue that we are permitted to play God in every instance except at the beginning of life. I suspect, thousands of mothers whose sons are among the "disappeared" in Chile would certainly not argue so.

Reconciliation means repentance; it means restitution; it means recovery; it means atonement in the sense of "at/one/ment"—and not in the sense of sacrifice, expiation, appeasement, or propitiation. Paul's notion of reconciliation has nothing to do with cultic rituals of sacrifice; it has to do, rather, with recovering relationships in the personal, social, and political spheres. *Reconcilition* (καταλλαγή, "making otherwise") is the word that describes what happens when husbands and wives resolve their differences; when individuals choose friendship, love, and intimacy over hostility, anger, and alienation; when societies voluntarily renounce social policy based on getting, having, and hoarding and choose justice, mercy, generosity, and inclusion in their stead. We cannot live as a reconciling church if we are self-congratualtory exclusionists, or if we claim to have PhDs in victim studies while we silently condone hate groups.

Reconciliation means recovery, and one of the first steps in recovery is facing our fears. *What are we afraid of—and why are we afraid of it?* If, as a recovering, reconciling church we are going to tell others "what it was like, what happened, and what it is like now," we need to find and face those fears. The German theologian Dorothee Sölle once asked: "Why do [we] human beings adore a God whose main attribute is power, whose interest is [or seems to be] subjugation, who is afraid of equal rights? A being treated as Lord, who has received from his theologians a certificate of omnipotence, simple power being insufficient?"[5] When I first read Sölle's questions, I felt very uncomfortable until it occurred to me that I was feeling uneasy *because I did not have the answers.* I felt the panic that every male feels when confronted by the possibility that he might—just *might*—have to stop and ask somebody directions. Imagine my horror, then, when I then read Ivone Gebara's commentary on Dorothee Sölle's questions:

> The liberator God [she writes], in spite of the attractiveness of the concept, sometimes seems as dangerous as the God of reason, who governs the world from a throne of glory. In practice, this image of God as liberator excludes women as much as does the image of God as "The Other," insofar as women continue to be the *pietás* of war games, accepting on their knees the murdered bodies of husbands, lovers, brothers, sisters, children, parents . . .
>
> I am suspicious of this omnipotent god, this self-sufficient god, this god beyond the earth and the cosmos, the god beyond humans and at the same time very much like humans, the celestial "double" of powerful men, whether of the right or the left.
>
> The god on high, in heaven, on a throne, the father of men, the god of blind obedience, the god who punishes and saves, is no longer useful—even when he presents a liberator's face—to our world, to the humanization of the human, to women, to the future of the poor. He too is the fruit of an authoritarian religion . . . is religion that produces sentimentalism and consolation as faith's response to the nonsense of existence reduced to survival, the existence today of thousands of humans scrabbling for a wretched loaf [just] to exist.[6]

Tough words, important words, for those of us hoping to live as a church of reconcilers. Ivone Gebara suggests that if we hope to live as a church in recovery, we have to reimagine what God's

---

[5] Cited in Ivone Gebara, "The Face of Transcendence as a Challenge to the Reading of the Bible in Latin America," in Elisabeth Schüssler Fiorenza, ed., *Searching the Scriptures, Vol I: A Feminist Introduction* (New York: Crossroad, 1995), 175.

[6] Ibid., 175.

"transcendence" means. Traditionally, we have defined transcendence as "omnipotence, self-sufficiency, grandeur, magnitude, hyper-masculinity." Suppose, however, we reaffirm transcendence not as "superiority" but as *relationship*, as *relation* present to everything, *relation* articulated among all human beings, animals, plants, earth, air, fire, water, cosmos. Everything that exists is relation and lives in *relation*, a vital energy in which we exist, a primary mystery that simply *is*.[7] If God is *transcendent*, and if transcendence is *relationship*, then we can say (indeed, we *must* say) that God is the One in our universe who makes a difference to all things and to whom all things make a difference. God's transcendent "otherness" is, in fact, the mystery of God's profound *relatedness*—to us, to all that *is*, to all that lives and moves and has being. Or to put it another way, God's transcendence is an all-inclusive relatedness that, nevertheless, lets each individual person or thing retain its difference, its distinctiveness, its uniqueness, its integrity.

God's transcendence is not domination or subjugation or remoteness; it is *relatedness*—a relatedness so profound and pervasive that it is inescapable in all of life. As the American poet A.R. Ammons once put it, I know that if I find You, I must go *up* and *out* and *over*—"over the sea marshes . . . over the hills of tall hickory . . . over the crater lakes and canyons . . . on up through the spheres of diminishing air . . . up farther than the loss of sight." And yet, at the same time, I know that

> . . . if I find you I will have to stay [here] with the earth,
> inspecting with thin tools and ground eyes
> trusting the microvilli sporangia and simplest coelenterates
> and praying for a nerve cell
> with all the soul of my chemical reactions . . .
> You are everywhere partial and entire
> You are on the inside of everything and on the outside.[8]

[7] Gebara, "The Face of Transcendence," 178.

[8] A. R. Ammons, *The Selected Poems*, expanded edition (NY: W. W. Norton & Co., 1986), 9.

Finally, Ammons admits, finding God means I must "walk down the path down the hill where the sweetgum / has begun to ooze spring sap at the cut." Finding God means staying *"here* with the separate leaves."[9]

Or, as Yvone Gebara suggests, we must redefine transcendence in two fundamental ways: (1) First, we have to acknowledge that transcendence is *experience*. It is that experience we have (at the birth of a child, perhaps, or the death of a parent) that we can never fully dominate life, that we can never understand it in its wholeness, that there is always a "surplus" of meaning, value, truth, reality, love—a surplus that reminds us that power resides in powerlessness. We are limited creatures whose desire is limit*less*. Desire drives us into the arms of a mystery that grows greater the harder we press it close to ourselves. We are "answers" always searching for deeper, larger, questions. We are not human beings trying to have a spiritual experience; we are spiritual beings having a human experience. (2) Second, we have to acknowledge that transcendence is *ethical experience*. If God's transcendence means God's intimate relatedness to all that is, then God is not only an object of worship but a call "to live life as an absolute value," to live justly, to live beyond egoism and lethargy. "It is an experience that puts us in solidarity, in a state of mercy and love, with those who are different, with neighbors fallen on the byways of life. It is an experience of profound joy, of gracious action for acts of tenderness done in our midst."[10] It is a life that courts "the erotic excitement of the earth and the intensity of life which arises everywhere in any absolutely unpredictable and mysterious way."[11]

Reconciliation means repentance, restitution, and recovery—and recovery has its source in Jesus' cross, death, and resurrection (the paschal mystery). Resurrection is not merely an event that once-upon-a-time happened to Jesus (at Easter) or to Christians (at baptism). Resurrection is also the name for what Christians *practice*, for how they live. Now you know why every Christian gathering is

[9] Ibid.; emphasis added.
[10] Gebara, "The Face of Transcendence," 180.
[11] Ibid., 181.

always, inevitably, an act of reconciliation. Gathering is what resurrection was and is—a gathering up into God's life (at God's initiative) all that was dead, destroyed, denied, delayed, deprived, depressed, deferred.

That is why, when we gather as reconciling church, we always gather in *someone else's name*, and not our own. We gather "in the name of the Father, and of the Son, and of the Holy Spirit." We gather "in the grace and peace of our Lord Jesus Christ"; we gather "in the communion of the Holy Spirit." We commence our journey forward travelling on somebody else's passport, using somebody else's visa. We literally "put on" the Lord Jesus, put on his love and vulnerability, put on his justice and mercy, put on his death and his life, put on his cross and passion, put on his heart and hands so we can be in the world what he was: bread of life, broken in mercy for the poor, broken so that the world may have life, and have it more abundantly.

Conclusion

Undoubtedly, our greatest challenge has been to pick and choose the nine Amen Corners that form the backbone of the present volume. Over twenty years, Nathan has written one hundred and twenty-three of them, for a total of approximately half a million words. If the job of a theologian is precisely to find words that reveal to us something about God's presence, then Nathan's columns are truly a remarkable achievement, if only for the range of topics covered: from Vatican II to Keith Haring; from doxology to poverty; from Aquinas to Emily Dickinson's poetry. In a unique attempt to embrace the widest possible spectrum of issues and attitudes experienced in our local churches, Nathan's eclectic meditations and lucid analyses represent an extraordinary tool to unlock the mysteries of God's salvific beauty in this temporal and chaotic world of ours.

Faced with such a daunting task, we relied on two guides who could legitimately be called the Amen Corner "founding fathers": Kevin Seasoltz, OSB, and Robert Hovda. In 1991, Seasoltz introduced Nathan's Amen Corner tenure by writing: "[H]e too will be both 'refreshing and provocative.'"[1] In effect, no other words seem to us more appropriate than these to reflect on Nathan's contribution to *Worship*. If a unifying thread must be found in Nathan's columns, it certainly is the persistent way in which, in his own inimitable style, he challenges his readers with the most complex issues that have characterized the church in these last twenty years. The columns gathered here, therefore, represent in our view the ones that more *refreshingly* and *provocatively* point to new directions

---

[1] Kevin Seasoltz, "The Amen Corner: Liturgy and Culture," Introduction, *Worship* 65, no. 4 (July 1991): 363.

for present and future reflections on the church, its worship, and its mission to belong to Christ.

The other guiding principle adopted is the one brilliantly delineated by Hovda when in 1983, in his "Apologia for a New Column," he offered the rationale behind the name "Amen Corner." Among other reasons, he writes: " 'Amen' continues to be . . . one of the most important words in our liturgical vocabulary. It suggests no mere passive acquiescence but, rather, like 'right on!' and 'You said it!' and 'Sing it again, sister!', an active, responsible, even enthusiastic joining in a deed that *needs* our participation. In liturgy, this translates as a summoning of one's full baptismal dignity and responsibility to transform the texts and movements of the tradition into the here-and-now symbolic action of the whole assembly—in other words, to create liturgy."[2] We think that the columns we chose indeed require *our* participation in a transformative act that *creates* liturgy, here-and-now.

Yet, this volume has not simply been a collection of columns by Nathan. Rather, it includes contributions by Nathan's former students—those who seek novel vistas for incarnating his thought anew. Among these essays, the careful reader will begin to notice a burgeoning research agenda for those who will follow in Nathan's footsteps. Readers of Nathan over the years will not be surprised to discern that such research includes attention to the body, a liturgically robust understanding of the proclamation of the Word in the preaching act, the liturgy of the poor, the role of women in the life of the church, the healing dimension of the aesthetic, ecumenism, and the inclusion of postmodern philosophical questions in a liturgically-inscribed sacramental theology. To remain at this level of abstraction, nonetheless, is to perform a disservice to Nathan as theological educator (not to mention it is anathema to the logic of Nathan's own thought).

As former students of Nathan can attest, his lectures were often occasions in which we might hear the latest version of an *Amen Corner* performed in our midst. What makes Nathan such a re-

---

[2] Robert Hovda, *Worship* 57, no. 2 (March 1983): 151.

markable writer and mentor alike is that his speech and prose alike empowered the student to perceive anew texts, historical developments, ritual actions that seemed so mundane upon first glance. Nathan as a teacher was never interested in self-replication, in creating dozens of "Mitchells" populating academic departments throughout the world. Rather, he wanted to form liturgical historians, theologians, and practitioners who could embody in their own writing, research, and liturgical ministry the reality that worship sought to make present: the sweetness of divine love still becoming flesh in the worship of the church. And whatever sources were made present to him, he baptized into his project of fostering this liturgical vision.

If there is an aesthetic dimension running across the companion essays in this volume, it is because Nathan's students have become adept at replicating this sensibility in their own writing. They too have become teachers and writers who invite students into an understanding of liturgical celebration that might heal the logic of power and violence endemic in church and society alike. They cross disciplinary boundaries with ease, all the while remaining grounded in the liturgical histories of the church. And they do so as a form of faith seeking understanding, inviting the reader to become what they receive in liturgical prayer. Thus, we close this edited collection with a note of gratitude to Nathan for his years of teaching and writing, incarnate in his *Amen Corners*. For those who have picked up the grammar of Nathan's discourse through these columns, we have no doubt that Nathan's aesthetic pedagogy, one grounded in liturgical history, will continue to influence countless generations of those who take up the study of liturgy. And for this, we are grateful.

Timothy P. O'Malley
Demetrio S. Yocum

Contributors

Kimberly Hope Belcher is an assistant professor of liturgical studies in the Department of Theology, University of Notre Dame.

Katharine E. Harmon is a lecturer in the Theology & Philosophy Department of Marian University in Indianapolis and a music minister serving the Archdiocese of Indianapolis.

Clare V. Johnson is senior lecturer in liturgical studies and sacramental theology at Australian Catholic University, Strathfield NSW, Australia.

Anne McGowan is an adjunct assistant professor at Saint John's School of Theology and Seminary who has offered classes in liturgy at the Yale Institute of Sacred Music and the University of Notre Dame.

Melanie C. Ross is an assistant professor of liturgical studies at Yale Divinity School and Yale Institute of Sacred Music.

Joél Z. Schmidt is an assistant professor in the Department of Religious and Theological Studies at Salve Regina University.

Editors

Maxwell E. Johnson is professor of liturgy at the University of Notre Dame and a pastor in the Evangelical Lutheran Church in America. He is the author, coauthor, or editor of more than nineteen books, including *The Rites of Christian Initiation*; *The Origins of Feasts, Fasts, and Seasons in Early Christianity*; *The Eucharistic Liturgies*, and *Praying and Believing in Early Christianity* (all from Liturgical Press). He is currently president of the North American Academy of Liturgy, and a member of Societas Liturgica, and the Society of Oriental Liturgy.

Timothy P. O'Malley is director of the Notre Dame Center for Liturgy and a concurrent assistant professional specialist in the Department of Theology, University of Notre Dame.

Demetrio S. Yocum is a research associate in the Department of Romance Languages and Literatures at the University of Notre Dame.